# The Family Tree

## Classic Essays on Family and Ancestors

Janet Marting
The University of Akron

*NTC Publishing Group*
*a division of* NTC/CONTEMPORARY PUBLISHING COMPANY
Lincolnwood, Illinois  USA

Executive Editor: Marisa L. L'Heureux
Development Editor: Lisa A. De Mol
Project Editor: Heidi L. Hedstrom
Cover and interior design: Ophelia M. Chambliss
Cover art: Celia Johnson/Gerald & Cullen Rapp, Inc.
Production Manager: Margo Goia

Acknowledgments begin on page 305, which is to be considered an extension of this copyright page.

ISBN: 0-8442-5303-0 (student text)
ISBN: 0-8442-5304-9 (instructor's edition)

Published by NTC Publishing Group
© 1998 NTC/Contemporary Publishing Company, 4255 West Touhy Avenue,
Lincolnwood (Chicago), Illinois 60646-1975 U.S.A.

**Library of Congress Cataloging-in-Publication Data**
The family tree : classic essays on family and ancestors / [edited by]
    Janet Marting.
            p.    cm. — (NTC's library of classic essays)
        Includes index.
        Summary: Explores how each person is shaped in part by family
    members and ancestors. Includes biographical headnotes on writers,
    discussion questions, and writing assignments.
        ISBN 0-8442-5303-0 (pbk.)
        1. Biography—Juvenile literature.  2. Genealogy—Juvenile
    literature. 3. Family—Juvenile literature.  [1. Biography.
    2. Genealogy. 3. Family.]    I. Marting, Janet.    II. Series.
    CT107.F37    1997
    920.02—dc21                                          97-351
                                                            CIP
                                                             AC

5 6 7 8 9 VP 0 9 8 7 6 5 4 3 2 1

# Contents

# Classic Essays on Husbands and Wives    IOI

# Classic Essays on Children    125

# Classic Essays on Grandparents and Ancestors    199

# Classic Essays on Families 249

# Preface

## NTC's Library of Classic Essays

This is a six-volume collection of some of the finest essays ever written, providing a broad yet in-depth overview of the development and scope of the genre. In essence, an essay is a short prose composition, usually exploring one subject and often presenting the personal view of the author. An essay may take a variety of forms (from narration to description to autobiography) and may reflect any number of moods (from critical to reflective to whimsical).

Although we recognize a few early works by Plato, Aristotle, and others as essays, it was really Michel de Montaigne, a French philosopher and writer, who substantially defined the form when he published two volumes of his own essays under the title Essais in 1580. Montaigne considered himself to be representative of humankind in general: thus, his essays, though they are to be read as general treatises on the human condition, are largely reflective of Montaigne's own attitudes and experiences.

The essay proved to be a most adaptable form. In the eighteenth century, both journalists and philosophers in England and pamphleteers and patriots in the American colonies quickly discovered the power of a well-crafted and provocative essay. By the middle of the nineteenth century, the essay was the form of choice for such brilliant writers as the American Ralph Waldo Emerson and the British George Eliot. In the twentieth century, the essay has become the most widely read genre—from personal essays in periodicals to scholarly essays in scientific journals to argumentative essays on the editorial pages of newspapers worldwide.

# The Family Tree:
## Classic Essays on Family and Ancestors

This volume contains thirty-four classic essays that illustrate the richness of the family in its many forms. Organized by family members, these essays explore how the family connects people across time and space. If, however, one of your favorites is not included here, it may well be in one of the other volumes: *From the Cradle to the Grave: Classic Essays on Coming of Age and Aging; Plato's Heirs: Classic Essays; Daughters of the Revolution: Classic Essays by Women; Diverse Identities: Classic Multicultural Essays;* or *Of Bunsen Burners, Bones, and Belles Lettres: Classic Essays across the Curriculum.*

This volume brings you essays that explore how writers think and write about the way in which their families have influenced who they are and established their place in an endless chain of people, spanning past, present, and future generations. It is our hope that this collection will allow you to examine who you are and better enable you to explore your place—and the place of others—in the universe.

# CLASSIC ESSAYS ON

# Brothers and Sisters

# from The Autobiography of Benjamin Franklin

## BENJAMIN FRANKLIN

Benjamin Franklin (1706–1790) was born in Boston, Massachusetts. At the age of twelve, he apprenticed to his older brother, a printer and newspaper editor. Using the pseudonym Silence Dogood, Franklin published his first essays before he was seventeen years old. In 1723, Franklin moved to Philadelphia to pursue a career in printing, and, by 1730, he had become the owner of a successful printing shop. One of Franklin's most memorable books is *Poor Richard's Almanack* (1733). Some of his other significant accomplishments include creating the first circulating library in North America, inventing the stove, and helping set up a school, which later became the University of Pennsylvania. Franklin moved to Great Britain, where he lived for a time, speaking on behalf of the American colonies. In 1775, he returned to America when he was chosen to be a delegate to the Second Continental Congress. Franklin served on the committee that drafted the Declaration of Independence. In 1776, he was appointed minister to France, and, in 1781, he became part of the commission that ended the Revolutionary War and secured independence for the United States. Franklin's notable achievements include having been president of the Pennsylvania Antislavery Society, which petitioned

3

Congress to oppose the slave trade. Franklin began writing his auto-biography in 1771, and later installments appeared in 1784, 1788, and 1789. Though incomplete at the time of his death, Franklin's autobiography was published in 1818. It is a classic autobiography that provides revealing information on one of the most influential Americans of the eighteenth century. In the following selection from his autobiography, Franklin recounts his rather contentious relationship with his older brother James—a relationship that helped to produce Franklin's first published essays.

1      My brother had, in 1720 or 21, begun to print a newspaper. It was the second that appeared in America, and was called the *New England Courant*. The only one before it was the *Boston News-Letter*. I remember his being dissuaded by some of his friends from the undertaking, as not likely to succeed, one newspaper being, in their judgment, enough for America. At this time (1771) there are not less than five-and-twenty. He went on, however, with the under-taking, and after having worked in composing the types and printing off the sheets, I was employed to carry the papers through the streets to the customers.

2      He had some ingenious men among his friends, who amused themselves by writing little pieces for this paper, which gained it credit and made it more in demand, and these gentlemen often vis-ited us. Hearing their conversations, and their accounts of the approbation their papers were received with, I was excited to try my hand among them; but, being still a boy, and suspecting that my brother would object to printing anything of mine in his paper if he knew it to be mine, I contrived to disguise my hand and, writing an anonymous paper, I put it in at night under the door of the printing house. It was found in the morning and communicated to his writ-ing friends when they called in as usual. They read it, commented on it in my hearing, and I had the exquisite pleasure of finding it met with their approbation, and that, in their different guesses at the author, none was named but men of some character among us for

learning and ingenuity. I suppose now that I was rather lucky in my judges, and that perhaps they were not really so very good ones as I then esteemed them.

3    Encouraged, however, by this, I wrote and conveyed in the same way to the press several more papers which were equally approved; and I kept my secret till my small fund of sense for such performances was pretty well exhausted, and then I discovered it, when I began to be considered a little more by my brother's acquaintance, and in a manner that did not quite please him, as he thought, probably with reason, that it tended to make me too vain. And perhaps this might be one occasion of the differences that we began to have about this time. Though a brother, he considered himself as my master, and me as his apprentice, and accordingly expected the same services from me as he would from another, while I thought he demeaned me too much in some he required of me, who from a brother expected more indulgence. Our disputes were often brought before our father, and I fancy I was either generally in the right, or else a better pleader, because the judgment was generally in my favor. But my brother was passionate, and had often beaten me, which I took extremely amiss; and, thinking my apprenticeship very tedious, I was continually wishing for some opportunity of shortening it, which at length offered in a manner unexpected.*

4    One of the pieces in our newspaper on some political point, which I have now forgotten, gave offense to the Assembly. He was taken up, censured, and imprisoned for a month, by the speaker's warrant, I suppose because he would not discover his author. I too was taken up and examined before the council; but, though I did not give them any satisfaction, they contented themselves with admonishing me, and dismissed me, considering me, perhaps, as an apprentice who was bound to keep his master's secrets.

5    During my brother's confinement, which I resented a good deal, notwithstanding our private differences, I had the management of the paper; and I made bold to give our rulers some rubs in it, which my brother took very kindly, while others began to consider me in an unfavorable light, as a young genius that had a turn for libeling

---

*I fancy his harsh and tyrannical treatment of me might be a means of impressing me with that aversion to arbitrary power that has stuck to me through my whole life.

and satire. My brother's discharge was accompanied with an order of the House (a very odd one) that "James Franklin should no longer print the paper called the *New England Courant.*"

6  There was a consultation held in our printing-house among his friends what he should do in this case. Some proposed to evade the order by changing the name of the paper; but my brother seeing inconveniences in that, it was finally concluded on as a better way to let it be printed for the future under the name of *Benjamin Franklin;* and to avoid the censure of the Assembly, that might fall on him as still printing it by his apprentice, the contrivance was that my old indenture should be returned to me, with a full discharge on the back of it, to be shown on occasion; but to secure to him the benefit of my service, I was to sign new indentures for the remainder of the term, which were to be kept private. A very flimsy scheme it was; however, it was immediately executed, and the paper went on accordingly under my name for several months.

7  At length, a fresh difference arising between my brother and me, I took upon me to assert my freedom, presuming that he would not venture to produce the new indentures. It was not fair in me to take this advantage, and this I therefore reckon one of the first errata of my life; but the unfairness of it weighed little with me when under the impressions of resentment for the blows his passion too often urged him to bestow upon me, though he was otherwise not an ill-natured man; perhaps I was too saucy and provoking.

8  When he found I would leave him, he took care to prevent my getting employment in any other printing-house of the town, by going round and speaking to every master, who accordingly refused to give me work. I then thought of going to New York, as the nearest place where there was a printer; and I was the rather inclined to leave Boston when I reflected that I had already made myself a little obnoxious to the governing party, and, from the arbitrary proceedings of the Assembly in my brother's case, it was likely I might, if I stayed, soon bring myself into scrapes; and farther, that my indiscreet disputations about religion began to make me pointed at with horror by good people as an infidel or atheist. I determined on the point, but my father now siding with my brother, I was sensible that, if I attempted to go openly, means would be used to prevent me. My friend Collins, therefore, undertook to manage a little for me. He agreed with the captain of a New York sloop for my pas-

sage, under the notion of my being a young acquaintance of his, that had got a naughty girl with child, whose friends would compel me to marry her, and therefore I could not appear or come away publicly. So I sold some of my books to raise a little money, was taken on board privately, and as we had a fair wind, in three days I found myself in New York, near three hundred miles from home, a boy of but seventeen, without the least recommendation to, or knowledge of, any person in the place, and with very little money in my pocket.

## Discussion Questions

1. Why did Franklin anonymously submit his writing to his brother's newspaper? Evaluate his reasons for doing so. What would you have done in Franklin's position?
2. In small groups, discuss the strengths and weaknesses of Franklin's relationship with his brother. How was it typical of relations between brothers?
3. What do you think Franklin's brother would have said in his own defense?
4. What are your impressions of Franklin from this excerpt from his autobiography? Explain.
5. Explain what this reading contributes to your understanding of Franklin as a historical figure.

## Writing Assignments

1. Imagine you are Franklin and, in a letter, confront your brother about his behavior toward you.
2. Write a journal entry that examines the ways in which Franklin's relationship with his brother is fairly typical of sibling relationships.
3. In a paper, explain how one can learn more about famous people by reading their autobiographies rather than more conventional historical accounts.

# from *Memoirs of a Dutiful Daughter*

## SIMONE DE BEAUVOIR

Simone de Beauvoir (1908–1986) was born in Paris. A student at the Catholic Cours Désir and then at the Sorbonne, Beauvoir was a member of the first generation of European women to receive a formal education. The death of her lifelong friend Elisabeth Mabille (Zaza) in 1929 moved Beauvoir to begin her writing career in earnest. Much of her writing dealt with institutions and social ideas with which she fervently disagreed. In 1929, Beauvoir met the famed existentialist Jean-Paul Sartre, with whom she was paired until his death in 1980. She is the author of four memoirs that document not only her coming of age but also her career as a writer: *Memoirs of a Dutiful Daughter* (1958), *The Prime of Life* (1960), *The Force of Circumstance* (1963), and *All Said and Done* (1972). She is also the author of *The Second Sex* (1949), her acclaimed treatise on patriarchy; *Old Age* (1970), an examination of aging; and *A Very Easy Death* (1964), a moving account of her mother's death. Beauvoir's novels include *She Came to Stay* (1943), *The Blood of Others* (1945), *All Men Are Mortal* (1946), *The Mandarins* (1954), and *Les Belles Images* (1966). Beauvoir's work is characterized by her attempts to reconcile the need for social, economic, and personal freedom with a need for the approval of others and self-approval. A staunch feminist and existentialist, Beauvoir was a leading figure in the 1930s and 1940s. In the following selection from *Memoirs of a Dutiful Daughter*, Beauvoir recounts the rivalry and the closeness of her relationship with Poupette, her younger sister.

1    My situation in the family resembled that of my father in his childhood and youth: he had found himself suspended between the airy scepticism of my grandfather and the bourgeois earnestness of my grandmother. In my own case, too, my father's individualism and pagan ethical standards were in complete contrast to the rigidly moral conventionalism of my mother's teaching. This imbalance, which made my life a kind of endless disputation, is the main reason why I became an intellectual.

2    For the time being, I felt I was being protected and guided both in matters of this life and of the life beyond. I was glad, too, that I was not entirely at the mercy of grown-ups; I was not alone in my children's world; I had an equal: my sister, who began to play a considerable role in my life about my sixth birthday.

3    We called her Poupette; she was two and a half years younger than me. People said she took after Papa. She was fair-haired, and in the photographs taken during our childhood her blue eyes always appear to be filled with tears. Her birth had been a disappointment, because the whole family had been hoping for a boy; certainly no one ever held it against her for being a girl, but it is perhaps not altogether without significance that her cradle was the centre of regretful comment. Great pains were taken to treat us both with scrupulous fairness; we wore identical clothes, we nearly always went out together; we shared a single existence, though as the elder sister I did in fact enjoy certain advantages. I had my own room, which I shared with Louise, and I slept in a big bed, an imitation antique in carved wood over which hung a reproduction of Murillo's *Assumption of the Blessed Virgin*. A cot was set up for my sister in a narrow corridor. While Papa was undergoing his army training, it was I who accompanied Mama when she went to see him. Relegated to a secondary position, the 'little one' felt almost superfluous. I had been a new experience for my parents: my sister found it much more difficult to surprise and astonish them; I had never been compared

with anyone: she was always being compared with me. At the Cours
Désir the ladies in charge made a habit of holding up the older children as examples to the younger ones; whatever Poupette might do,
and however well she might do it, the passing of time and the subli-
mation of a legend all contributed to the idea that I had done everything much better. No amount of effort and success was sufficient to
break through that impenetrable barrier. The victim of some
obscure malediction, she was hurt and perplexed by her situation,
and often in the evening she would sit crying on her little chair. She
was accused of having a sulky disposition; one more inferiority she
had to put up with. She might have taken a thorough dislike to me,
but paradoxically she only felt sure of herself when she was with me.
Comfortably settled in my part of elder sister, I plumed myself only
on the superiority accorded to my greater age; I thought Poupette
was remarkably bright for her years; I accepted her for what she
was—someone like myself, only a little younger; she was grateful for
my approval, and responded to it with an absolute devotion. She
was my liegeman, my *alter ego*, my double; we could not do without
one another.

⁴    I was sorry for children who had no brother or sister; solitary
amusements seemed insipid to me; no better than a means of killing
time. But when there were two, hopscotch or a ball game were
adventurous undertakings, and bowling hoops an exciting competi-
tion. Even when I was just doing transfers or daubing a catalogue
with water-colours I felt the need of an associate. Collaborating and
vying with one another, we each found a purpose in our work that
saved it from all gratuitousness. The games I was fondest of were
those in which I assumed another character; and in these I had to
have an accomplice. We hadn't many toys; our parents used to lock
away the nicest ones—the leaping tiger and the elephant that could
stand on his hind legs; they would occasionally bring them out to
show to admiring guests. I didn't mind. I was flattered to possess
objects which could amuse grown-ups; and I loved them because
they were precious: familiarity would have bred contempt. In any
case the rest of our playthings—grocer's shop, kitchen utensils,
nurse's outfit—gave very little encouragement to the imagination. A
partner was absolutely essential to me if I was to bring my imaginary
stories to life.

5     A great number of the anecdotes and situations which we dramatized were, we realized, rather banal; the presence of the grown-ups did not disturb us when we were selling hats or defying the Boche's artillery fire. But other scenarios, the ones we liked best, required to be performed in secret. They were, on the surface, perfectly innocent, but, in sublimating the adventure of our childhood, or anticipating the future, they drew upon something secret and intimate within us which would not bear the searching light of adult gazes. I shall speak later of those games which, from my point of view, were the most significant. In fact, I was always the one who expressed myself through them; I imposed them upon my sister, assigning her the minor roles which she accepted with complete docility. At that evening hour when the stillness, the dark weight, and the tedium of our middle-class domesticity began to invade the hall, I would unleash my fantasms; we would make them materialize with great gestures and copious speeches, and sometimes, spellbound by our play, we succeeded in taking off from the earth and leaving it far behind until an imperious voice suddenly brought us back to reality. Next day we would start all over again. 'We'll play *you know what*,' we would whisper to each other as we prepared for bed. The day would come when a certain theme, worked over too long, would no longer have the power to inspire us; then we would choose another, to which we would remain faithful for a few hours or even for weeks.

6     I owe a great debt to my sister for helping me to externalize many of my dreams in play: she also helped me to save my daily life from silence; through her I got into the habit of wanting to communicate with people. When she was not there I hovered between two extremes: words were either insignificant noises which I made with my mouth, or, whenever I addressed my parents, they became deeds of the utmost gravity; but when Poupette and I talked together, words had a meaning yet did not weigh too heavily upon us. I never knew with her the pleasure of sharing or exchanging things, because we always held everything in common; but as we recounted to one another the day's incidents and emotions, they took on added interest and importance. There was nothing wrong in what we told one another; nevertheless, because of the importance we both attached to our conversations, they created a bond between us which isolated

us from the grown-ups; when we were together, we had our own secret garden.

7    We found this arrangement very useful. The traditions of our family compelled us to take part in a large number of duty visits, especially around the New Year; we had to attend interminable family dinners with aunts and first cousins removed to the hundredth degree, and pay visits to decrepit old ladies. We often found release from boredom by running into the hall and playing at 'you know what'. In summer, Papa was very keen on organizing expeditions to the woods at Chaville or Meudon; the only means we had of enlivening the boredom of these long walks was our private chatter; we would make plans and recall all the things that had happened to us in the past; Poupette would ask me questions; I would relate episodes from French or Roman history, or stories which I made up myself.

8    What I appreciated most in our relationship was that I had a real hold over her. The grown-ups had me at their mercy. If I demanded praise from them, it was still up to them to decide whether to praise me or not. Certain aspects of my behaviour seemed to have an immediate effect upon my mother, an effect which had not the slightest connexion with what I had intended. But between my sister and myself things happened naturally. We would disagree, she would cry, I would become cross, and we would hurl the supreme insult at one another: 'You *fool!*' and then we'd make it up. Her tears were real, and if she laughed at one of my jokes, I knew she wasn't trying to humour me. She alone endowed me with authority; adults sometimes gave in to me: she obeyed me.

9    One of the most durable bonds that bound us together was that which exists between master and pupil. I loved studying so much that I found teaching enthralling. Playing at school with my dolls did not satisfy me at all: I didn't just want to go through the motions of teaching: I really wanted to pass on the knowledge I had acquired.

10   Teaching my sister to read, write, and count gave me, from the age of six onwards, a sense of pride in my own efficiency. I liked scrawling phrases or pictures over sheets of paper: but in doing so I was only creating imitation objects. When I started to change ignorance into knowledge, when I started to impress truths upon a virgin mind, I felt I was at last creating something real. I was not just imitating grown-ups: I was on their level, and my success had noth-

ing to do with their good pleasure. It satisfied in me an aspiration that was more than mere vanity. Until then, I had contented myself with responding dutifully to the care that was lavished upon me: but now, for the first time, I, too, was being of service to someone. I was breaking away from the passivity of childhood and entering the great human circle in which everyone is useful to everyone else. Since I had started working seriously time no longer fled away, but left its mark on me: by sharing my knowledge with another, I was fixing time on another's memory, and so making it doubly secure.

## Discussion Questions

1. What does Beauvoir think children miss in not having brothers or sisters? Explain why you agree or disagree with her thinking.
2. What role did games have in Beauvoir's childhood?
3. In small groups, discuss how the relationship Beauvoir had with her immediate family members was typical of most children's. Explain.
4. Would Beauvoir have cherished her relationship with her sister if *she* had been the younger child? Why?
5. What does Beauvoir mean when she states in the last paragraph "by sharing my knowledge with another, I was fixing time on another's memory, and so making it doubly secure"?

## Writing Assignments

1. Write a letter to a sibling explaining how the closeness (or the estrangement) of your relationship with him or her has had an impact on your life. If you have no siblings, write an essay explaining how you "missed out" on something important. If you have siblings, write an essay claiming that being an only child is preferable to having brothers and sisters. The essay need not be serious: you may use sarcasm, exaggeration, and so forth to make your case.

2. Do you think that single-children families create more or less hardship for the child? Write a paper that supports your stance.
3. Research some of the studies conducted on birth order. In a paper, argue whether commonly held theories about birth order (for example, the oldest child is independent, the middle child is the problem child, the youngest child is the baby in the family) are correct.

# Sibling Rivalry

## ANNA QUINDLEN

Anna Quindlen (b. 1952) was born in Philadelphia, Pennsylvania, and graduated from Barnard College in 1974. A journalist by trade, she began her career as a part-time reporter for the *New York Post* during her first year in college. After graduation, she became a full-time reporter for the *Post* for three years. She then worked at *The New York Times*, first as a general assignment and city hall reporter, then as the author of the "About New York" column, and later as deputy metropolitan editor. From 1986 to 1988, she wrote the syndicated "Life in the Thirties" column for the *Times*. In 1990, she started another column, "Public and Private," for the newspaper. At the end of 1994, Quindlen left the *Times* to become a full-time novelist. Her two novels are *Object Lessons* (1991) and *One True Thing* (1994). She has also written a children's book, *The Tree That Came to Stay* (1992). Her popular and much acclaimed newspaper columns are assembled in two books: *Living Out Loud* (1988), in which the following essay appears, and *Thinking Out Loud: On the Personal, the Political, the Public and the Private* (1993). In 1992, Quindlen was awarded a Pulitzer Prize for commentary. In the following selection, Quindlen reflects on the nature of sibling rivalry.

1    The boys are playing in the back room, a study in brotherly love. The younger one has the fire engine and the older one has the tow truck and although entire minutes have passed, neither has made a grab for the other's toy. The younger one is babbling to himself in pidgin English and the older is singing ceaselessly, tonelessly, as though chanting a mantra. It is not until I move closer to the two of them, toe to toe on the tile floor, that I catch the lyrics to the melody: "Get out of here. Get out of here. Get out of here."

2    Later the older one will explain that he picked up this particular turn of phrase from me, when I was yelling at one of the dogs. (In a similar phenomenon, he always says "Jesus, Mary, and Joseph" when I apply the brakes of the car hard in traffic.) When I said it to the dogs, I meant it figuratively; how Quin means it is less easily classified. I know, because I know where he is coming from. I have vivid memories of being a small girl reading in a club chair, and of having my brother, a year younger than I, enter the room and interrupt me. An emotion as big and as bang-bang-banging as a second heart would fill my ribs. It was, trust me, pure hatred.

3    This house is full of sibling rivalry right now, as colorful and everpresent as my children's Lego blocks. The preschool class is full of it, too, filled with three-year-olds in various stages of shell shock because their moms and dads came home in the car one day with a receiving blanket full of turf battles, emotional conflicts, and divided love.

4    Realization has come slowly for some of them; I think it began one day when the younger one needed me more and I turned to him and said, "You know, Quin, I'm Christopher's mommy too." The look that passed over his face was the one I imagine usually accompanies the discovery of a dead body in the den: shock, denial, horror. "And Daddy is Christopher's daddy?" he gasped. When I confirmed this he began to cry—wet, sad sobbing.

5    I cannot remember which of my books described sibling rivalry thus: Imagine that one night your husband comes home and tells you that he has decided to have a second wife. She will be younger than you, cuter than you, and will demand much more of his time and attention. That doesn't mean, however, that he will love you any the less. Covers the down side pretty well, doesn't it?

6    And yet the down side is not the only one; if it were, "Get out of here" would not have such a sweet little melody. My son loves his

brother, who is immensely lovable; at the same time, he dislikes his brother intensely. He wants him to be around, but only sometimes, and only on his terms. He is no different from a lot of us, who have fantasies about the things we want and who are surprised by the realities when we get them. He likes the idea of a brother, but not always the brother himself. When his brother is hurt and helpless, he calls him "my baby." "I don't want my baby to cry, Mommy," he says, which is the kind of line you get into this business to hear.

7    But when there is a tussle over the fire engine, his baby develops a name, an identity, a reality that is infuriating. "Christopher," he says then, shaking an index finger as short as a pencil stub in the inflated baby face "you don't touch my truck, Christopher. O.K.? O.K., CHRISTOPHER?"

8    He actually likes babies; he even wants to bring one home, the two-month-old brother of his friend Sonia. Eric, he thinks, is perfect: he cannot walk, cannot talk, has no interest in Maurice Sendak books, Lego blocks, the trucks, the sandbox, or any of the other things that make life worth living, including—especially including—me. One day at Sonia's house he bent over Eric's bassinet to say hello, but what came out instead was a triumphant "You can't catch me!" as he sailed away from him.

9    His baby can't catch him yet, but it's only a matter of time. Then he will have to make a choice: a partner, an accomplice, an opponent, or, perhaps most likely, a mixture of the three. At some point his fantasy of a brother may dovetail with the reality; mine did when my younger brother, the insufferable little nerd with the Coke-bottle glasses whom I loathed, turned into a good-looking teenage boy who interested my girlfriends, had some interesting boyfriends of his own, and was a first-rate dancer. But it's not as simple as that, either. In his bones now my elder son probably knows the awful, wonderful truth: that he and his brother are yoked together for life, blood of each other's blood, joined as surely as if they were Siamese twins. Whether the yoke is one of friendship or resentment, it will inevitably shadow both their lives. That is certainly something to bear, as good a reason as any to look at someone and wish that he could, impossibly, occasionally, go someplace else.

# Discussion Questions

1. In small groups, generate a definition of sibling rivalry and then discuss how accurately Quindlen describes the term, particularly in paragraph 5.
2. Discuss the effectiveness of Quindlen's beginning her essay with a description of her children playing.
3. Do you agree with Quindlen in the last paragraph when she posits the idea that her children's sibling relationship will "inevitably shadow both their lives"? Why?
4. Does sibling rivalry pose a danger to children, that is, have a negative, permanent impact on their lives? Or is it just a natural stage in life that most children live through unharmed?

# Writing Assignments

1. Write a journal entry recounting an incident from your childhood in which sibling rivalry (either yours or that of a friend) got out of hand.
2. Write a letter to your sibling (if you are an only child, write to an imaginary sibling) in which you explain why sibling rivalry was detrimental in your relationship.
3. Sibling rivalry can be viewed as valuable preparation for life as an adult. Write a paper in which you examine the benefits that can be derived from sibling rivalry.
4. Write an essay that explores how your life would be different if you had no siblings (or if you are an only child, if you had siblings).

# *from* Brothers and Keepers

## JOHN EDGAR WIDEMAN

John Edgar Wideman (b. 1941) was born in Pittsburgh, Pennsylvania. He attended the University of Pennsylvania, where he was inducted into the honor society Phi Beta Kappa. He earned a B.A. from Oxford University, where he was the second African American to be named a Rhodes scholar. Wideman was a Kent fellow at the University of Iowa's creative writing program before joining the faculty of the University of Pennsylvania. A fiction writer, Wideman is the author of *A Glance Away* (1967), *Hurry Home* (1969), *The Lynchers* (1973), *Hiding Place* (1981), *Damballah* (1981), *Sent for You Yesterday* (1983), *Rueben* (1987), *Fever* (1989), *Philadelphia Fire* (1990), *The Stories of John Edgar Wideman* (1992), and *The Cattle Killing* (1997). Wideman has also written two memoirs: *Brothers and Keepers* (1984), which explores the markedly different life he has led from that of his brother, an inmate charged with murder; and *Fatheralong* (1994), an examination of his father and a look at Wideman himself as a father. Wideman is one of the most distinguished contemporary African American fiction writers, as evidenced by his winning the P.E.N./Faulkner Award in 1984 and again in 1991. In the following selection from *Brothers and Keepers*, Wideman describes a visit to the penitentiary to visit his younger brother, Robby. The writing, reminiscent of his fiction, is as richly descriptive of Wideman's thoughts and emotions as it is of the people, places, and events he encounters.

*Summer 1982*

1          ONE MORE TIME. Summer 1982. The weather in Pittsburgh is unbearably hot. Two weeks of high temperatures and high humidity. Nights not much better than the days. Nights too hot for sleeping, days sapping what's left of the strength the sleepless nights don't replenish. You get sopping wet climbing in or out of a car. Especially if your car's little and not air-conditioned, like my mother's Chevette. Nobody remembers the last time they felt a cool breeze, nobody remembers pulling on clothes and not sweating through them in five minutes. "Unbearable" is my mother's word. She uses it often but never lightly. In her language it means the heat is something you can't escape. The sticky heat's a burden you wake up to every morning and carry till you're too exhausted to toss and turn anymore in your wet sheets. Unbearable doesn't mean a weight that gets things over with, that crushes you once and for all, but a burden that exerts relentless pressure. Whether you're lifting a bag of groceries from a shopping cart into the furnace your car becomes after sitting closed for twenty minutes in the Giant Eagle parking lot, or celebrating the birth of a new baby in the family, the heat is there. A burden touching, flawing everything. Unbearable is not that which can't be borne, but what must be endured forever.

2          Of course the July dog days can't last forever. Sooner or later they'll end. Abruptly. Swept away by one of those violent lightning-and-thunder storms peculiar to Pittsburgh summers. The kind signaled by a sudden disappearance of air, air sucked away so quickly you feel you're falling. Then nothing. A vast emptiness rubbing your skin. The air's gone. You're in a vacuum, a calm, still, vacated space waiting for the storm to rush in. You know the weather must turn, but part of the discomfort of being in the grip of a heat wave or any

grave trouble is the fear that maybe it won't end. Maybe things will stay as miserable as they are.

3      Nothing changes. Nothing remains the same. One more visit to the prison, only this time, after I dropped my mother off at work, I tried a new route. The parkway had been undergoing repairs for two years. I'd used it anyway, in spite of detours and traffic jams. But this time I tried a shortcut my buddy Scott Payne had suggested. Scott was right; his way was quicker and freer of hassles. I'd arrived at Western Penitentiary in record time. Yet something was wrong. The new route transported me to the gates but I wasn't ready to pass through. Different streets, different buildings along the way hadn't done the trick, didn't have the power to take me where I needed to go because the journey to visit my brother in prison was not simply a matter of miles and minutes. Between Homewood and Woods Run, the flat, industrialized wasteland beside the river where the prison's hidden, there is a vast, uncharted space, a no-man's-land where the traveler must begin to forget home and begin to remember the alien world inside "The Walls." At some point an invisible line is crossed, the rules change. Visitors must take leave of the certainties underpinning their everyday lives.

4      Using the parkway to reach Woods Run had become part of the ritual I depended upon to get me ready to see my brother. Huge green exit signs suspended over the highway, tires screaming on gouged patches of road surface, the darkness and claustrophobia of Squirrel Hill Tunnel, miles of abandoned steel-mill sheds, a mosque's golden cupola, paddle-wheeled pleasure boats moored at the riverbank, the scenes and sensations I catalogue now as I write were stepping stones. They broke the journey into stages, into moments I could anticipate. Paying attention to the steps allowed me to push into the back of my mind their inevitable destination, the place where the slide show of images was leading me.

5      I'd missed all that; so when I reached the last few miles of Ohio River Boulevard Scott's shortcut shared with my usual route, the shock of knowing the prison was just minutes away hit me harder than usual. I wasn't prepared to step through the looking glass.

6      Giving up one version of reality for another. That's what entering the prison was about. Not a dramatic flip-flop of values. That would be too easy. If black became white and good became bad and fast

became slow, the players could learn the trick of reversing labels, and soon the upside-down world would seem natural. Prison is more perverse. Inside the walls nothing is certain, nothing can be taken for granted except the arbitrary exercise of absolute power. Rules engraved in stone one day will be superseded the next. What you don't know can always hurt you. And the prison rules are designed to keep you ignorant, keep you guessing, insure your vulnerability. Think of a fun-house mirror, a floor-to-ceiling sheet of undulating glass. Images ripple across its curved surface constantly changing. Anything caught in the mirror is bloated, distorted. Prison's like that mirror. Prison rules and regulations, the day-to-day operation of the institution, confront the inmate with an image of himself that is grotesque, absurd. A prisoner who refuses to internalize this image, who insists upon seeing other versions of himself, is in constant danger.

7    Somebody with a wry sense of humor had a field day naming the cluster of tiny streets bordering Western Penitentiary. Doerr, Refuge, Ketchum. When I reached the left turn at Doerr that would take me along the south wall of the prison to the parking-lot entrance, I still wasn't ready to go inside. I kept driving past the prison till the street I was on dead-ended. A U-turn in the lot of a chemical factory pointed me back toward the penitentiary and then for a few long minutes I sat in the car. . . .

8    In the half mile back to the prison as the walls loom higher and nearer I asked the question I always must when a visit is imminent: Is Rob still alive? The possibility of sudden, violent death hangs over my brother's head every minute of every day so when I finally reach the guard's cage and ask for P3468, my heart stands still and I'm filled with the numbing irony of wishing, of praying that the guard will nod his head and say, *Yes*, your brother's still inside.

9    Robby hugs me, we clasp hands. My arm goes round his body and I hug him back. Our eyes meet. What won't be said, can't be said no matter how long we talk, how much I write, hovers in his eyes and mine. We know where we are, what's happening, how soon this tiny opening allowing us to touch will be slammed shut. All that in our eyes, and I can't take seeing it any longer than he can. The glance we exchange is swift, is full of fire, of unsayable rage and pain. Neither of us can hold it more than a split second. He sees in me

what I see in him. The knowledge that this place is bad, worse than bad. That the terms under which we are meeting stink. That living under certain conditions is less than no life at all, and what we have to do, *ought* to do, is make our stand here, together. That dying with your hands on an enemy's throat is better than living under his boot. Just a flash. The simplest, purest solution asserting itself. I recognize what Rob is thinking. I know he knows what's rushing through my mind. Fight. Forget the games, the death by inches buying time. Fight till they kill us or let us go. If we die fighting, it will be a good day to die. The right day. The right way.

10     After that first contact, after that instant of threat and consolation and promise flickers out as fast as it came, my eyes drop to the vinyl-cushioned couches, rise again to the clutter of other prisoners and visitors. I force myself to pretend the eye conversation never took place, that Robby and I hadn't been talking about first things and last things and hadn't reached a crystal-clear understanding of what we must do. We'd lost the moment. The escape route closed down as he looked away or I looked away. We're going to deal with the visit now. We're going to talk, survive another day. I have to pretend the other didn't happen because if I don't, disappointment and shame will spoil the visit. And visits are all we have. All we're going to have for years and years, unless we choose the other way, the solution burning in Rob's eyes and mine before each visit begins.

11     The last iron gate, the last barred door. The visit proper doesn't begin until after we meet and touch and decide we'll do it their way one more time. Because the other way, the alternative is always there. I meet it every time. We know it's there and we consciously say, *No.* And the no lets everything else follow. Says yes to the visit. The words.

12     Whatever else the visit turns into, it begins as compromise, an acceptance of defeat. Maybe the rage, the urge to fight back doesn't rise from a truer, better self. Maybe what's denied is not the instinctual core of my being but an easily sidestepped, superficial layer of bravado, a ferocity I'd like to think is real but that winds up being no more than a Jonathan Jackson, George Jackson, Soledad-brother fantasy, a carryover from the old Wild West, shoot-em-up days as a kid. The Lone Ranger, Robin Hood, Zorro. Masked raiders attacking the bad guys' castle, rescuing rusty sidekicks in a swirl of swordplay, gunfire, thundering hooves. Maybe I needed to imagine myself

in that role because I knew how far from the truth it was. Kidding myself so I could take the visits seriously, satisfy myself that I was doing all I could, doing better than nothing.

13    Point is, each visit's rooted in denial, compromise, a sinking feeling of failure. I'm letting Robby down, myself down, the team. . . . Always that to get through. The last gate. Sometimes it never swings all the way open on its hinges. A visit can be haunted by a sense of phoniness, hollowness. Who am I? Why am I here? Listening to my brother, answering him, but also fighting the voice that screams that none of this matters, none of this is worth shit. You missed your chance to put your money where your mouth is. A good day to die but you missed it. You let them win again. Humiliate you again. You're on your knees again, scrambling after scraps.

14    Sometimes we occupy one of the lawyer-client tables, but today a guard chases us away. Robby's had trouble with him before. I commit the guard's name to memory just in case. My personal shit list for close watching or revenge or whatever use it would serve if something suspicious happens to my brother. I consider making a fuss. After all, I'm a professional writer. Don't I have just as much right as a lawyer or social worker to the convenience of a table where I can set down the tools of my trade, where my brother and I can put a little distance between ourselves and the babble of twenty or thirty simultaneous conversations?

15    The guard's chest protrudes like there's compressed air instead of flesh inside the gray blouse of his uniform. A square head. Pale skin except on his cheeks, which are bluish and raw from razor burn. His mustache and short curly hair are meticulously groomed, too perfect to be real. The stylized hair of comic-book superheroes. A patch of blue darkness etched with symmetrical accent lines. His eyes avoid mine. He had spoken in a clipped, mechanical tone of voice. Not one man talking to another but a peremptory recital of rules droned at some abstraction in the middle distance where the guard's eyes focus while his lips move. I think, Nazi Gestapo Frankenstein robot . . . , but he's something worse. He's what he is and there's no way to get around that or for the moment get around him because he's entrenched in this no-man's-land and he is what he is and that's worse than any names I can call him. He's laying down the law and that's it. The law. No matter that all three tables are unoccupied. No matter that I tell him we've sat at them before. No matter that we'll

vacate if and when the lawyers need them. No matter that I might have a case, make a case that my profession, my status means something outside the walls. No matter, my pride and anger and barely concealed scorn. I move on. We obey because the guard's in power. Will remain in power when I have to leave and go about my business. Then he'll be free to take out on my brother whatever revenge he couldn't exact from me and my smart mouth. So I take low. Shake my head but stroll away (just enough nigger in my walk to tell the guard I know what he thinks of me but that I think infinitely less of him) toward the least crowded space in the row of benches against the wall.

16     Not much news to relate. Robby cares about family business and likes to keep up with who's doing what, when, how, etc., but he also treats the news objectively, cold-bloodedly. Family affairs have everything and nothing to do with him. He's in exile, powerless to influence what goes on outside the walls, so he maintains a studied detachment; he hears what I say and quickly mulls it over, buries the worrisome parts, grins at good news. When he comments on bad news it's usually a grunt, a nod, or a gesture with his hands that says all there is to say and says, A million words wouldn't make any difference, would they. Learning to isolate himself, to build walls within the walls enclosing him is a matter of survival. If he doesn't insulate himself against those things he can't change, if he can't discipline himself to ignore and forget, to narrow the range of his concerns to what he can immediately, practically effect, he'll go crazy. The one exception is freedom. Beneath whatever else Robby says or does or thinks, the dream of freedom pulses. The worst times, the lowest times are when the pulse seems extinguished. Like in the middle of the night, the hour of the wolf when even the joint is quiet and the earth stops spinning on its axis and he bursts from sleep, the deathly sleep that's the closest thing to mercy prison ever grants, starts from sleep and for a moment hears nothing. In the shadow of that absolute silence he can't imagine himself ever leaving prison alive. For hours, days, weeks, the mood of that moment can oppress him. He needs every ounce of willpower he possesses to pick up the pieces of his life, to animate them again with the hope that one day the arbitrary, bitter, little routines he manufactures to sustain himself will make sense because one day he'll be free.

17    I arrange my pens and yellow pad atop the table. But before we begin working on the book I tell Robby my sawing dream.

18    I am a man, myself but not myself. The man wakes up and can't see the stars. The smell of death surrounds him. Fifteen hundred other men sleep in the honeycomb of steel that is his home forever. The fitful stirrings, clattering bars, groaning, the sudden outcries of fear, rage, madness, and God knows what else are finally over at this hour of the night or morning as he lies in his cell listening to other men sleep. The monotonous sawing sound reminds him of the funny papers, the little cloud containing saw and log drawn above a character's head so you can see the sound of sleeping. Only the man doesn't see logs floating above the prisoner's heads. As he listens and shuts his eyes and gets as close to praying as he ever does anymore, praying for sleep, for blessed oblivion, the cartoon he imagines behind his closed eyes is himself sawing away the parts of his own body. Doggedly, without passion or haste, drawing a dull saw up and back, up and back through his limbs. Slices drop away on the concrete floor. The man is cutting himself to pieces, there is less of him every time he saws through a section. He is lopping off his own flesh and blood but works methodically, concentrating on the up-and-back motion of the saw. When there's nothing left, he'll be finished. He seems almost bored, almost asleep, ready to snore like the saw's snoring as it chews through his body.

19    Robby shakes his head and starts to say something but doesn't, and we both leave the dream alone. Pass on to the book, the tasks still to be accomplished.

20    Robby had said he liked what he'd seen of the first draft. Liked it fine, but something was missing. Trouble was, he hadn't been able to name the missing ingredient. I couldn't either but I knew I had to try and supply it. By the book's conclusion I wanted a whole, rounded portrait of my brother. I'd envisioned a climactic scene in the final section, an epiphany that would reveal Robby's character in a powerful burst of light and truth. As the first draft evolved, I seemed to settle for much less. One early reader had complained of a "sense of frustration . . . By the end of the book I want to know more about Robby than I actually know. I know a lot of facts about his life but most of his inner self escapes me." On target or not, the reaction of this early reader, coupled with Robby's feeling that something crucial was lacking, had destroyed any complacency I had

about the book's progress. I reread Robby's letters, returned to the books and articles that had informed my research into prisons and prisoners. I realized no apotheosis of Robby's character could occur in the final section because none had transpired in my dealings with my brother. The first draft had failed because it attempted to impose a dramatic shape on a relationship, on events and people too close to me to see in terms of beginning, middle, and end. My brother was in prison. A thousand books would not reduce his sentence one day. And the only denouement that might make sense of his story would be his release from prison. I'd been hoping to be a catalyst for change in the world upon which the book could conceivably have no effect at all. I'd been waiting to record dramatic, external changes in Robby's circumstances when what I should have been attuned to were the inner changes, his slow, internal adjustment day by day to an unbearable situation. The book was no powerful engine being constructed to set my brother free; it was dream, wish, song.

21     No, I could not create a man whose qualities were self-evident cause for returning him to the world of free people. Prison had changed my brother, not broken him, and therein lay the story. The changes were subtle, incremental; bit by bit he had been piecing himself together. He had not become a model human being with a cure for cancer at his fingertips if only the parole board would just give him a chance, turn him loose again on the streets of Homewood. The character traits that landed Robby in prison are the same ones that have allowed him to survive with dignity and pain and a sense of himself as infinitely better than the soulless drone prison demands he become. Robby knows his core is intact; his optimism, his intelligence, his capacity for love, his pride, his dream of making it big, becoming somebody special. And though these same qualities helped get him in trouble and could derail him again, I'm happy they are still there. I rejoice with him.

22     The problem with the first draft was my fear. I didn't let Robby speak for himself enough. I didn't have enough confidence in his words, his vision, his insights. I wanted to clean him up. Manufacture compelling before-and-after images. Which meant I made the bad too bad and good too good. I knew what I wanted; so, for fear I might not get what I needed, I didn't listen carefully, probe deeply enough. As I tried his story again I began to recognize patterns, a certain consistency in his responses, a basic impetuous

honesty that made him see himself and his world with unflinching clarity. He never stopped asking questions. He never allowed answers to stop him. The worst things he did followed from the same impulse as the best. He could be unbelievably dumb, corrupt, selfish, and destructive but those qualities could keep him down no more than his hope, optimism, his refusal to accept a dull, inferior portion could buoy him above the hell that engulfed black boys in the Homewood streets.

23      Robby watched it all. Ups and downs. Rises and falls. What was consistent was the watching, the consciousness, the vision in which he saw himself as counting, as being worth saving at any cost. If he had lost that vision, if he loses it now, then we will all matter a little less.

24      To repair the flawed first draft I had asked for more from Robby. He'd responded sporadically with poems, anecdotes, meditations on his time behind bars. What he was giving me helped me turn a corner. I was closer to him. I was beginning to understand what had been missing in the first version of his story. I was learning to respect my brother's touch, his vision. Learning what was at stake in this give-and-take between us, initiated by the idea of a book.

25      A letter from Robby had added this coda to Garth's story, the story he thought might be one place to begin telling his own:

> After Garth's funeral, me, Mike, and Cecil, our ladies, and Garth's lady sat in Mike's car and waited for all the other cars to leave. We weren't doing any talking, just crying and sniffling. It was raining outside and the silence was broken only by the pitter-patter of the rain on the car. Now I was always the oldest of our crew and Garth had always been my little brother though always taller. So when Mike finally started up the car the radio came on and a song by the group War was on the box. The name of the song was "Me and Baby Brother" and the chorus goes: "Me and baby brother used to run together. . . . Running over one another headed for the corner." It was like it was just for me. I sat there in the backseat with tears just running down my face.

26    His new girl friend Leslie claims Robby lives through the words of songs and movies. Robby admits maybe it's true. He's sent me the lyrics of a Sly and the Family Stone jam, "Family Affair." The song was popular at about the time Robby was breaking up with his first wife, Geraldine. For him the song says everything there is to say about that period in his life. Part of the magic's in the words, the line-by-line correspondence between what was happening to him and the situations and people the song described:

*Newlyweds a year ago but they're still*
*Checking each other*
*Nobody wants to blow*
*Nobody wants to be left out*
*You can't leave cause your heart is there.* . . .

But another part was the music itself, what transfigures the personal, the unique with universals of rhythm, tone, and harmony, what must always remain unspoken because words can't keep up with the flood of feeling, of experience music releases.

27    The music Robby loves is simple; the lyrics often seem sentimental, banal. Though rhythm and blues and rock 'n' roll are rooted in traditional African music, the soul sounds Robby listened to in the sixties had been heavily commercialized, exploited by whites. Fortunes were made by whites who produced, performed, wrote, and distributed this so-called black music. About the only thing whites didn't do to black music was destroy it. Miraculously, the best black singers and musicians transcended the destructive incursions on their turf. Afro-American musical styles passed through one more crucible and emerged on the other side modified externally but intact at the core. Robby could see himself, recognize his world in the music called soul.

28    Over 125 years before Robby discovered visions of himself reflected in "Family Affair," young Frederick Douglass learned in the music of fellow slaves truths about his life, about the ordeal of slavery and the capacity of the spirit to rise above it, truths that were articulated in the form of strange chants, cries, percussive clapping and stomping, call-and-response cadences created by black field

hands as they marched from one back-breaking job to another. "Their songs still follow me," Douglass later wrote; and certain songs continue to haunt my brother. Simple songs. Lyrics as uncomplicated, transparent as the poetry of the gospels and spirituals we sang in Homewood A.M.E. Zion church: *Let my people go. Farther along we'll understand why. Amazing Grace. How sweet the sound. One bright morning. His eye is on the sparrow so I know He watches me.*

29 The messages are simple. The mysteries they enfold are not. What Robby hears is the sound of what he has been, where he has been, the people he traveled with, the ones here, the ones there, the ones gone forever. The best, the authentic black music does not unravel the mysteries, but recalls them, gives them a particular form, a specific setting, attaches the mysteries to familiar words and ideas. Simple lyrics of certain songs follow us, haunt us because the words floating in the music are a way of eavesdropping on the mysteries, remembering the importance of who we are but also experiencing the immensity of Great Time and Great Space, the Infinite always at play around the edges of our lives.

30 *You are my sunshine, my only sunshine. You make me happy when skies are gray.* Our grandfather John French loved that song. Hummed it, crooned it high on Dago Red, beat out its rhythm on his knee, a table's edge, the bottom of a pot. *Froggy went a-courtin'* was another favorite, and we'd ride like Froggy jiggedy-jig, jiggedy-jig on Daddy John's thigh while he sang. Those songs had survived. John French found them and stored them and toted them on his journey from Culpepper, Virginia, to Pittsburgh, Pennsylvania, the place where we began to know him as our mother's father. He saved those songs and they documented his survival. All of that hovered in the words and music when he passed them on to us.

31 Here are some more of the lines Robby remembered from "Family Affair":

> *One child grows up to be somebody*
> *who just loves to learn.*
> *And the other child grows up to be*
> *somebody who just loves to burn*
> *Mom loves the both of them*
> *You see it in the blood*

*Both kids are good to Mom*
*Blood thicker than the mud . . .*
*It's a family affair.*

32    What do these words tell me about my brother? Why did he share them with me? One reason may be his dissatisfaction with the picture of him I'd drawn in the first draft of this book. There will necessarily be distance, vast discrepancy between any image I create and the mystery of all my brother is, was, can be. We both know that. And he'll never be satisfied, but he's giving me the benefit of the doubt. Not complaining overtly, but reminding me that there's more, much, much more to know, to learn. He's giving me a song, holding open a door on a world I can never enter. Robby can't carry me over to the other side, but he can crack the door and I can listen.

33    Robby refuses to be beaten down. Sly said in another song that everybody wants to be a star. That wish contains the best of us and the worst. The thrust of ego and selfishness, the striving to be better than we are. If Robby fell because the only stardom he could reasonably seek was stardom in crime, then that's wrong. It's wrong not because Robby wanted more but because society closed off every chance of getting more, except through crime. So I'm glad to see Robby's best (worst) parts have survived. Can't have one without the other.

34    I let Robby know I've rewritten the book, virtually from start to finish. Plenty of blurred, gray space, lots of unfilled gaps and unanswered questions and people to interview, but the overall design is clearer now. I'm trying to explain to Robby how I feel released rather than constrained by the new pattern beginning to emerge. The breakthrough came when I started to hear what was constant, persistent beneath the changes in his life. The book will work if the reader participates, begins to grasp what I have. I hadn't been listening closely enough, so I missed the story announcing itself. When I caught on, there I was, my listening, waiting self part of the story, listening, waiting for me.

35    Yet I remained apprehensive about the prison section of the book. Robby wouldn't be able to help me as much in this last section as he had with the others. The method we'd evolved was this: Robby would tell his stories. I'd listen, take notes, reconstruct the

episodes after I'd allowed them time to sink in, then check my version with Rob to determine if it sounded right to him. Letters and talk about what I'd written would continue until we were both satisfied. We'd had lots of practice performing that operation and I was beginning to feel a measure of confidence in the results it eventually produced. "Doing Time" was a different matter. The book would end with this section. Since I was writing the book, one way or another I'd be on center stage. Not only would the prison section have to pull together many loose ends, but new material had to surface and be resolved. Aside from logical and aesthetic considerations, finishing the book as object, completing the performance, there was the business of both rendering and closing down the special relationship between my brother and myself that writing the book had precipitated. All the questions I'd decided to finesse or sidestep or just shrug off in order to get on with writing would now return, some in the form of issues to be addressed in concluding the book, some as practical dilemmas in the world outside the book, the world that had continued to chug along while I wrote.

Robby was still a prisoner. He was inside and I was outside. Success, fame, ten million readers wouldn't change that. The book, whether it flopped or became a best-seller, would belong to the world beyond the prison walls. Ironically, it would validate the power of the walls, confirm the distance between what transpired inside and outside. Robby's story would be "out there," but he'd still be locked up. Despite my attempts to identify with my brother, to reach him and share his troubles, the fact was, I remained on the outside. With the book. Though I never intended to steal his story, to appropriate it or exploit it, in a sense that's what would happen once the book was published.

His story would be out there in a world that ignored his existence. It could be put to whatever uses people chose. Of course I was hoping Robby would benefit from a book written about him, but the possible benefits did not alter the fact that imprisonment profoundly alienated him from the finished product of our collaboration.

Simple things like sharing financial profits could be handled; but how could I insure a return on the emotional investment my brother had made? Once I'd gotten the book I'd come for, would I be able to sustain the bond that had grown between us? Would I continue to listen with the same attention to his stories? Would he still possess a story? Much of what he'd entrusted to me had nothing to do with putting a book together. Had I identified with him because I discovered that was the best way to write the book? Would the identification I'd achieved become a burden, too intense, too pressurized to survive once the book was completed? Was the whole thing between us about a book or had something finer, truer been created? And even if a finer, truer thing had come into being, would it be shattered by the noisy explosion (or dull thud) of the book's appearance in the world beyond walls?

39      Some of these questions could be asked outright. Others were too intimidating, too close to the bone to raise with my brother. Yet we had to deal with all of them. In the world and in the prison section. The book, if there was to be a book, must end, must become in some senses an artifact. I wanted to finish it but I didn't want to let it go. I might be losing much more than a book.

40      The fears I could put into words I tried to share with Robby. He nodded, clenched and unclenched his big hands, smiled at the funny parts, the blackly comic pratfalls and cul de sacs neither of us nor anybody in the world can avoid. Yeah, shit's gon hit the fan. Yeah, sounds like it might get rough . . . but then again . . . what can you do but do? Many of my worries clearly were not his. I was the writer, that was *my* kitchen, *my* heat. He'd thought about some of the stuff worrying me but I could tell he hadn't spent lots of time fretting over it. And wouldn't. Many of the troubles I anticipated were too far down the line to tease out Robby's concern. In prison he had learned to walk a very fine line. On one side of the line was the minute-by-minute, day-by-day struggle for survival to which he must devote his undivided attention. On the other side his vision of something better, a life outside the walls, an existence he could conceive only if he allowed himself the luxury of imagination, of formulating plans in a future divorced from his present circumstances. The line was thin, was perilous because any energy he squandered on envisioning the future was time away, a lapse in the eternal vigilance he must maintain to stay alive in his cage. Yet the struggle to survive, the heightened awareness he must sustain to get through each moment, each day made no sense unless his efforts were buying something other than more chunks of prison routine. And plans for the future were pipe dreams unless he could convince himself he

possessed the stamina and determination to make it step by step through the withering prison regimen. These options, realities, consequences defined the straight and narrow path Robby was forced to tread. Like Orpheus ascending from Hades or Ulysses chained to the mast or a runaway slave abandoning his family and fleeing toward the North Star, my brother knew the only way he might get what he desperately wanted was to turn his back on it, pretend it didn't exist.

41   Walking the line, leaning neither too far to the left nor too far to the right, balancing, always balancing the pulls of heart and head in one direction against the tugs wrenching him in the other—that was Robby's unbearable burden, made more unbearable because to escape it all he had to do was surrender, tilt one way or the other, and let the weight on his shoulders drag him down.

42   The source of my brother's strength was a mystery to me. When I put myself in his shoes, tried to imagine how I'd cope if I were sentenced to life imprisonment, I couldn't conceive of any place inside myself from which I could draw the courage and dignity he displayed. In prison Robby had achieved an inner calm, a degree of self-sufficiency and self-reliance never apparent when he was running the streets. I didn't know many people, inside or out, who carried themselves the way he did now. Like my mother, he'd grown accustomed to what was unbearable, had named it, tamed it. He'd fallen, but he'd found the strength to rise again. Inch by inch, hand over hand, he'd pulled himself up on a vine he'd never known was there, a vine still invisible to me. I knew the vine was real because I'd watched my brother grasp it, because I could feel its absence in the untested air when I thought of myself in his situation. To discover the source of my brother's strength I found myself comparing what I'd accomplished outside the walls with what he'd managed inside. The comparison made me uncomfortable.

43   I didn't envy my brother. I'd learned enough about the hell of prison life not to mistake what I was feeling for envy. No, I wouldn't trade my problems for his. I'd take my chances on the outside. Yet something like envy was stirring. Worse than envy. The ancient insatiability of ego kicking up. Why hadn't I ever been able to acknowledge a talent, success, or capacity in another person without

feeling that person's accomplishment either diminished me or pointed to some crucial deficiency in my constitution? What compound of greed, insecurity, and anger forced me always to compare, compete? Why couldn't I just leave myself out of it and celebrate Robby's willpower, his grace under pressure? Why couldn't I simply applaud and be grateful for whatever transformation of self he'd performed? Were my visits to prison about freeing him or freeing myself from the doubt that perhaps, after all, in spite of it all, maybe my brother has done more with his life than I've done with mine. Maybe he's the better man and maybe the only way I can face that truth about him, about myself, is to demystify the secret of his survival. Maybe I'm inside West Pen to warm myself by his fire, to steal it. Perhaps in my heart of hearts or, better, my ego of egos, I don't really want to tear down the walls, but tear my brother down, bring him back to the soft, uncertain ground where my feet are planted.

44     If somebody has sung the praises of a book or movie, I go in looking for flaws, weaknesses. No matter how good these books or movies, my pleasure is never unalloyed because I'm searching for the bad parts, groping for them even when they're not there; so I usually come away satisfied by my dissatisfaction. I'm stuck with a belief that nothing can stand too close an examination. The times when I experience the world as joy, as song, some part of me insists even in the midst of the joy, the song, that these moments will pass and nothing, nothing promises they will ever come again. My world is fallen. It's best to be suspicious, not to trust anything, anyone too far. Including myself. Especially the treacherous, layered reality of being whatever I think I am at a given moment. It's a fallen world. My brother is rising from the ashes but because he is my brother, another fall is as certain as this rising and my particular burden is to see both always. I can't help it.

45     Does what he's achieved in the narrow confines of a cell mock the cage I call freedom? What would I do in his place? How would I act? Are the walls between us permanent? Do we need them, want them? Is there a better place without barred windows and steel doors and locked cells where there's room for both of us, all of us?

46     What it comes down to is saying yes. Yes to the blood making us brothers. Blood bonding us, constraining us to the unspoken faith that I'm trying to do my best and he's trying to do his best but

nothing we do can insure the worst won't happen so we keep at it, as best we can, doing the book and hoping it will turn out okay.

47 He's been thinking a lot about the time on the road, the three months as a fugitive when he and his partners crisscrossed the country, playing hide and seek with the law. He's tried to write some of it down but he's been too busy. Too much's been happening. School. He'll graduate in January. A little ceremony for the few guys who made it all the way through the program. An associate degree in engineering technology and three certificates. Rough. Real rough. The math he'd never had in high school. The slow grind of study. Hours relearning to be a student. Learning to take the whole business seriously while you hear the madness of the prison constantly boiling outside your cell. But I'm gon get it, Bruh. Few more weeks. These last exams kicking my ass but I'm gon get it. Most the fellows dropped out. Only three of us completed the program. It'll look good on my record, too. But I ain't had time to do nothing else. Them books you sent. I really enjoy reading them but lately I ain't been doing nothing but studying.

## Discussion Questions

1. What is Wideman's purpose in devoting an entire paragraph (paragraph 1) to define the word *unbearable*? How convincing do you find his definition? Explain.
2. Wideman frequently uses sentence fragments in his essay. Explain why you think he uses this stylistic technique and what impact it has on the writing.
3. What is Wideman referring to in paragraph 3 when he states, "Nothing changes. Nothing remains the same"?
4. Wideman claims that Robby's calmness is a mystery to him. How do you account for Robby's calmness?
5. What do you learn about Wideman's character from this essay? Cite specific passages that contribute to your response.
6. In small groups, discuss what emotion—and for whom—Wideman wants to evoke in his readers.

# Writing Assignments

1. Imagine you are Robby and, in a letter to Wideman, convey your reactions to the essay.
2. In an essay, describe a time when you felt protective of a sibling or a friend's sibling. What prompted your feelings and behavior? What did you learn about the relationship and about yourself?
3. Is it harder for brothers to have a close relationship than it is for sisters? Write a paper that explores this question.

# A Brother's Murder

## BRENT STAPLES

Brent Staples (b. 1951) grew up in Chester, Pennsylvania. He
earned his B.A. from Widener College in 1973 and his Ph.D. from
the University of Chicago in 1982. Staples began his writing career
as a reporter for the *Chicago-Sun Times* before joining the staff of
*The New York Times,* where he has been the first assistant metropolitan editor since 1985. In 1994, Staples wrote *Parallel Time:
Growing Up in Black and White,* which chronicles his experiences as
a child, adolescent, and adult. His main focus in that book, as well
as in his other essays, is growing up as an African American in a
white world. The book centers around the murder of Staples's
younger brother Blake, a twenty-two-year-old drug dealer. Staples
tries to reconcile his own life, one far different from his brother's,
with his unsuccessful attempts to reach Blake. The following essay,
published in *The New York Times Magazine* in 1986, not only
describes an encounter with his brother but emerges as a tribute to
him as well. By reporting on his brother's life and their relationship,
Staples is motivated to analyze his own life.

1    It has been more than two years since my telephone rang with the news that my younger brother Blake—just 22 years old—had been murdered. The young man who killed him was only 24. Wearing a ski mask, he emerged from a car, fired six times at close range with a massive .44 Magnum, then fled. The two had once been inseparable friends. A senseless rivalry—beginning, I think, with an argument over a girlfriend—escalated from posturing, to threats, to violence, to murder. The way the two were living, death could have come to either of them from anywhere. In fact, the assailant had already survived multiple gunshot wounds from an incident much like the one in which my brother lost his life.

2    As I wept for Blake I felt wrenched backward into events and circumstances that had seemed light-years gone. Though a decade apart, we both were raised in Chester, Pa., an angry, heavily black, heavily poor, industrial city southwest of Philadelphia. There, in the 1960's, I was introduced to mortality, not by the old and failing, but by beautiful young men who lay wrecked after sudden explosions of violence. The first, I remember from my 14th year—Johnny, brash lover of fast cars, stabbed to death two doors from my house in a fight over a pool game. The next year, my teen-age cousin, Wesley, whom I loved very much, was shot dead. The summers blur. Milton, an angry young neighbor, shot a crosstown rival, wounding him badly. William, another teen-age neighbor, took a shotgun blast to the shoulder in some urban drama and displayed his bandages proudly. His brother, Leonard, severely beaten, lost an eye and donned a black patch. It went on.

3    I recall not long before I left for college, two local Vietnam veterans—one from the Marines, one from the Army—arguing fiercely, nearly at blows about which outfit had done the most in the war. The most killing, they meant. Not much later, I read a magazine article that set that dispute in a context. In the story, a noncommissioned officer—a sergeant, I believe—said he would pass up any number of affluent, suburban-born recruits to get hard-core soldiers from the inner city. They jumped into the rice paddies with "their manhood on their sleeves," I believe he said. These two items—the veterans arguing and the sergeant's words—still characterize for me the circumstances under which black men in their teens and 20's kill one another with such frequency. With a touchy paranoia born of living battered lives, they are desperate to

be *real* men. Killing is only *machismo* taken to the extreme. Incursions to be punished by death were many and minor, and they remain so: they include stepping on the wrong toe, literally; cheating in a drug deal; simply saying "I dare you" to someone holding a gun; crossing territorial lines in a gang dispute. My brother grew up to wear his manhood on his sleeve. And when he died, he was in that group—black, male and in its teens and early 20's—that is far and away the most likely to murder or be murdered.

4    I left the East Coast after college, spent the mid- and late-1970's in Chicago as a graduate student, taught for a time, then became a journalist. Within 10 years of leaving my hometown, I was overeducated and "upwardly mobile," ensconced on a quiet, tree-lined street where voices raised in anger were scarcely ever heard. The telephone, like some grim umbilical, kept me connected to the old world with news of deaths, imprisonings and misfortune. I felt emotionally beaten up. Perhaps to protect myself, I added a psychological dimension to the physical distance I had already achieved. I rarely visited my hometown. I shut it out.

5    As I fled the past, so Blake embraced it. On Christmas of 1983, I traveled from Chicago to a black section of Roanoke, Va., where he then lived. The desolate public housing projects, the hopeless, idle young men crashing against one another—these reminded me of the embittered town we'd grown up in. It was a place where once I would have been comfortable, or at least sure of myself. Now, hearing of my brother's forays into crime, his scrapes with police and street thugs, I was scared, unsteady on foreign terrain.

6    I saw that Blake's romance with the street life and the hustler image had flowered dangerously. One evening that late December, standing in some Roanoke dive among drug dealers and grim, hair-trigger losers, I told him I feared for his life. He had affected the image of the tough he wanted to be. But behind the dark glasses and the swagger, I glimpsed the baby-faced toddler I'd once watched over. I nearly wept. I wanted desperately for him to live. The young think themselves immortal, and a dangerous light shone in his eyes as he spoke laughingly of making fools of the policemen who had raided his apartment looking for drugs. He cried out as I took his right hand. A line of stitches lay between the thumb and index fin-

ger. Kickback from a shotgun, he explained, nothing serious. Gunplay had become part of his life.

7    I lacked the language simply to say: Thousands have lived this for you and died. I fought the urge to lift him bodily and shake him. This place and the way you are living smells of death to me, I said. Take some time away, I said. Let's go downtown tomorrow and buy a plane ticket anywhere, take a bus trip, anything to get away and cool things off. He took my alarm casually. We arranged to meet the following night—an appointment he would not keep. We embraced as though through glass. I drove away.

8    As I stood in my apartment in Chicago holding the receiver that evening in February 1984, I felt as though part of my soul had been cut away. I questioned myself then, and I still do. Did I not reach back soon or earnestly enough for him? For weeks I awoke crying from a recurrent dream in which I chased him, urgently trying to get him to read a document I had, as though reading it would protect him from what had happened in waking life. His eyes shining like black diamonds, he smiled and danced just beyond my grasp. When I reached for him, I caught only the space where he had been.

## Discussion Questions

1. In small groups, discuss how close Staples was to his brother.
2. Why does Staples recount the deaths of people other than his brother in paragraph 2, and what does he mean when he writes, "It went on"?
3. Explain the meaning of Staples's statement in paragraph 3: "My brother grew up to wear his manhood on his sleeve."
4. How do you account for Staples's being unable to tell his brother what he was thinking (paragraph 7)?
5. Explain the symbolism of Staples's dream.
6. Throughout the essay, Staples uses analogies and images to convey his point. Select three that you find especially powerful and explain why they are an effective rhetorical device.
7. Did Staples feel guilty about his brother's death? Why?

# Writing Assignments

1. Imagine you are Staples and write a letter to Blake in which you explain the reasons for your behavior toward him.
2. To what extent should a person be his/her brother's/sister's keeper? Write a paper that supports your stance.
3. Write an essay describing an incident with a sibling or an imaginary sibling that illustrates "hindsight is 20/20."
4. Compare Staples's feelings toward Blake with Wideman's toward Robby. In an essay, describe how the two relationships are similar though the circumstances surrounding them are different.

# CLASSIC ESSAYS ON

# Mothers and Fathers

# My Father

## DORIS LESSING

Doris Lessing (b. 1919) was born in Persia to British parents and educated in Salisbury, Southern Rhodesia. After spending twenty-five years in South Africa, she moved to England in 1949. Lessing worked as a nursemaid, secretary, and typist before becoming a full-time writer. Primarily a fiction writer, Lessing is the author of *The Grass Is Singing* (1950), *A Proper Marriage* (1954), *Retreat to Innocence* (1956), *The Golden Notebook* (1962), *Landlocked* (1965), *The Four-Gated City* (1969), *Briefing for a Descent into Hell* (1971), *The Summer before the Dark* (1973), *Memoirs of a Survivor* (1974), *The Good Terrorist* (1986), and *The Fifth Child* (1988). Her books of nonfiction include *Going Home* (1957), *In Pursuit of the English* (1961), *Particularly Cats* (1967), *Prisons We Choose to Live Inside* (1967), *A Small Personal Voice: Essays, Reviews, Interviews* (1975), *The Wind Blows Away Our Words* (1987), *Under My Skin* (1994), and *Love, Again* (1996). Lessing is the recipient of numerous awards, including the Somerset Maugham Award in 1954, the Austrian State Prize for European Literature in 1981, the Shakespeare Prize in 1982, W. H. Smith Literary Award in 1986, Palermo Prize in 1987, L.A. Times Book Prize in 1995, and the James Tait Memorial Prize in 1995. In the following essay, written in 1963 and published in *A Small Personal Voice*, Lessing undertakes the difficult task of writing a sensitive and loving portrait of a father she grew to know "when his best years were over."

1    We use our parents like recurring dreams, to be entered into
when needed; they are always there for love or for hate; but it occurs
to me that I was not always there for my father. I've written about
him before, but novels, stories, don't have to be "true." Writing this
article is difficult because it has to be "true." I knew him when his
best years were over.

2    There are photographs of him. The largest is of an officer in the
1914–18 war. A new uniform—buttoned, badged, strapped,
tabbed—confines a handsome, dark young man who holds himself
stiffly to confront what he certainly thought of as his duty. His eyes
are steady, serious, and responsible, and show no signs of what he
became later. A photograph at sixteen is of a dark, introspective
youth with the same intent eyes. But it is his mouth you notice—a
heavily-jutting upper lip contradicts the rest of a regular face. His
moustache was to hide it: "Had to do something—a damned fleshy
mouth. Always made me uncomfortable, that mouth of mine."

3    Earlier a baby (eyes already alert) appears in a lace waterfall that
cascades from the pillowy bosom of a fat, plain woman to her feet.
It is the face of a head cook. "Lord, but my mother was a practical
female—almost as bad as you!" as he used to say, or throw at my
mother in moments of exasperation. Beside her stands, or droops,
arms dangling, his father, the source of the dark, arresting eyes, but
otherwise masked by a long beard.

4    The birth certificate says: Born 3rd August, 1886, Walton Villa,
Creffield Road, S. Mary at the Wall, R.S.D. Name, Alfred Cook.
Name and surname of Father: Alfred Cook Tayler. Name and
maiden name of Mother: Caroline May Batley. Rank or Profession:
Bank Clerk. Colchester, Essex.

5    They were very poor. Clothes and boots were a problem. They
"made their own amusements." Books were mostly the Bible and
The Pilgrim's Progress. Every Saturday night they bathed in a hip-
bath in front of the kitchen fire. No servants. Church three times on
Sundays. "Lord, when I think of those Sundays! I dreaded them all
week, like a nightmare coming at you full tilt and no escape." But he
rabbited with ferrets along the lanes and fields, bird-nested, stole
fruit, picked nuts and mushrooms, paid visits to the blacksmith and
the mill and rode a farmer's carthorse.

6    They ate economically, but when he got diabetes in his forties
and subsisted on lean meat and lettuce leaves, he remembered suet

puddings, treacle puddings, raisin and currant puddings, steak and kidney puddings, bread and butter pudding, "batter cooked in the gravy with the meat," potato cake, plum cake, butter cake, porridge with treacle, fruit tarts and pies, brawn, pig's trotters and pig's cheek and homesmoked ham and sausages. And "lashings of fresh butter and cream and eggs." He wondered if this diet had produced the diabetes, but said it was worth it.

7   There was an elder brother described by my father as: "Too damned clever by half. One of those quick, clever brains. Now I've always had a slow brain, but I get there in the end, damn it!"

8   The brothers went to a local school and the elder did well, but my father was beaten for being slow. They both became bank clerks in, I think, the Westminster Bank, and one must have found it congenial, for he became a manager, the "rich brother," who had cars and even a yacht. But my father did not like it, though he was conscientious. For instance, he changed his writing, letter by letter, because a senior criticised it. I never saw his unregenerate hand, but the one he created was elegant, spiky, careful. Did this mean he created a new personality for himself, hiding one he did not like, as he hid his "damned fleshy mouth"? I don't know.

9   Nor do I know when he left home to live in Luton or why. He found family life too narrow? A safe guess—he found everything too narrow. His mother was too down-to-earth? He had to get away from his clever elder brother?

10   Being a young man in Luton was the best part of his life. It ended in 1914, so he had a decade of happiness. His reminiscences of it were all of pleasure, the delight of physical movement, of dancing in particular. All his girls were "a beautiful dancer, light as a feather." He played billiards and ping-pong (both for his country); he swam, boated, played cricket and football, went to picnics and horse races, sang at musical evenings. One family of a mother and two daughters treated him "like a son only better. I didn't know whether I was in love with the mother or the daughters, but oh I did love going there; we had such good times." He was engaged to one daughter, then, for a time, to the other. An engagement was broken off because she was rude to a waiter. "I could not marry a woman who allowed herself to insult someone who was defenseless." He used to say to my wryly smiling mother: "Just as well I didn't marry either of them; they would never have stuck it out the way you have, old girl."

11   Just before he died he told me he had dreamed he was standing in a kitchen on a very high mountain holding X in his arms. "Ah, yes, that's what I've missed in my life. Now don't you let yourself be cheated out of life by the old dears. They take all the colour out of everything if you let them."

12   But in that decade—"I'd walk 10, 15 miles to a dance two or three times a week and think nothing of it. Then I'd dance every dance and walk home again over the fields. Sometimes it was moonlight, but I liked the snow best, all crisp and fresh. I loved walking back and getting into my digs just as the sun was rising. My little dog was so happy to see me, and I'd feed her, and make myself porridge and tea, then I'd wash and shave and go off to work."

13   The boy who was beaten at school, who went too much to church, who carried the fear of poverty all his life, but who nevertheless was filled with the memories of country pleasures; the young bank clerk who worked such long hours for so little money, but who danced, sang, played, flirted—this naturally vigorous, sensuous being was killed in 1914, 1915, 1916. I think the best of my father died in that war, that his spirit was crippled by it. The people I've met, particularly the women, who knew him young, speak of his high spirits, his energy, his enjoyment of life. Also of his kindness, his compassion and—a word that keeps recurring—his wisdom. "Even when he was just a boy he understood things that you'd think even an old man would find it easy to condemn." I do not think these people would have easily recognised the ill, irritable, abstracted, hypochondriac man I knew.

14   He "joined up" as an ordinary soldier out of a characteristically quirky scruple: it wasn't right to enjoy officers' privileges when the Tommies had such a bad time. But he could not stick the communal latrines, the obligatory drinking, the collective visits to brothels, the jokes about girls. So next time he was offered a commission he took it.

15   His childhood and young man's memories, kept fluid, were added to, grew, as living memories do. But his war memories were congealed in stories that he told again and again, with the same words and gestures, in stereotyped phrases. They were anonymous, general, as if they had come out of a communal war memoir. He met a German in no-man's-land, but both slowly lowered their rifles and smiled and walked away. The Tommies were the salt of the earth, the

British fighting men the best in the world. He had never known such comradeship. A certain brutal officer was shot in a sortie by his men, but the other officers, recognising rough justice, said nothing. He had known men intimately who saw the Angels at Mons. He wished he could force all the generals on both sides into the trenches for just one day, to see what the common soldiers endured . . . *that* would have ended the war at once.

16    There was an undercurrent of memories, dreams, and emotions much deeper, more personal. This dark region in him, fate-ruled, where nothing was true but horror, was expressed inarticulately, in brief, bitter exclamations or phrases of rage, incredulity, betrayal. The men who went to fight in that war believed it when they said it was to end war. My father believed it. And he was never able to reconcile his belief in his country with his anger at the cynicism of its leaders. And the anger, the sense of betrayal, strengthened as he grew old and ill.

17    But in 1914 he was naive, the German atrocities in Belgium inflamed him, and he enlisted out of idealism, although he knew he would have a hard time. He knew because a fortuneteller told him. (He could be described as uncritically superstitious or as psychically gifted.) He would be in great danger twice, yet not die—he was being protected by a famous soldier who was his ancestor. "And sure enough, later I heard from the Little Aunties that the church records showed we were descended the backstairs way from the Duke of Wellington, or was it Marlborough? Damn it, I forget. But one of them would be beside me all through the war, she said." (He was romantic, not only about this solicitous ghost, but also about being a descendant of the Huguenots, on the strength of the "e" in Tayler; and about "the wild blood" in his veins from a great uncle who, sent unjustly to prison for smuggling, came out of a ten-year sentence and earned it, very efficiently, along the coasts of Cornwall until he died.)

18    The luckiest thing that ever happened to my father, he said, was getting his leg shattered by shrapnel ten days before Passchendaele. His whole company was killed. He knew he was going to be wounded because of the fortuneteller, who had said he would know. "I did not understand what she meant, but both times in the trenches, first when my appendix burst and I nearly died, and then just before Passchendaele, I felt for some days as if a thick, black vel-

vet pall was settled over me. I can't tell you what it was like. Oh, it was awful, awful, and the second time it was so bad I wrote to the old people and told them I was going to be killed."

19    His leg was cut off at mid-thigh, he was shell-shocked, he was very ill for many months, with a prolonged depression afterwards. "You should always remember that sometimes people are all seething underneath. You don't know what terrible things people have to fight against. You should look at a person's eyes, that's how you tell. . . . When I was like that, after I lost my leg, I went to a nice doctor man and said I was going mad, but he said, don't worry, everyone locks up things like that. You don't know—horrible, horrible, awful things. I was afraid of myself, of what I used to dream. I wasn't myself at all."

20    In the Royal Free Hospital was my mother, Sister McVeagh. He married his nurse which, as they both said often enough (though in different tones of voice), was just as well. That was 1919. He could not face being a bank clerk in England, he said, not after the trenches. Besides, England was too narrow and conventional. Besides, the civilians did not know what the soldiers had suffered, they didn't want to know, and now it wasn't done even to remember "The Great Unmentionable." He went off to the Imperial Bank of Persia, in which country I was born.

21    The house was beautiful, with great stone-floored high-ceilinged rooms whose windows showed ranges of snow-streaked mountains. The gardens were full of roses, jasmine, pomegranates, walnuts, Kermanshah he spoke of with liking, but soon they went to Teheran, populous with "Embassy people," and my gregarious mother created a lively social life about which he was irritable even in recollection.

22    Irritableness—that note was first struck here, about Persia. He did not like, he said, "the graft and the corruption." But here it is time to try and describe something difficult—how a man's good qualities can also be his bad ones, or if not bad, a danger to him.

23    My father was honourable—he always knew exactly what that word meant. He had integrity. His "one does not do that sort of thing," his "no, it is *not* right," sounded throughout my childhood and were final for all of us. I am sure it was true he wanted to leave Persia because of "the corruption." But it was also because he was already unconsciously longing for something freer, because as a

bank official he could not let go into the dream-logged personality that was waiting for him. And later in Rhodesia, too, what was best in him was also what prevented him from shaking away the shadows: it was always in the name of honesty or decency that he refused to take this step or that out of the slow decay of the family's fortunes.

24    In 1925 there was leave from Persia. That year in London there was an Empire Exhibition, and on the Southern Rhodesian stand some very fine maize cobs and a poster saying that fortunes could be made on maize at 25/-a bag. So on an impulse, turning his back forever on England, washing his hands of the corruption of the East, my father collected all his capital, £800, I think, while my mother packed curtains from Liberty's, clothes from Harrods, visiting cards, a piano, Persian rugs, a governess and two small children.

25    Soon, there was my father in a cigar-shaped house of thatch and mud on the top of a kopje that overlooked in all directions a great system of mountains, rivers, valleys, while overhead the sky arched from horizon to empty horizon. This was a couple of hundred miles south from the Zambesi, a hundred or so west from Mozambique, in the district of Banket, so called because certain of its reefs were of the same formation as those called *banket* on the Rand. Lomagundi—gold country, tobacco country, maize country—wild, almost empty. (The Africans had been turned off it into reserves.) Our neighbours were four, five, seven miles off. In front of the house . . . no neighbours, nothing; no farms, just wild bush with two rivers but no fences to the mountains seven miles away. And beyond these mountains and bush again to the Portuguese border, over which "our boys" used to escape when wanted by the police for pass or other offences.

26    And then? There was bad luck. For instance, the price of maize dropped from 25/- to 9/- a bag. The seasons were bad, prices bad, crops failed. This was the sort of thing that made it impossible for him ever to "get off the farm," which, he agreed with my mother, was what he most wanted to do.

27    It was an absurd country, he said. A man could "own" a farm for years that was totally mortgaged to the Government and run from the Land Bank, meanwhile employing half-a-hundred Africans at 12/-a month and none of them knew how to do a day's work. Why, two farm labourers from Europe could do in a day what twenty of these ignorant black savages would take a week to do. (Yet he was proud

that he had a name as a just employer, that he gave "a square deal.") Things got worse. A fortuneteller had told him that her heart ached when she saw the misery ahead for my father: this was the misery.

28 But it was my mother who suffered. After a period of neurotic illness, which was a protest against her situation, she became brave and resourceful. But she never saw that her husband was not living in a real world, that he had made a captive of her common sense. We were always about to "get off the farm." A miracle would do it—a sweepstake, a goldmine, a legacy. And then? What a question! We would go to England where life would be normal with people coming in for musical evenings and nice supper parties at the Trocadero after a show. Poor woman, for the twenty years we were on the farm, she waited for when life would begin for her and for her children, for she never understood that what was a calamity for her was for them a blessing.

29 Meanwhile my father sank towards his death (at 61). Everything changed in him. He had been a dandy and fastidious, now he hated to change out of shabby khaki. He had been sociable, now he was misanthropic. His body's disorders—soon diabetes and all kinds of stomach ailments—dominated him. He was brave about his wooden leg, and even went down mine shafts and climbed trees with it, but he walked clumsily and it irked him badly. He greyed fast, and slept more in the day, but would be awake half the night pondering about. . . .

30 It could be gold divining. For ten years he experimented on private theories to do with the attractions and repulsions of metals. His whole soul went into it but his theories were wrong or he was *unlucky*—after all, if he had found a mine he would have had to leave the farm. It could be the relation between the minerals of the earth and of the moon; his decision to make infusions of all the plants on the farm and drink them himself in the interests of science; the criminal folly of the British Government in not realising that the Germans and the Russians were conspiring as Anti-Christ to . . . the inevitability of war because no one would listen to Churchill, but it would be all right because God (by then he was a British Israelite) had destined Britain to rule the world; a prophecy said 10 million dead would surround Jerusalem—how would the corpses be cleared away?; people who wished to abolish flogging should be flogged; the natives understood nothing but a good beating; hanging must not be abolished because the Old Testament said "an eye for an eye and a tooth for a tooth. . . ."

31    Yet, as this side of him darkened, so that it seemed all his thoughts were of violence, illness, war, still no one dared to make an unkind comment in his presence or to gossip. Criticism of people, particularly of women, made him more and more uncomfortable till at last he burst out with: "It's all very well, but no one has the right to say that about another person."

32    In Africa, when the sun goes down, the stars spring up, all of them in their expected places, glittering and moving. In the rainy season, the sky flashed and thundered. In the dry season, the great dark hollow of night was lit by veld fires: the mountains burned through September and October in chains of red fire. Every night my father took out his chair to watch the sky and the mountains, smoking, silent, a thin shabby fly-away figure under the stars. "Makes you think—there are so many worlds up there, wouldn't really matter if we did blow ourselves up—plenty more where we came from."

33    The Second World War, so long foreseen by him, was a bad time. His son was in the Navy and in danger, and his daughter a sorrow to him. He became very ill. More and more often it was necessary to drive him into Salisbury with him in a coma, or in danger of one, on the back seat. My mother moved him into a pretty little suburban house in town near the hospitals, where he took to his bed and a couple of years later died. For the most part he was unconscious under drugs. When awake he talked obsessively (a tongue licking a nagging sore place) about "the old war." Or he remembered his youth. "I've been dreaming—Lord, to see those horses come lickety-split down the course with their necks stretched out and the sun on their coats and everyone shouting. . . . I've been dreaming how I walked along the river in the mist as the sun was rising. . . . Lord, lord, lord, what a time that was, what good times we all had then, before the old war."

## Discussion Questions

1. What do you think Lessing means when she writes in the first paragraph, "We use our parents like recurring dreams . . ."?
2. Why is the first sentence an appropriate opening line for the essay? Explain.

3. What details are most successful in revealing Lessing's father? Cite specific lines.

4. Explain what Lessing means in paragraph 13 when she writes ". . . this naturally vigorous, sensuous being was killed in 1914, 1915, 1916."

5. Although this essay is about her father, Lessing also reveals details about herself. Characterize Lessing from these details.

6. In what way can the war in which Lessing's father fought be seen as a character in her essay? Explain.

7. In small groups, discuss anything you would like to know more about Lessing's father that she omits in her portrait.

## Writing Assignments

1. Imagine you are Lessing's father. Write a letter to your daughter that reports on the most significant events of your life.

2. Write an essay that vividly describes a family member, as Lessing did in this essay.

3. In a paper, examine the inherent difficulties of writing about people with whom you are close. How do you think writers, such as Lessing, confront such problems?

# Finding
# a Voice

## EUDORA
## WELTY

Eudora Welty was born in Mississippi in 1909 and received her edu-
cation at the University of Wisconsin and the Columbia Business
School. She began her career as a journalist and copywriter, and during the Great Depression she worked for the Works Progress
Administration as a writer and photographer. She later wrote stories
and novels about the people she met in Mississippi during the
Depression. The recipient of a Pulitzer Prize, a PEN/Malamud
Award, and the National Endowment for the Humanities Frankel
Prize, Welty is the author of the novels *The Robber Bridegroom*
(1942), *Delta Wedding* (1946), and *The Optimist's Daughter*
(1972). Her stories are collected in *Thirteen Stories* (1965), and in
*The Collected Stories of Eudora Welty* (1980). *The Eye of the Story*
(1978) is a collection of Welty's literary nonfiction. Welty's evocative
portrayal of characters and the Southern experience has earned her
the reputation as one of the leading contemporary American fiction
writers of the South. Welty's nonfiction pieces are reminiscent of her
stories: they often use narration as a way to present her ideas. In *One
Writer's Beginnings* (1984), a series of lectures originally presented at
Harvard University in 1983, she details the people and events that
influenced her life as a writer. The following selection, from that
book, describes the powerful impact Welty's parents had on her life.

1     I never saw until after he was dead a small keepsake book given to my father in his early childhood. On one page was a message of one sentence written to him by his mother on April 15, 1886. The date is the day of her death. "My dearest Webbie: I want you to be a good boy and to meet me in heaven. Your loving Mother." Webb was his middle name—her maiden name. She always called him by it. He was seven years old, her only child.

2     He had other messages in his little book to keep and read over to himself. "May your life, though short, be pleasant / As a warm and melting day" is from "Dr. Armstrong," and as it follows his mother's message may have been entered on the same day. Another entry reads: "Dear Webbie, if God send thee a cross, take it up willingly and follow Him. If it be light, slight it not. If it be heavy, murmur not. After the cross is the crown. Your aunt, Nina Welty." This is dated earlier—he was then three years old. The cover of the little book is red and embossed with baby ducklings falling out of a basket entwined with morning glories. It is very rubbed and worn. It had been given him to keep and he had kept it; he had brought it among his possessions to Mississippi when he married; my mother had put it away. . . .

3     I think now, in looking back on these summer trips—this one and a number later, made in the car and on the train—that another element in them must have been influencing my mind. The trips were wholes unto themselves. They were stories. Not only in form, but in their taking on direction, movement, development, change. They changed something in my life: each trip made its particular revelation, though I could not have found words for it. But with the passage of time, I could look back on them and see them bringing me news, discoveries, premonitions, promises—I still can; they still do. When I did begin to write, the short story was a shape that had already formed itself and stood waiting in the back of my mind. Nor is it surprising to me that when I made my first attempt at a novel I entered its world—that of the mysterious Yazoo-Mississippi Delta— as a child riding there on a train: "From the warm windowsill the endless fields glowed like a hearth in firelight, and Laura, looking out, leaning on her elbows with her head between her hands, felt what an arriver in a land feels—that slow hard pounding in the breast."

4    The events in our lives happen in a sequence in time, but in their significance to ourselves they find their own order, a timetable not necessarily—perhaps not possibly—chronological. The time as we know it subjectively is often the chronology that stories and novels follow: it is the continuous thread of revelation. . . .

5    I had the window seat. Beside me, my father checked the progress of our train by moving his finger down the timetable and springing open his pocket watch. He explained to me what the position of the arms of the semaphore meant; before we were to pass through a switch we would watch the signal lights change. Along our track, the mileposts could be read; he read them. Right on time by Daddy's watch, the next town sprang into view, and just as quickly was gone.

6    Side by side and separately, we each lost ourselves in the experience of not missing anything, of seeing everything, of knowing each time what the blows of the whistle meant. But of course it was not the same experience: what was new to me, not older than ten, was a landmark to him. My father knew our way mile by mile; by day or by night, he knew where we were. Everything that changed under our eyes, in the flying countryside, was the known world to him, the imagination to me. Each in our own way, we hungered for all of this: my father and I were in no other respect or situation so congenial.

7    In Daddy's leather grip was his traveler's drinking cup, collapsible; a lid to fit over it had a ring to carry it by; it traveled in a round leather box. This treasure would be brought out at my request, for me to bear to the water cooler at the end of the Pullman car, fill to the brim, and bear back to my seat, to drink water over its smooth lip. The taste of silver could almost be relied on to shock your teeth.

8    After dinner in the sparkling dining car, my father and I walked back to the open-air observation platform at the end of the train and sat on the folding chairs placed at the railing. We watched the sparks we made fly behind us into the night. Fast as our speed was, it gave us time enough to see the rose-red cinders turn to ash, each one, and disappear from sight. Sometimes a house far back in the empty hills showed a light no bigger than a star. The sleeping countryside seemed itself to open a way through for our passage, then close again behind us.

9     The swaying porter would be making ready our berths for the night, pulling the shade down just so, drawing the green fishnet hammock across the window so the clothes you took off could ride along beside you, turning down the tight-made bed, standing up the two snowy pillows as high as they were wide, switching on the eye of the reading lamp, starting the tiny electric fan—you suddenly saw its blades turn into gauze and heard its insect murmur; and drawing across it all the pair of thick green theaterlike curtains—billowing, smelling of cigar smoke—between which you would crawl or dive headfirst to button them together with yourself inside, to be seen no more that night.

10     When you lay enclosed and enwrapped, your head on a pillow parallel to the track, the rhythm of the rail clicks pressed closer to your body as if it might be your heart beating, but the sound of the engine seemed to come from farther away than when it carried you in daylight. The whistle was almost too far away to be heard, its sound wavering back from the engine over the roofs of the cars. What you listened for was the different sound that ran under you when your own car crossed on a trestle, then another sound on an iron bridge; a low or a high bridge—each had its pitch, or drumbeat, for your car.

11     Riding in the sleeper rhythmically lulled me and waked me. From time to time, waked suddenly, I raised my window shade and looked out at my own strip of the night. Sometimes there was unexpected moonlight out there. Sometimes the perfect shadow of our train, with our car, with me invisibly included, ran deep below, crossing a river with us by the light of the moon. Sometimes the encroaching walls of mountains woke me by clapping at my ears. The tunnels made the train's passage resound like the "loud" pedal of a piano, a roar that seemed to last as long as a giant's temper tantrum.

12     But my father put it all into the frame of regularity, predictability, that was his fatherly gift in the course of our journey. I saw it going by, the outside world, in a flash. I dreamed over what I could see as it passed, as well as over what I couldn't. Part of the dream was what lay beyond, where the path wandered off through the pasture, the red clay road climbed and went over the hill or made a turn and was hidden in trees, or toward a river whose bridge I could see but whose name I'd never know. A house back at its distance at night

showing a light from an open doorway, the morning faces of the children who stopped still in what they were doing, perhaps picking blackberries or wild plums, and watched us go by—I never saw with the thought of their continuing to be there just the same after we were out of sight. For now, and for a long while to come, I was proceeding in fantasy.

13     I learned much later—after he was dead, in fact, the time when we so often learn fundamental things about our parents—how well indeed he knew the journey, and how he happened to do so. He fell in love with my mother, and she with him, in West Virginia when she was a teacher in the mountain schools near her home and he was a young man from Ohio who'd gone over to West Virginia to work in the office of a lumber construction company. When they decided to marry, they saw it as part of the adventure of starting a new life to go to a place far away and new to both of them, and that turned out to be Jackson, Mississippi. From rural Ohio and rural West Virginia, that must have seemed, in 1904, as far away as Bangkok might possibly seem to young people today. My father went down and got a job in a new insurance company being formed in Jackson. This was the Lamar Life. He was promoted almost at once, made secretary and one of the directors, and he was to stay with the company for the rest of his life. He set about first thing finding a house in Jackson, then a town of six or eight thousand people, for them to live in until they could build a house of their own. So during the engagement, he went the thousand miles to see her when he could afford it. The rest of the time—every day, sometimes twice a day—the two of them sent letters back and forth by this same train.

14     Their letters had all been kept by that great keeper, my mother; they were in one of the trunks in the attic—the trunk that used to go on the train with us to West Virginia and Ohio on summer trips. I didn't in the end feel like a trespasser when I came to open the letters: they brought my parents before me for the first time as young, as inexperienced, consumed with the strength of their hopes and desires, as *living* on these letters. I would have known my mother's voice in her letters anywhere. But I wouldn't have so quickly known my father's. Annihilating those miles between them—the miles I came along to travel with him, that first time on the train—those

miles he knew nearly altogether by heart, he wrote more often than only once a day, and mailed his letters directly onto the mail car— letters that are so ardent, so direct and tender in expression, so urgent, that they seemed to bare, along with his love, the rest of his whole life to me.

15      On the train I saw that world passing my window. It was when I came to see it was *I* who was passing that my self-centered child-hood was over. But it was not until I began to write, as I seriously did only when I reached my twenties, that I found the world out there revealing, because (as with my father now) *memory* had become attached to seeing, love had added itself to discovery, and because I recognized in my own continuing longing to keep going, the need I carried inside myself to know—the apprehen-sion, first, and then the passion, to connect myself to it. Through travel I first became aware of the outside world; it was through travel that I found my own introspective way into becoming a part of it.

16      This is, of course, simply saying that the outside world is the vital component of my inner life. My work, in the terms in which I see it, is as dearly matched to the world as its secret sharer. My imagination takes its strength and guides its direction from what I see and hear and learn and feel and remember of my living world. But I was to learn slowly that both these worlds, outer and inner, were different from what they seemed to me in the beginning. . . .

17      It seems to me, writing of my parents now in my seventies, that I see continuities in their lives that weren't visible to me when they were living. Even at the times that have left me my most vivid mem-ories of them, there were connections between them that escaped me. Could it be because I can better see their lives—or any lives I know—today because I'm a fiction writer? See them not as fiction, certainly—see them, perhaps, as even greater mysteries than I knew. Writing fiction has developed in me an abiding respect for the unknown in a human lifetime and a sense of where to look for the threads, how to follow, how to connect, find in the thick of the tan-gle what clear line persists. The strands are all there: to the memory nothing is ever really lost.

18      The little keepsake book given to my father so long ago, of which I never heard a word spoken by anybody, has grown in eloquence to

me. The messages that were meant to "go with him"—and which did—the farewell from his mother on the day of her death; and the doctor's following words that the child's own life would be short; the admonition from his Aunt Penina to bear his cross and murmur not—made a sum that he had been left to ponder over from the time he had learned to read. It seems to me that my father's choosing life insurance as his work, and indeed he exhausted his life for it, must have always had a deeper reason behind it than his conviction, strong as it was, in which he joined the majority in the twenties, that success in business was the solution to most of the problems of living—security of the family, their ongoing comfort and welfare, and especially the certainty of education for the children. This was partly why the past had no interest for him. He saw life in terms of the future, and he worked to provide that future for his children.

19    Right along with the energetic practice of optimism, and deeper than this, was an abiding awareness of mortality itself—most of all the mortality of a parent. This care, this caution, that ruled his life in the family, and in the business he chose and succeeded in expanding so far, began very possibly when he was seven years old, when his mother, asking him with perhaps literally her last words to be a good boy and meet her in heaven, died and left him alone.

20    Strangely enough, what Ned Andrews had extolled too, in all his rhetoric, was the future works of man and the leaving of the past behind. No two characters could have been wider apart than those of Ned Andrews and Christian Welty, or more different in their self-expression. They never knew each other, and the only thing they had in common was my mother's love. Who knows but that this ambition for the betterment of mankind in the attainable future was the quality in them both that she loved first? She would have responded to the ardency of their beliefs. I'm not sure she succeeded in having faith in their predictions. Neither got to live their lives out; the hurt she felt in this was part of her love for both.

21    My father of course liberally insured his own life for the future provision of his family, and had cause to believe that all was safe ahead. Then the Great Depression arrived. And in 1931 a disease that up to then even he had never heard of, leukemia, caused his death in a matter of weeks, at the age of fifty-two.

# Discussion Questions

1. Explain the importance of Welty's summer trips with her father.
2. In paragraph 4, Welty discusses the significance of events not necessarily remembered in a chronological sequence. Cite specific examples from your own life of this observation.
3. Welty likens the trips to stories. How effective is this analogy? Explain.
4. Why does Welty state in paragraph 13 that after they die, "we so often learn fundamental things about our parents"? What does Welty learn that confirms this observation?
5. In paragraph 15, Welty explains the moment when her "self-centered childhood was over." Does Welty's distinction between watching the world pass versus her passing warrant her newfound revelation? Why or why not?
6. What do you learn about Welty's father and Welty from this essay? Identify specific passages that inform your answer.
7. In small groups, discuss who this essay is really about: Welty or her father.

# Writing Assignments

1. Write a letter to your father or mother describing the impact he or she had on your life.
2. Write an essay about a time you spent with your father or mother when you learned something important about yourself.
3. In a paper, explain how time helps to develop perspective and understanding. Cite specific examples to support your point.

# The Seam of the Snail

## CYNTHIA OZICK

Cynthia Ozick (b. 1928) was born to Russian immigrants in New York City and reared in the Bronx. The recipient of a B.A. from New York University in 1949 and an M.A. from Ohio State University the following year, Ozick is a prolific poet, novelist, short fiction writer, essayist, and translator (from Yiddish). Her novels include *Trust* (1966), *The Cannibal Galaxy* (1983), and *The Messiah of Stockholm* (1987), and her translations appear in the *Penguin Book of Yiddish Verse* (1987). Her collections of short fiction are *The Pagan Rabbi and Other Stories* (1971), *Bloodshed and Three Novellas* (1976), and *Levitation: Five Fictions* (1981). Her play is entitled *The Shawl* (1990). Ozick has also published five collections of essays: *Art and Ardor* (1983), *Metaphor and Memory* (1989), *What Henry James Knew and Other Essays* (1993) and its companion book *Portrait of the Artist as a Bad Character and Other Essays on Writing* (1996), and *Fame and Folly* (1996). In the following essay, written in 1985 and published in *Metaphor and Memory*, Ozick uses meticulous description as she examines her mother's life in comparison to her own.

1    In my Depression childhood, whenever I had a new dress, my cousin Sarah would get suspicious. The nicer the dress was, and

especially the more expensive it looked, the more suspicious she would get. Finally she would lift the hem and check the seams. This was to see if the dress had been bought or if my mother had sewed it. Sarah could always tell. My mother's sewing had elegant outsides, but there was something catch-as-catch-can about the insides. Sarah's sewing, by contrast, was as impeccably finished inside as out; not one stray thread dangled.

2    My uncle Jake built meticulous grandfather clocks out of rosewood; he was a perfectionist, and sent to England for the clockworks. My mother built serviceable radiator covers and a serviceable cabinet, with hinged doors, for the pantry. She built a pair of bookcases for the living room. Once, after I was grown and in a house of my own, she fixed the sewer pipe. She painted ceilings, and also landscapes; she reupholstered chairs. One summer she planted a whole yard of tall corn. She thought herself capable of doing anything, and did everything she imagined. But nothing was perfect. There was always some clear flaw, never visible head-on. You had to look underneath, where the seams were. The corn thrived, though not in rows. The stalks elbowed one another like gossips in a dense little village.

3    "Miss Brrrroooobaker," my mother used to mock, rolling her Russian *r*'s, whenever I crossed a *t* she had left uncrossed, or corrected a word she had misspelled, or became impatient with a v that had tangled itself up with a *w* in her speech. ("*Vvv*entriloquist," I would say. "*Vvv*entriloquist," she would obediently repeat. And the next time it would come out "wiolinist.") Miss Brubaker was my high school English teacher, and my mother invoked her name as an emblem of raging finical obsession. "Miss Brrrroooobaker," my mother's voice hoots at me down the years, as I go on casting and recasting sentences in a tiny handwriting on monomaniacally uniform paper. The loops of my mother's handwriting—it was the Palmer Method—were as big as soup bowls, spilling generous splashy ebullience. She could pull off, at five minutes' notice, a satisfying dinner for ten concocted out of nothing more than originality and panache. But the napkin would be folded a little off center, and the spoon might be on the wrong side of the knife. She was an optimist who ignored trifles; for her, God was not in the details but in the intent. And all these culinary and agricultural efflorescences were extracurricular, accomplished in the crevices and niches of a fourteen-hour business day. When she scribbled out her family

memoirs, in heaps of dog-eared notebooks, or on the backs of old bills, or on the margins of last year's calendar, I would resist typing them; in the speed of the chase she often omitted words like "the," "and," "will." The same flashing and bountiful hand fashioned and fired ceramic pots, and painted brilliant autumn views and vases of imaginary flowers and ferns, and decorated ordinary Woolworth platters with lavish enameled gardens. But bits of the painted petals would chip away.

4    Lavish: my mother was as lavish as nature. She woke early and saturated the hours with work and inventiveness, and read late into the night. She was all profusion, abundance, fabrication. Angry at her children, she would run after us whirling the cord of the electric iron, like a lasso or a whip; but she never caught us. When, in seventh grade, I was afraid of failing the Music Appreciation final exam because I could not tell the difference between "To a Wild Rose" and "Barcarole," she got the idea of sending me to school with a gauze sling rigged up on my writing arm, and an explanatory note that was purest fiction. But the sling kept slipping off. My mother gave advice like mad—she boiled over with so much passion for the predicaments of strangers that they turned into permanent cronies. She told intimate stories about people I had never heard of.

5    Despite the gargantuan Palmer loops (or possibly because of them), I have always known that my mother's was a life of—intricately abashing word!—excellence: insofar as excellence means ripe generosity. She burgeoned, she proliferated; she was endlessly leafy and flowering. She wore red hats, and called herself a gypsy. In her girlhood she marched with the suffragettes and for Margaret Sanger and called herself a Red. She made me laugh, she was so varied: like a tree on which lemons, pomegranates, and prickly pears absurdly all hang together. She had the comedy of prodigality.

6    My own way is a thousand times more confined. I am a pinched perfectionist, the ultimate fruition of Miss Brubaker; I attend to crabbed minutiae and am self-trammeled through taking pains. I am a kind of human snail, locked in and condemned by my own nature. The ancients believed that the moist track left by the snail as it crept was the snail's own essence, depleting its body little by little; the farther the snail toiled, the smaller it became, until it finally rubbed itself out. That is how perfectionists are. Say to us Excellence, and we will show you how we use up our substance and wear ourselves

away, while making scarcely any progress at all. The fact that I am an exacting perfectionist in a narrow strait only, and nowhere else, is hardly to the point, since nothing matters to me so much as a comely and muscular sentence. It is my narrow strait, this snail's road; the track of the sentence I am writing now; and when I have eked out the wet substance, ink or blood, that is its mark, I will begin the next sentence. Only in treading out sentences am I perfectionist; but then there is nothing else I know how to do, or take much interest in. I miter every pair of abutting sentences as scrupulously as Uncle Jake fitted one strip of rosewood against another. My mother's worldly and bountiful hand has escaped me. The sentence I am writing is my cabin and my shell, compact, self-sufficient. It is the burnished horizon—a merciless planet where flawlessness is the single standard, where even the inmost seams, however hidden from a laxer eye, must meet perfection. Here "excellence" is not strewn casually from a tipped cornucopia, here disorder does not account for charm, here trifles rule like tyrants.

7    I measure my life in sentences pressed out, line by line, like the lustrous ooze on the underside of the snail, the snail's secret open seam, its wound, leaking attar. My mother was too mettlesome to feel the force of a comma. She scorned minutiae. She measured her life according to what poured from the horn of plenty, which was her own seamless, ample, cascading, elastic, susceptible, inexact heart. My narrower heart rides between the tiny twin horns of the snail, dwindling as it goes.

8    And out of this thinnest thread, this ink-wet line of words, must rise a visionary fog, a mist, a smoke, forging cities, histories, sorrows, quagmires, entanglements, lives of sinners, even the life of my furnacehearted mother: so much wilderness, waywardness, plenitude on the head of the precise and impeccable snail, between the horns. (Ah, if this could be!)


# Discussion Questions

1. In small groups, discuss what the title of Ozick's essay means.
2. Explain the significance of the first two paragraphs mentioning Sarah and Uncle Jake.

3. In small groups, discuss what the essay reveals about Ozick's relationship with her mother.

4. Explain what Ozick means in paragraph 3 when she describes her mother as "an optimist who ignored trifles; for her, God was not in the details but in the intent." What examples in the essay support this observation?

5. In paragraph 6, Ozick describes herself as "a kind of human snail." How effective do you find this analogy? Explain your answer.

6. What does Ozick mean in paragraph 7 when she states, "I measure my life in sentences pressed out . . ."?

7. Why do you think Ozick ends her essay with a parenthetical statement? Comment on the effectiveness of that technique.

## Writing Assignments

1. Write an essay that describes the way in which a family member performed a household chore that you found especially memorable.

2. In an essay, compare and contrast your method of work with that of a relative, as Ozick did with her mother.

3. Write an essay using a metaphor to reveal who you are.

4. In a paper, examine the importance of performing an activity with care and perfection. Describe the activity and discuss the significance to the attention given to it.

# Discovery of a Father

## SHERWOOD ANDERSON

Sherwood Anderson (1876–1941) was born in Camden, Ohio. He dropped out of school to work a series of odd jobs. He commenced his writing career at the age of thirty-six. Widely traveled, Anderson eventually settled in West Virginia where he edited two local newspapers. Anderson is the author of numerous books, including *Windy McPherson's Son* (1916), *Marching Men* (1917), *Winesburg, Ohio* (1919), *Horses and Men* (1923), *Tar: A Midwest Childhood* (1926), and *Dark Laughter* (1927). The following essay, which originally appeared in Anderson's *Memoirs*, examines "one of the strangest relationships in the world": that between a father and a son. In it, Anderson describes how he came to love his father.

1    One of the strangest relationships in the world is that between father and son. I know it now from having sons of my own.

2    A boy wants something very special from his father. You hear it said that fathers want their sons to be what they feel they cannot themselves be, but I tell you it also works the other way. I know that as a small boy I wanted my father to be a certain thing he was not. I wanted him to be a proud, silent, dignified father. When I was with other boys and he passed along the street, I wanted to feel a glow of pride: "There he is. That is my father."

3    But he wasn't such a one. He couldn't be. It seemed to me then
that he was always showing off. Let's say someone in our town had
got up a show. They were always doing it. The druggist would be
in it, the shoestore clerk, the horse doctor, and a lot of women and
girls. My father would manage to get the chief comedy part. It was,
let's say, a Civil War play and he was a comic Irish soldier. He had
to do the most absurd things. They thought he was funny, but I
didn't.

4    I thought he was terrible. I didn't see how Mother could stand it.
She even laughed with the others. Maybe I would have laughed if it
hadn't been my father.

5    Or there was a parade, the Fourth of July or Decoration Day.
He'd be in that, too, right at the front of it, as Grand Marshal or
something, on a white horse hired from a livery stable.

6    He couldn't ride for shucks. He fell off the horse and everyone
hooted with laughter, but he didn't care. He even seemed to like it.
I remember once when he had done something ridiculous, and right
out on Main Street, too. I was with some other boys and they were
laughing and shouting at him and he was shouting back and having
as good a time as they were. I ran down an alley back of some stores
and there in the Presbyterian Church sheds I had a good long cry.

7    Or I would be in bed at night and Father would come home a little lit up and bring some men with him. He was a man who was
never alone. Before he went broke, running a harness shop, there
were always a lot of men loafing in the shop. He went broke, of
course, because he gave too much credit. He couldn't refuse it and
I thought he was a fool. I had got to hating him.

8    There'd be men I didn't think would want to be fooling around
with him. There might even be the superintendent of our schools
and a quiet man who ran the hardware store. Once, I remember,
there was a white-haired man who was a cashier of the bank. It was
a wonder to me they'd want to be seen with such a windbag. That's
what I thought he was. I know now what it was that attracted them.
It was because life in our town, as in all small towns, was at times
pretty dull and he livened it up. He made them laugh. He could tell
stories. He'd even get them to singing.

9    If they didn't come to our house they'd go off, say at night, to
where there was a grassy place by a creek. They'd cook food there
and drink beer and sit about listening to his stories.

10      He was always telling stories about himself. He'd say this or that
wonderful thing happened to him. It might be something that made
him look like a fool. He didn't care.

11      If an Irishman came to our house, right away father would say he
was Irish. He'd tell what county in Ireland he was born in. He'd tell
things that happened there when he was a boy. He'd make it seem
so real that, if I hadn't known he was born in southern Ohio, I'd
have believed him myself.

12      If it was a Scotchman, the same thing happened. He'd get a burr
into his speech. Or he was a German or a Swede. He'd be anything
the other man was. I think they all knew he was lying, but they
seemed to like him just the same. As a boy that was what I couldn't
understand.

13      And there was Mother. How could she stand it? I wanted to ask
but never did. She was not the kind you asked such questions.

14      I'd be upstairs in my bed, in my room above the porch, and
Father would be telling some of his tales. A lot of Father's stories
were about the Civil War. To hear him tell it he'd been in about
every battle. He'd known Grant, Sherman, Sheridan and I don't
know how many others. He'd been particularly intimate with
General Grant so that when Grant went East, to take charge of all
the armies, he took Father along.

15      "I was an orderly at headquarters and Sam Grant said to me,
'Irve,' he said, 'I'm going to take you along with me.'"

16      It seems he and Grant used to slip off sometimes and have a quiet
drink together. That's what my father said. He'd tell about the day
Lee surrendered and how, when the great moment came, they
couldn't find Grant.

17      "You know," my father said, "about General Grant's book, his
memoirs. You've read of how he said he had a headache and how,
when he got word that Lee was ready to call it quits, he was suddenly and miraculously cured.

18      "Huh," said Father. "He was in the woods with me.

19      "I was there with my back against a tree. I was pretty well corned.
I had got hold of a bottle of pretty good stuff.

20      "They were looking for Grant. He had got off his horse and
come into the woods. He found me. He was covered with mud.

21      "I had the bottle in my hand. What'd I care? The war was over. I
knew we had them licked."

22     My father said that he was the one who told Grant about Lee. An orderly riding by had told him, because the orderly knew how thick he was with Grant. Grant was embarrassed.

23     "But, Irve, look at me. I'm all covered with mud," he said to Father.

24     And then, my father said, he and Grant decided to have a drink together. They took a couple of shots and then, because he didn't want Grant to show up potted before the immaculate Lee, he smashed the bottle against the tree.

25     "Sam Grant's dead now and I wouldn't want it to get out on him," my father said.

26     That's just one of the kind of things he'd tell. Of course, the men knew he was lying, but they seemed to like it just the same.

27     When we got broke, down and out, do you think he ever brought anything home? Not he. If there wasn't anything to eat in the house, he'd go off visiting around at farm houses. They all wanted him. Sometimes he'd stay away for weeks, Mother working to keep us fed, and then home he'd come bringing, let's say, a ham. He'd got it from some farmer friend. He'd slap it on the table in the kitchen. "You bet I'm going to see that my kids have something to eat," he'd say, and Mother would just stand smiling at him. She'd never say a word about all the weeks and months he'd been away, not leaving us a cent for food. Once I heard her speaking to a woman in our street. Maybe the woman had dared to sympathize with her. "Oh," she said, "it's all right. He isn't ever dull like most of the men in this street. Life is never dull when my man is about."

28     But often I was filled with bitterness, and sometimes I wished he wasn't my father. I'd even invent another man as my father. To protect my mother I'd make up stories of a secret marriage that for some strange reason never got known. As though some man, say the president of a railroad company or maybe a Congressman, had married my mother, thinking his wife was dead and then it turned out she wasn't.

29     So they had to hush it up but I got born just the same. I wasn't really the son of my father. Somewhere in the world there was a very dignified, quite wonderful man who was really my father. I even made myself half believe these fancies.

30     And then there came a certain night. Mother was away from home. Maybe there was church that night. Father came in. He'd

been off somewhere for two or three weeks. He found me alone in the house, reading by the kitchen table.

31    It had been raining and he was very wet. He sat and looked at me for a long time, not saying a word. I was startled, for there was on his face the saddest look I had ever seen. He sat for a time, his clothes dripping. Then he got up.

32    "Come on with me," he said.

33    I got up and went with him out of the house. I was filled with wonder but I wasn't afraid. We went along a dirt road that led down into a valley, about a mile out of town, where there was a pond. We walked in silence. The man who was always talking had stopped his talking.

34    I didn't know what was up and had the queer feeling that I was with a stranger. I don't know whether my father intended it so. I don't think he did.

35    The pond was quite large. It was still raining hard and there were flashes of lightning followed by thunder. We were on a grassy bank at the pond's edge when my father spoke, and in the darkness and rain his voice sounded strange.

36    "Take off your clothes," he said. Still filled with wonder, I began to undress. There was a flash of lightning and I saw that he was already naked.

37    Naked, we went into the pond. Taking my hand, he pulled me in. It may be that I was too frightened, too full of a feeling of strangeness, to speak. Before that night my father had never seemed to pay any attention to me.

38    "And what is he up to now?" I kept asking myself. I did not swim very well, but he put my hand on his shoulder and struck out into the darkness.

39    He was a man with big shoulders, a powerful swimmer. In the darkness I could feel the movements of his muscles. We swam to the far edge of the pond and then back to where we had left our clothes. The rain continued and the wind blew. Sometimes my father swam on his back, and when he did he took my hand in his large powerful one and moved it over so that it rested always on his shoulder. Sometimes there would be a flash of lightning, and I could see his face quite clearly.

40    It was as it was earlier, in the kitchen, a face filled with sadness. There would be the momentary glimpse of his face, and then again the darkness, the wind and the rain. In me there was a feeling I had never known before.

41    It was a feeling of closeness. It was something strange. It was as though there were only we two in the world. It was as though I had been jerked suddenly out of myself, out of my world of the schoolboy, out of a world in which I was ashamed of my father.

42    He had become blood of my blood; he the strong swimmer and I the boy clinging to him in the darkness. We swam in silence, and in silence we dressed in our wet clothes and went home.

43    There was a lamp lighted in the kitchen, and when we came in, the water dripping from us, there was my mother. She smiled at us. I remember that she called us "boys." "What have you boys been up to?" she asked, but my father did not answer. As he had begun the evening's experience with me in silence, so he ended it. He turned and looked at me. Then he went, I thought, with a new and strange dignity, out of the room.

44    I climbed the stairs to my room, undressed in darkness and got into bed. I couldn't sleep and did not want to sleep. For the first time I knew that I was the son of my father. He was a storyteller as I was to be. It may be that I even laughed a little softly there in the darkness. If I did, I laughed knowing that I would never again be wanting another father.

## Discussion Questions

1. Anderson begins his essay with the contention that "one of the strangest relationships in the world is that between father and son." What in his essay supports that observation?

2. What is the purpose of paragraph 13 in which Anderson offers four short lines about his mother?

3. In small groups, discuss whether you find Anderson's changed opinion of his father believable.

4. Why do you think it was only after Anderson had sons of his own that he was able to reach the observation about the "strangest relationships in the world"?

5. Explain your reasons for agreeing or disagreeing with Anderson's statement in paragraph 2, "A boy wants something very special from his father."

6. Although his essay is ostensibly about his father, Anderson reveals details about himself. Citing specific passages, explain what you learn about him.
7. Explain the symbolism of Anderson and his father swimming in the nude.

# Writing Assignments

1. Imagine you are Anderson. Write a letter to your son explaining the importance of your relationship with him.
2. Write an essay in which you describe an event that changed your view of a close relative.
3. Explore the connections among three generations; that is, what can a man learn about his father from becoming a father himself? Or what can a boy learn about his father from seeing him relate to the grandfather?

# The Inheritance of Tools

## SCOTT RUSSELL SANDERS

Scott Russell Sanders (b. 1945) was born in Tennessee. He earned a B.A. from Brown University and a Ph.D. from Cambridge University in England. A professor of English at Indiana University, Sanders writes children's stories, essays, science fiction, folktales, and historical novels. His work has been published in such publications as *North American Review, Georgia Review, The Ohio Review, Omni, Transatlantic Review,* and *New Dimensions.* He is also the author of *Wilderness Plots: Tales about the Settlement of American Land* (1983), *Fetching the Dead: Stories* (1984), *Stone Country* (1985), *Hear the Wind Blow: American Folkstories Retold* (1985), *Bad Man Ballad* (1985), *The Paradise of Bombs* (1987), *Staying Put: Making a Home in a Restless World* (1993), and *Writing from the Center* (1995). Sanders is especially interested in and recognized for his personal essays about the Midwest, writing in which he explores his life and observations of the world. Sanders has received a Woodrow Wilson Fellowship, a Marshall scholarship, and a Bennett Fellowship in creative writing. In the following essay, which was first published in *North American Review*, Sanders focuses on his father's tools as a way to recall the lessons his father taught him—about carpentry and about life.

1    At just about the hour when my father died, soon after dawn one February morning when ice coated the windows like cataracts, I banged my thumb with a hammer. Naturally I swore at the hammer, the reckless thing, and in the moment of swearing I thought of what my father would say: "If you'd try hitting the nail it would go in a whole lot faster. Don't you know your thumb's not as hard as that hammer?" We both were doing carpentry that day, but far apart. He was building cupboards at my brother's place in Oklahoma; I was at home in Indiana putting up a wall in the basement to make a bedroom for my daughter. By the time my mother called with news of his death—the long distance wires whittling her voice until it seemed too thin to bear the weight of what she had to say—my thumb was swollen. A week or so later a white scar in the shape of a crescent moon began to show above the cuticle, and month by month it rose across the pink sky of my thumbnail. It took the better part of a year for the scar to disappear, and every time I noticed it I thought of my father.

2    The hammer had belonged to him, and to his father before him. The three of us have used it to build houses and barns and chicken coops, to upholster chairs and crack walnuts, to make doll furniture and bookshelves and jewelry boxes. The head is scratched and pockmarked, like an old plowshare that has been working rocky fields, and it gives off the sort of dull sheen you see on fast creek water in the shade. It is a finishing hammer, about the weight of a bread loaf, too light really for framing walls, too heavy for cabinetwork, with a curved claw for pulling nails, a rounded head for pounding, a fluted neck for looks, and a hickory handle for strength.

3    The present handle is my third one, bought from a lumberyard in Tennessee down the road from where my brother and I were helping my father build his retirement house. I broke the previous one by trying to pull sixteen-penny nails out of floor joists—a foolish thing to do with a finishing hammer, as my father pointed out. "You ever hear of a crowbar?" he said. No telling how many handles he and my grandfather had gone through before me. My grandfather used to cut down hickory trees on his farm, saw them into slabs, cure the planks in his hayloft, and carve handles with a drawknife. The grain in hickory is crooked and knotty, and therefore tough, hard to split, like the grain in the two men who owned this hammer before me.

4    After proposing marriage to a neighbor girl, my grandfather used this hammer to build a house for his bride on a stretch of river bottom in northern Mississippi. The lumber for the place, like the hickory for the handle, was cut on his own land. By the day of the wedding he had not quite finished the house, and so right after the ceremony he took his wife home and put her to work. My grandmother had worn her Saturday dress for the wedding, with a fringe of lace tacked on around the hem in honor of the occasion. She removed this lace and folded it away before going out to help my grandfather nail siding on the house. "There she was in her good dress," he told me some fifty-odd years after that wedding day, "holding up them long pieces of clapboard while I hammered, and together we got the place covered up before dark." As the family grew to four, six, eight, and eventually thirteen, my grandfather used this hammer to enlarge his house room by room, like a chambered nautilus expanding his shell.

5    By and by the hammer was passed along to my father. One day he was up on the roof of our pony barn nailing shingles with it, when I stepped out the kitchen door to call him for supper. Before I could yell, something about the sight of him straddling the spine of that roof and swinging the hammer caught my eye and made me hold my tongue. I was five or six years old, and the world's commonplaces were still news to me. He would pull a nail from the pouch at his waist, bring the hammer down, and a moment later the *thunk* of the blow would reach my ears. And that is what had stopped me in my tracks and stilled my tongue, that momentary gap between seeing and hearing the blow. Instead of yelling from the kitchen door, I ran to the barn and climbed two rungs up the ladder—as far as I was allowed to go—and spoke quietly to my father. On our walk to the house he explained that sound takes time to make its way through air. Suddenly the world seemed larger, the air more dense, if sound could be held back like any ordinary traveler.

6    By the time I started using this hammer, at about the age when I discovered the speed of sound, it already contained houses and mysteries for me. The smooth handle was one my grandfather had made. In those days I needed both hands to swing it. My father would start a nail in a scrap of wood, and I would pound away until I bent it over.

7 "Looks like you got ahold of some of those rubber nails," he would tell me. "Here, let me see if I can find you some stiff ones." And he would rummage in a drawer until he came up with a fistful of more cooperative nails. "Look at the head," he would tell me. "Don't look at your hands, don't look at the hammer. Just look at the head of that nail and pretty soon you'll learn to hit it square."

8 Pretty soon I did learn. While he worked in the garage cutting dovetail joints for a drawer or skinning a deer or tuning an engine, I would hammer nails. I made innocent blocks of wood look like porcupines. He did not talk much in the midst of his tools, but he kept up a nearly ceaseless humming, slipping in and out of a dozen tunes in an afternoon, often running back over the same stretch of melody again and again, as if searching for a way out. When the humming did cease, I knew he was faced with a task requiring great delicacy or concentration, and I took care not to distract him.

9 He kept scraps of wood in a cardboard box—the ends of two-by-fours, slabs of shelving and plywood, odd pieces of molding—and everything in it was fair game. I nailed scraps together to fashion what I called boats or houses, but the results usually bore only faint resemblance to the visions I carried in my head. I would hold up these constructions to show my father, and he would turn them over in his hands admiringly, speculating about what they might be. My cobbled-together guitars might have been alien spaceships, my barns might have been models of Aztec temples, each wooden contraption might have been anything but what I had set out to make.

10 Now and again I would feel the need to have a chunk of wood shaped or shortened before I riddled it with nails, and I would clamp it in a vice and scrape at it with a handsaw. My father would let me lacerate the board until my arm gave out, and then he would wrap his hand around mine and help me finish the cut, showing me how to use my thumb to guide the blade, how to pull back on the saw to keep it from binding, how to let my shoulder do the work.

11 "Don't force it," he would say, "just drag it easy and give the teeth a chance to bite."

12 As the saw teeth bit down the wood released its smell, each kind with its own fragrance, oak or walnut or cherry or pine—usually pine, because it was the softest and the easiest for a child to work. No matter how weathered and gray the board, no matter how warped and cracked, inside there was this smell waiting, as of some-

thing freshly baked. I gathered every smidgen of sawdust and stored it away in coffee cans, which I kept in a drawer of the workbench. When I did not feel like hammering nails I would dump my sawdust on the concrete floor of the garage and landscape it into highways and farms and towns, running miniature cars and trucks along miniature roads. Looming as huge as a colossus, my father worked over and around me, now and again bending down to inspect my work, careful not to trample my creations. It was a landscape that smelled dizzyingly of wood. Even after a bath my skin would carry the smell, and so would my father's hair, when he lifted me for a bedtime hug.

13    I tell these things not only from memory but also from recent observation, because my own son now turns blocks of wood into nailed porcupines, dumps cans full of sawdust at my feet and sculpts highways on the floor. He learns how to swing a hammer from the elbow instead of the wrist, how to lay his thumb beside the blade to guide a saw, how to tap a chisel with a wooden mallet, how to mark a hole with an awl before starting a drill bit. My daughter did the same before him, and even now, on the brink of teenage aloofness, she will occasionally drag out my box of wood scraps and carpenter something. So I have seen my apprenticeship to wood and tools reenacted in each of my children, as my father saw his own apprenticeship renewed in me.

14    The saw I used belonged to him, as did my level and both of my squares, and all four tools had belonged to his father. The blade of the saw is the bluish color of gun barrels, and the maple handle, dark from the sweat of hands, is inscribed with curving leaf designs. The level is a shaft of walnut two feet long, edged with brass and pierced by three round windows in which air bubbles float in oil-filled tubes of glass. The middle window serves for testing whether a surface is horizontal, the others for testing whether it is plumb or vertical. My grandfather used to carry this level on the gun rack behind the seat in his pickup, and when I rode with him I would turn around to watch the bubbles dance. The larger of the two squares is called a framing square, a flat steel elbow so beat up and tarnished you can barely make out the rows of numbers that show how to figure the cuts on rafters. The smaller one is called a try square, for marking right angles, with a blued steel blade for the shank and a brass-faced block of cherry for the head.

15    I was taught early on that a saw is not to be used apart from a square: "If you're going to cut a piece of wood," my father insisted, "you owe it to the tree to cut it straight."

16    Long before studying geometry, I learned there is a mystical virtue in right angles. There is an unspoken morality in seeking the level and the plumb. A house will stand, a table will bear weight, the sides of a box will hold together only if the joints are square and the members upright. When the bubble is lined up between two marks etched in the glass tube of a level, you have aligned yourself with the forces that hold the universe together. When you miter the corners of a picture frame, each angle must be exactly forty-five degrees, as they are in the perfect triangles of Pythagoras, not a degree more or less. Otherwise the frame will hang crookedly, as if ashamed of itself and of its maker. No matter if the joints you are cutting do not show. Even if you are butting two pieces of wood together inside a cabinet, where no one except a wrecking crew will ever see them, you must take pains to insure that the ends are square and the studs are plumb.

17    I took pains over the wall I was building on the day my father died. Not long after that wall was finished—paneled with tongue-and-groove boards of yellow pine, the nail holes filled with putty and the wood all stained and sealed—I came close to wrecking it one afternoon when my daughter ran howling up the stairs to announce that her gerbils had escaped from their cage and were hiding in my brand-new wall. She could hear them scratching and squeaking behind her bed. Impossible! I said. How on earth could they get inside by drum-tight wall? Through the heating vent, she answered. I went downstairs, pressed my ear to the honey-colored wood, and heard the scritch scratch of tiny feet.

18    "What can we do?" my daughter wailed. "They'll starve to death, they'll die of thirst, they'll suffocate."

19    "Hold on," I soothed. "I'll think of something."

20    While I thought and she fretted, the radio on her bedside table delivered us the headlines. Several thousand people had died in a city in India from a poisonous cloud that had leaked overnight from a chemical plant. A nuclear-powered submarine had been launched. Rioting continued in South Africa. An airplane had been hijacked in the Mediterranean. Authorities calculated that several thousand homeless people slept on the streets within sight of the Washington

Monument. I felt my usual helplessness in face of all these calamities. But here was my daughter weeping because her gerbils were holed up in a wall. This calamity I could handle.

21   "Don't worry," I told her. "We'll set food and water by the heating vent and lure them out. And if that doesn't do the trick, I'll tear the wall apart until we find them."

22   She stopped crying and gazed at me. "You'd really tear it apart? Just for my gerbils? The *wall?*" Astonishment slowed her down only for a second, however, before she ran to the workbench and began tugging at drawers, saying, "Let's see, what'll we need? Crowbar. Hammer. Chisels. I hope we don't have to use them—but just in case."

23   We didn't need the wrecking tools. I never had to assault my handsome wall, because the gerbils eventually came out to nibble at a dish of popcorn. But for several hours I studied the tongue-and-groove skin I had nailed up on the day of my father's death, considering where to begin prying. There were no gaps in that wall, no crooked joints.

24   I had botched a great many pieces of wood before I mastered the right angle with a saw, botched even more before I learned to miter a joint. The knowledge of these things resides in my hands and eyes and the webwork of muscles, not in the tools. There are machines for sale—powered miter boxes and radial arm saws, for instance—that will enable any casual soul to cut proper angles in boards. The skill is invested in the gadget instead of the person who uses it, and this is what distinguishes a machine from a tool. If I had to earn my keep by making furniture or building houses, I suppose I would buy powered saws and pneumatic nailers; the need for speed would drive me to it. But since I carpenter only for my own pleasure or to help neighbors or to remake the house around the ears of my family, I stick with hand tools. Most of the ones I own were given to me by my father, who also taught me how to wield them. The tools in my workbench are a double inheritance, for each hammer and level and saw is wrapped in a cloud of knowing.

25   All of these tools are a pleasure to look at and to hold. Merchants would never paste NEW NEW NEW! signs on them in stores. Their designs are old because they work, because they serve their purpose well. Like folksongs and aphorisms and the grainy bits of language, these tools have been pared down to essentials. I look at my claw hammer, the distillation of a hundred generations of carpenters, and

consider that it holds up well beside those other classics—Greek vases, Gregorian chants, *Don Quixote*, barbed fishhooks, candles, spoons. Knowledge of hammering stretches back to the earliest humans who squatted beside fires chipping flints. Anthropologists have a lovely name for those unworked rocks that served as the earliest hammers. "Dawn stones" they are called. Their only qualification for the work, aside from hardness, is that they fit the hand. Our ancestors used them for grinding corn, tapping awls, smashing bones. From dawn stones to this claw hammer is a great leap in time, but no great distance in design or imagination.

26    On that iced-over February morning when I smashed my thumb with the hammer, I was down in the basement framing the wall that my daughter's gerbils would later hide in. I was thinking of my father, as I always did whenever I built anything, thinking how he would have gone about the work, hearing in memory what he would have said about the wisdom of hitting the nail instead of my thumb. I had the studs and plates nailed together all square and trim, and was lifting the wall into place when the phone rang upstairs. My wife answered, and in a moment she came to the basement door and called down softly to me. The stillness in her voice made me drop the framed wall and hurry upstairs. She told me my father was dead. Then I heard the details over the phone from my mother. Building a set of cupboards for my brother in Oklahoma, he had knocked off work early the previous afternoon because of cramps in his stomach. Early this morning, on his way into the kitchen of my brother's trailer, maybe going for a glass of water, so early that no one else was awake, he slumped down on the linoleum and his heart quit.

27    For several hours I paced around inside my house, upstairs and down, in and out of every room, looking for the right door to open and knowing there was no such door. My wife and children followed me and wrapped me in arms and backed away again, circling and staring as if I were on fire. Where was the door, the door, the door? I kept wondering. My smashed thumb turned purple and throbbed, making me furious. I wanted to cut it off and rush outside and scrape away the snow and hack a hole in the frozen earth and bury the shameful thing.

28    I went down into the basement, opened a drawer in my workbench, and stared at the ranks of chisels and knives. Oiled and sharp, as my father would have kept them, they gleamed at me like teeth. I

took up a clasp knife, pried out the longest blade, and tested the edge on the hair of my forearm. A tuft came away cleanly, and I saw my father testing the sharpness of tools on his own skin, the blades of axes and knives and gouges and hoes, saw the red hair shaved off in patches from his arms and the backs of his hands. "That will cut bear," he would say. He never cut a bear with his blades, now my blades, but he cut deer, dirt, wood. I closed the knife and put it away. Then I took up the hammer and went back to work on my daughter's wall, snugging the bottom plate against a chalkline on the floor, shimming the top plate against the joists overhead, plumbing the studs with my level, making sure before I drove the first nail that every line was square and true.

# Discussion Questions

1. For what jobs and by whom had Sanders's hammer previously been used? Why is it important that Sanders provide this information?
2. How would you characterize Sanders's father from the incidents described in the essay? Provide specific examples to support your answer.
3. Describe the relationship Sanders had with his father.
4. What is the symbolism of the essay's title?
5. Explain the importance of the incident with Sanders's daughter's gerbils.
6. What does Sanders mean in paragraph 24 when he writes, "The tools in my workbench are a double inheritance, for each hammer and level and saw is wrapped in a cloud of knowing"?
7. In small groups, discuss why Sanders wrote about the hammer, as opposed to another tool or belonging of his father.

# Writing Assignments

1. Choose an item you have inherited from a relative. In an essay, discuss its history and importance to you.

2. Although we usually think of material items when we hear the word *inheritance*, we also inherit other, more important things from our relatives such as personality traits or interests. In an essay, describe such an inheritance, explaining how it is as much a part of you as it was the person from whom you inherited it.

3. If you had to choose something you would want your children to inherit from you, what would it be? Write an essay in which you explain the rationale for your choice.

# My Father's Life

## RAYMOND CARVER

Raymond Carver (1938–1988) was born in Oregon and graduated from California State University at Humboldt in 1963. He spent a year at the Writer's Workshop at the University of Iowa where he earned an M.F.A. in 1966 and studied creative writing under the tutelage of John Gardner at Chico State College. Carver taught writing at the University of California at Santa Cruz. A fiction writer and poet, Carver is the author of *Will You Please Be Quiet, Please?* (1976), *What We Talk about When We Talk about Love* (1981), *Fires: Essays, Poems, Stories* (1983), *Cathedral* (1984), *Saints* (1987), and *Where I'm Calling From: New and Selected Stories* (1988). Carver's poetry collections include *Where Water Comes Together with Other Water* (1985), *Ultramarine* (1986), *In a Marine Light: Selected Poems* (1987), and *A New Path to the Waterfall*, published posthumously in 1989. His poetry and short stories have been published in *Esquire, Harper's, The New Yorker*, and the *Atlantic*. Among his many awards for writing are a Guggenheim fellowship in 1977 and a National Endowment for the Arts Award in Fiction in 1979. In 1993, film director Robert Altman compiled some of Carver's stories into a film entitled *Short Cuts*, for which he was nominated for an Academy Award for best director. Married to the writer Tess Gallagher, Carver lived in the small town of Port Angeles, Washington. He had surgery for lung cancer in 1987, but the cancer returned to his brain the next year. In the following essay, which originally appeared in *Esquire* in 1984, Carver offers an honest, yet loving, portrait of his alcoholic father.

1    My dad's name was Clevie Raymond Carver. His family called him Raymond and friends called him C. R. I was named Raymond Clevie Carver Jr. I hated the "Junior" part. When I was little my dad called me Frog, which was okay. But later, like everybody else in the family, he began calling me Junior. He went on calling me this until I was thirteen or fourteen and announced that I wouldn't answer to that name any longer. So he began calling me Doc. From then until his death, on June 17, 1967, he called me Doc, or else Son.

2    When he died, my mother telephoned my wife with the news. I was away from my family at the time, between lives, trying to enroll in the School of Library Science at the University of Iowa. When my wife answered the phone, my mother blurted out, "Raymond's dead!" For a moment, my wife thought my mother was telling her that I was dead. Then my mother made it clear *which* Raymond she was talking about and my wife said, "Thank God. I thought you meant *my* Raymond."

3    My dad walked, hitched rides, and rode in empty boxcars when he went from Arkansas to Washington State in 1934, looking for work. I don't know whether he was pursuing a dream when he went out to Washington. I doubt it. I don't think he dreamed much. I believe he was simply looking for steady work at decent pay. Steady work was meaningful work. He picked apples for a time and then landed a construction laborer's job on the Grand Coulee Dam. After he'd put aside a little money, he bought a car and drove back to Arkansas to help his folks, my grandparents, pack up for the move west. He said later that they were about to starve down there, and this wasn't meant as a figure of speech. It was during that short while in Arkansas, in a town called Leola, that my mother met my dad on the sidewalk as he came out of a tavern.

4    "He was drunk," she said. "I don't know why I let him talk to me. His eyes were glittery. I wish I'd had a crystal ball." They'd met once, a year or so before, at a dance. He'd had girlfriends before her,

my mother told me. "Your dad always had a girlfriend, even after we married. He was my first and last. I never had another man. But I didn't miss anything."

5    They were married by a justice of the peace on the day they left for Washington, this big, tall country girl and a farmhand-turned-construction worker. My mother spent her wedding night with my dad and his folks, all of them camped beside the road in Arkansas.

6    In Omak, Washington, my dad and mother lived in a little place not much bigger than a cabin. My grandparents lived next door. My dad was still working on the dam, and later, with the huge turbines producing electricity and the water backed up for a hundred miles into Canada, he stood in the crowd and heard Franklin D. Roosevelt when he spoke at the construction site. "He never mentioned those guys who died building that dam," my dad said. Some of his friends had died there, men from Arkansas, Oklahoma, and Missouri.

7    He then took a job in a sawmill in Clatskanie, Oregon, a little town alongside the Columbia River. I was born there, and my mother has a picture of my dad standing in front of the gate to the mill, proudly holding me up to face the camera. My bonnet is on crooked and about to come untied. His hat is pushed back on his forehead, and he's wearing a big grin. Was he going in to work or just finishing his shift? It doesn't matter. In either case, he had a job and a family. These were his salad days.

8    In 1941 we moved to Yakima, Washington, where my dad went to work as a saw filer, a skilled trade he'd learned in Clatskanie. When war broke out, he was given a deferment because his work was considered necessary to the war effort. Finished lumber was in demand by the armed services, and he kept his saws so sharp they could shave the hair off your arm.

9    After my dad had moved us to Yakima, he moved his folks into the same neighborhood. By the mid-1940s the rest of my dad's family—his brother, his sister, and her husband, as well as uncles, cousins, nephews, and most of their extended family and friends— had come out from Arkansas. All because my dad came out first. The men went to work at Boise Cascade, where my dad worked, and the women packed apples in the canneries. And in just a little while, it seemed—according to my mother—everybody was better off than my dad. "Your dad couldn't keep money," my mother said. "Money burned a hole in his pocket. He was always doing for others."

10    The first house I clearly remember living in, at 1515 South Fifteenth Street, in Yakima, had an outdoor toilet. On Halloween night, or just any night, for the hell of it, neighbor kids, kids in their early teens, would carry our toilet away and leave it next to the road. My dad would have to get somebody to help him bring it home. Or these kids would take the toilet and stand it in somebody else's backyard. Once they actually set it on fire, but ours wasn't the only house that had an outdoor toilet. When I was old enough to know what I was doing, I threw rocks at the other toilets when I'd see someone go inside. This was called bombing the toilets. After a while, though, everyone went to indoor plumbing until, suddenly, our toilet was the last outdoor one in the neighborhood. I remember the shame I felt when my third-grade teacher, Mr. Wise, drove me home from school one day. I asked him to stop at the house just before ours, claiming I lived there.

11    I can recall what happened one night when my dad came home late to find that my mother had locked all the doors on him from the inside. He was drunk, and we could feel the house shudder as he rattled the door. When he'd managed to force open a window, she hit him between the eyes with a colander and knocked him out. We could see him down there on the grass. For years afterward, I used to pick up this colander—it was as heavy as a rolling pin—and imagine what it would feel like to be hit in the head with something like that.

12    It was during this period that I remember my dad taking me into the bedroom, sitting me down on the bed, and telling me that I might have to go live with my Aunt LaVon for a while. I couldn't understand what I'd done that meant I'd have to go away from home to live. But this, too—whatever prompted it—must have blown over, more or less, anyway, because we stayed together, and I didn't have to go live with her or anyone else.

13    I remember my mother pouring his whiskey down the sink. Sometimes she'd pour it all out and sometimes, if she was afraid of getting caught, she'd only pour half of it out and then add water to the rest. I tasted some of his whiskey once myself. It was terrible stuff, and I don't see how anybody could drink it.

14    After a long time without one, we finally got a car, in 1949 or 1950, a 1938 Ford. But it threw a rod the first week we had it, and my dad had to have the motor rebuilt.

15  "We drove the oldest car in town," my mother said. "We could have had a Cadillac for all he spent on car repairs." One time she found someone else's tube of lipstick on the floorboard, along with a lacy handkerchief. "See this?" she said to me. "Some floozy left this in the car."

16  Once I saw her take a pan of warm water into the bedroom where my dad was sleeping. She took his hand from under the covers and held it in the water. I stood in the doorway and watched. I wanted to know what was going on. This would make him talk in his sleep, she told me. There were things she needed to know, things she was sure he was keeping from her.

17  Every year or so, when I was little, we would take the North Coast Limited across the Cascade Range from Yakima to Seattle and stay in the Vance Hotel and eat, I remember, at a place called the Dinner Bell Cafe. Once we went to Ivar's Acres of Clams and drank glasses of warm clam broth.

18  In 1956, the year I was to graduate from high school, my dad quit his job at the mill in Yakima and took a job in Chester, a little sawmill town in northern California. The reasons given at the time for his taking the job had to do with a higher hourly wage and the vague promise that he might, in a few years' time, succeed to the job of head filer in this new mill. But I think, in the main, that my dad had grown restless and simply wanted to try his luck elsewhere. Things had gotten a little too predictable for him in Yakima. Also, the year before, there had been the deaths, within six months of each other, of both his parents.

19  But just a few days after graduation, when my mother and I were packed to move to Chester, my dad penciled a letter to say he'd been sick for a while. He didn't want us to worry, he said, but he'd cut himself on a saw. Maybe he'd got a tiny sliver of steel in his blood. Anyway, something had happened and he'd had to miss work, he said. In the same mail was an unsigned postcard from somebody down there telling my mother that my dad was about to die and that he was drinking "raw whiskey."

20  When we arrived in Chester, my dad was living in a trailer that belonged to the company. I didn't recognize him immediately. I guess for a moment I didn't want to recognize him. He was skinny and pale and looked bewildered. His pants wouldn't stay up. He didn't look like my dad. My mother began to cry. My dad put his

arm around her and patted her shoulder vaguely, like he didn't know
what this was all about, either. The three of us took up life together
in the trailer, and we looked after him as best we could. But my dad
was sick, and he couldn't get any better. I worked with him in the
mill that summer and part of the fall. We'd get up in the mornings
and eat eggs and toast while we listened to the radio, and then go
out the door with our lunch pails. We'd pass through the gate
together at eight in the morning, and I wouldn't see him again until
quitting time. In November I went back to Yakima to be closer to
my girlfriend, the girl I'd made up my mind I was going to marry.

21      He worked at the mill in Chester until the following February,
when he collapsed on the job and was taken to the hospital. My
mother asked if I would come down there and help. I caught a bus
from Yakima to Chester, intending to drive them back to Yakima.
But now, in addition to being physically sick, my dad was in the
midst of a nervous breakdown, though none of us knew to call it
that at the time. During the entire trip back to Yakima, he didn't
speak, not even when asked a direct question. ("How do you feel,
Raymond?" "You okay, Dad?") He'd communicate, if he communicated at all, by moving his head or by turning his palms up as if to
say he didn't know or care. The only time he said anything on the
trip, and for nearly a month afterward, was when I was speeding
down a gravel road in Oregon and the car muffler came loose. "You
were going too fast," he said.

22      Back in Yakima a doctor saw to it that my dad went to a psychiatrist. My mother and dad had to go on relief, as it was called, and the
county paid for the psychiatrist. The psychiatrist asked my dad,
"Who is the President?" He'd had a question put to him that he
could answer. "Ike," my dad said. Nevertheless, they put him on the
fifth floor of Valley Memorial Hospital and began giving him elec-
troshock treatments. I was married by then and about to start my
own family. My dad was still locked up when my wife went into this
same hospital, just one floor down, to have our first baby. After she
had delivered, I went upstairs to give my dad the news. They let me
in through a steel door and showed me where I could find him. He
was sitting on a couch with a blanket over his lap. *Hey*, I thought.
*What in hell is happening to my dad?* I sat down next to him and told
him he was a grandfather. He waited a minute and then said, "I feel
like a grandfather." That's all he said. He didn't smile or move. He

was in a big room with a lot of other people. Then I hugged him, and he began to cry.

23 Somehow he got out of there. But now came the years when he couldn't work and just sat around the house trying to figure what next and what he'd done wrong in his life that he'd wound up like this. My mother went from job to crummy job. Much later she referred to that time he was in the hospital, and those years just afterward, as "when Raymond was sick." The word *sick* was never the same for me again.

24 In 1964, through the help of a friend, he was lucky enough to be hired on at a mill in Klamath, California. He moved down there by himself to see if he could hack it. He lived not far from the mill, in a one-room cabin not much different from the place he and my mother had started out living in when they went west. He scrawled letters to my mother, and if I called she'd read them aloud to me over the phone. In the letters, he said it was touch and go. Every day that he went to work, he felt like it was the most important day of his life. But every day, he told her, made the next day that much easier. He said for her to tell me he said hello. If he couldn't sleep at night, he said, he thought about me and the good times we used to have. Finally, after a couple of months, he regained some of his confidence. He could do the work and didn't think he had to worry that he'd let anybody down ever again. When he was sure, he sent for my mother.

25 He'd been off from work for six years and had lost everything in that time—home, car, furniture, and appliances, including the big freezer that had been my mother's pride and joy. He'd lost his good name too—Raymond Carver was someone who couldn't pay his bills—and his self-respect was gone. He'd even lost his virility. My mother told my wife, "All during that time Raymond was sick we slept together in the same bed, but we didn't have relations. He wanted to a few times, but nothing happened. I didn't miss it, but I think he wanted to, you know."

26 During those years I was trying to raise my own family and earn a living. But, one thing and another, we found ourselves having to move a lot. I couldn't keep track of what was going down in my dad's life. But I did have a chance one Christmas to tell him I wanted to be a writer. I might as well have told him I wanted to become a plastic surgeon. "What are you going to write about?" he wanted to know.

Then, as if to help me out, he said, "Write about stuff you know about. Write about some of those fishing trips we took." I said I would, but I knew I wouldn't. "Send me what you write," he said. I said I'd do that, but then I didn't. I wasn't writing anything about fishing, and I didn't think he'd particularly care about, or even necessarily understand, what I was writing in those days. Besides, he wasn't a reader. Not the sort, anyway, I imagined I was writing for.

27    Then he died. I was a long way off, in Iowa City, with things still to say to him. I didn't have the chance to tell him goodbye, or that I thought he was doing great at his new job. That I was proud of him for making a comeback.

28    My mother said he came in from work that night and ate a big supper. Then he sat at the table by himself and finished what was left of a bottle of whiskey, a bottle she found hidden in the bottom of the garbage under some coffee grounds a day or so later. Then he got up and went to bed, where my mother joined him a little later. But in the night she had to get up and make a bed for herself on the couch. "He was snoring so loud I couldn't sleep," she said. The next morning when she looked in on him, he was on his back with his mouth open, his cheeks caved in. *Graylooking*, she said. She knew he was dead—she didn't need a doctor to tell her that. But she called one anyway, and then she called my wife.

29    Among the pictures my mother kept of my dad and herself during those early days in Washington was a photograph of him standing in front of a car, holding a beer and a stringer of fish. In the photograph he is wearing his hat back on his forehead and has this awkward grin on his face. I asked her for it and she gave it to me, along with some others. I put it up on my wall, and each time we moved, I took the picture along and put it up on another wall. I looked at it carefully from time to time, trying to figure out some things about my dad, and maybe myself in the process. But I couldn't. My dad just kept moving further and further away from me and back into time. Finally, in the course of another move, I lost the photograph. It was then that I tried to recall it, and at the same time make an attempt to say something about my dad, and how I thought that in some important ways we might be alike. I wrote the poem when I was living in an apartment house in an urban area south of San Francisco, at a time when I found myself, like my dad, having trouble with alcohol. The poem was a way of trying to connect up with him.

### Photograph of My Father
### in His Twenty-Second Year

*October.* Here in this dank, unfamiliar kitchen
I study my father's embarrassed young man's face.
Sheepish grin, he holds in one hand a string
of spiny yellow perch, in the other
a bottle of Carlsberg beer.

In jeans and flannel shirt, he leans
against the front fender of a 1934 Ford.
He would like to pose brave and hearty for his
posterity,
wear his old hat cocked over his ear.
All his life my father wanted to be bold.

But the eyes give him away, and the hands
that limply offer the string of dead perch
and the bottle of beer. Father, I love you,
yet how can I say thank you, I who can't hold my
liquor either
and don't even know the places to fish.

30      The poem is true in its particulars, except that my dad died in
June and not October, as the first word of the poem says. I wanted
a word with more than one syllable to it to make it linger a little. But
more than that, I wanted a month appropriate to what I felt at the
time I wrote the poem—a month of short days and failing light,
smoke in the air, things perishing. June was summer nights and
days, graduations, my wedding anniversary, the birthday of one of
my children. June wasn't a month your father died in.

31      After the service at the funeral home, after we had moved outside, a woman I didn't know came over to me and said, "He's happier where he is now." I stared at this woman until she moved
away. I still remember the little knob of a hat she was wearing.
Then one of my dad's cousins—I didn't know the man's name—
reached out and took my hand, "We all miss him," he said, and I
knew he wasn't saying it just to be polite.

32    I began to weep for the first time since receiving the news. I hadn't been able to before. I hadn't had the time, for one thing. Now, suddenly, I couldn't stop. I held my wife and wept while she said and did what she could do to comfort me there in the middle of that summer afternoon.

33    I listened to people say consoling things to my mother, and I was glad that my dad's family had turned up, had come to where he was. I thought I'd remember everything that was said and done that day and maybe find a way to tell it sometime. But I didn't. I forgot it all, or nearly. What I do remember is that I heard our name used a lot that afternoon, my dad's name and mine. But I knew they were talking about my dad. *Raymond*, these people kept saying in their beautiful voices out of my childhood. *Raymond*.

# Discussion Questions

1. Why do you think Carver spends the entire first paragraph explaining his and his father's names?
2. How is Carver's character similar to and different from his father's? Cite specific examples from the essay.
3. What facts about Carver's father's life do you find most revealing? Why?
4. What is the importance of Carver's providing so many seemingly minute details about his father's life?
5. Explain why Carver included the poem in this essay. What does it add?
6. In small groups, discuss why Carver forgot "everything that was said and done that day [of his father's funeral]"? Why is it important for Carver to include that information and to end the essay with it?

# Writing Assignments

1. Imagine you are Carver. Write a letter to your father that explains the impact he had on your life.

2. Write an essay about the way someone has affected your life. Show the person in the way Carver does.

3. Write a paper that examines the importance of funeral rituals. Argue whether funerals are necessary for family and friends to reach closure.

4. Select three essays from this collection and analyze the ways in which the writers avoid sentimentality when writing about emotional situations.

# *from* Hunger of Memory

## RICHARD RODRIGUEZ

Richard Rodriguez (b. 1944) was born in San Francisco, the son of working-class Mexican parents. Spanish was his first language, and he barely spoke English when he started school at the age of five. He holds a B.A. from Stanford University, an M.A. from Columbia University, and a Ph.D. from the University of California at Berkeley. Along with serving as editor at Pacific News Services in San Francisco, being a contributing editor at *Harper's* magazine, and lecturing throughout the country on issues concerning affirmative action, Rodriguez is a full-time writer. He is the author of a series of highly acclaimed autobiographical essays, *Hunger of Memory: The Education of Richard Rodriguez* (1982), and *Days of Obligation: An Argument with My Mexican Father* (1992). Rodriguez has established himself as a critic of affirmative action programs and writes about the dangers of bilingual education programs. Rodriguez's thoughtful, honest, and courageous exploration of the issues surrounding bilingual education in the United States has made him one of the leading figures in the field. In the following essay from *Hunger of Memory*, Rodriguez details the many secrets that as a youth distanced him from his parents.

1    I am writing about those very things my mother has asked me not to reveal. Shortly after I published my first autobiographical essay seven years ago, my mother wrote me a letter pleading with me never again to write about our family life. 'Write about something else in the future. Our family life is private.' And besides: 'Why do you need to tell the *gringos* about how "divided" you feel from the family?'

2    I sit at my desk now, surrounded by versions of paragraphs and pages of this book, considering that question.

3    When I decided to compose this intellectual autobiography, a New York editor told me that I would embark on a lonely journey. Over the noise of voices and dishes in an East Side restaurant, he said, 'There will be times when you will think the entire world has forgotten you. Some mornings you will yearn for a phone call or a letter to assure you that you still are connected to the world.' There *have* been mornings when I've dreaded the isolation this writing requires. Mornings spent listless in silence and in fear of confronting the blank sheet of paper. There have been times I've rushed away from my papers to answer the phone; gladly gotten up from my chair, hearing the mailman outside. Times I have been frustrated by the slowness of words, the way even a single paragraph never seemed done.

4    I had known a writer's loneliness before, working on my dissertation in the British Museum. But that experience did not prepare me for the task of writing these pages where my own life is the subject. Many days I feared I had stopped living by committing myself to remember the past. I feared that my absorption with events in my past amounted to an immature refusal to live in the present. Adulthood seemed consumed by memory. I would tell myself otherwise. I would tell myself that the act of remembering is an act of the present. (In writing this autobiography, I am actually describing the man I have become—the man in the present.)

5    Times when the money ran out, I left writing for temporary jobs. Once I had a job for over six months. I resumed something like a conventional social life. But then I have turned away, come back to my San Francisco apartment to closet myself in the silence I both need and fear.

6    I stay away from late-night parties. (To be clearheaded in the morning.) I disconnect my phone for much of the day. I must avoid

complex relationships—a troublesome lover or a troubled friend. The person who knows me best scolds me for escaping from life. (*Am* I evading adulthood?) People I know get promotions at jobs. Friends move away. Friends get married. Friends divorce. One friend tells me she is pregnant. Then she has a baby. Then the baby has the formed face of a child. Can walk. Talk. And still I sit at this desk laying my words like jigsaw pieces, a fellow with ladies in housecoats and old men in slippers who watch TV. Neighbors in my apartment house rush off to work about nine. I hear their steps on the stairs. (They will be back at six o'clock.) Somewhere planes are flying. The door slams behind them.

7    'Why?' My mother's question hangs in the still air of memory.

8    The loneliness I have felt many mornings, however, has not made me forget that I am engaged in a highly public activity. I sit here in silence writing this small volume of words, and it seems to me the most public thing I ever have done. My mother's letter has served to remind me: I am making my personal life public. Probably I will never try to explain my motives to my mother and father. My mother's question will go unanswered to her face. Like everything else on these pages, my reasons for writing will be revealed instead to public readers I expect never to meet.

# I

9    It is to those whom my mother refers to as the *gringos* that I write. The *gringos*. The expression reminds me that she and my father have not followed their children all the way down the path to full Americanization. They were changed—became more easy in public, less withdrawn and uncertain—by the public success of their children. But something remained unchanged in their lives. With excessive care they continue today to note the difference between private and public life. And their private society remains only their family. No matter how friendly they are in public, no matter how firm their smiles, my parents never forget when they are in public. My mother must use a high-pitched tone of voice when she addresses people who are not relatives. It is a tone of voice I have all my life heard her use away from the house. Coming home from

grammar school with new friends, I would hear it, its reminder: My new intimates were strangers to her. Like my sisters and brother, over the years, I've grown used to hearing that voice. Expected to hear it. Though I suspect that voice has played deep in my soul, sounding a lyre, to recall my 'betrayal,' my movement away from our family's intimate past. It is the voice I hear even now when my mother addresses her son- or daughter-in-law. (They remain public people to her.) She speaks to them, sounding the way she does when talking over the fence to a neighbor.

10    It was, in fact, the lady next door to my parents—a librarian— who first mentioned seeing my essay seven years ago. My mother was embarrassed because she hadn't any idea what the lady was talking about. But she had heard enough to go to a library with my father to find the article. They read what I wrote. And then she wrote her letter.

11    It is addressed to me in Spanish, but the body of the letter is in English. Almost mechanically she speaks of her pride at the start. ('Your dad and I are very proud of the brilliant manner you have to express yourself.') Then the matter of most concern comes to the fore. 'Your dad and I have only one objection to what you write. You say too much about the family . . . Why do you have to do that? . . . Why do you need to tell the *gringos*? . . . Why do you think we're so separated as a family? Do you really think this, Richard?'

12    A new paragraph changes the tone. Soft, maternal. Worried for me she adds, 'Do not punish yourself for having to give up our culture in order to "make it" as you say. Think of all the wonderful achievements you have obtained. You should be proud. Learn Spanish better. Practice it with your dad and me. Don't worry so much. Don't get the idea that I am mad at you either.

13    'Just keep one thing in mind. Writing is one thing, the family is another. I don't want *tus hermanos* hurt by your writings. And what do you think the cousins will say when they read where you talk about how the aunts were maids? Especially I don't want the *gringos* knowing about our private affairs. Why should they? Please give this some thought. Please write about something else in the future. Do me this favor.'

14    Please.

# Discussion Questions

1. What is your impression of Rodriguez when he reveals in the first sentence that he is "writing about those very things my mother has asked me not to reveal"? Does your impression change by the end of the essay? Why?
2. Why did Rodriguez's editor call his writing "a lonely journey"?
3. In small groups, discuss whether Rodriguez's reasons for writing about his family are valid.
4. Characterize Rodriguez from what he reveals about himself in this essay.
5. What is the point of Rodriguez's essay?
6. What has Rodriguez learned by writing this essay? Explain.
7. How is this essay an example of "intellectual autobiography," the term Rodriguez uses in paragraph 3?

# Writing Assignments

1. Assume the role of Rodriguez's mother. Write a letter to him in which you explain why he should not reveal what he does in this essay.
2. In a journal entry, write about a time in your life when you could have been aptly named "Secrets."
3. Reflect on your childhood and write an essay examining the ways in which you have changed or stayed the same since childhood.
4. Write a chapter of your "intellectual autobiography"; that is, compose an essay in which you examine the way you learned something important.

# CLASSIC ESSAYS ON

# Husbands and Wives

# Of Marriage and Single Life

## FRANCIS BACON

Francis Bacon (1561–1626) was born in London, educated at Trinity College in Cambridge, and trained for the legal profession at Gray's Inn. During his life, he served as solicitor general and lord high chancellor of England. Bacon became Baron Verulam in 1618 and Viscount St. Albans in 1621. While sitting on the judicial bench, he was convicted by Parliament of having accepted bribes. His reputation as an important figure in the emergence of Western thought is the result of his philosophical texts *The Advancement of Learning* (1605), Novum Organum (1620), and *De Augmentis Scientiarum* (1623). These books reflect the change in thinking in the seventeenth century from Aristotelian logic, which favors deductive reasoning, to the inductive approach, which was employed by the physical sciences. Bacon is also the author of *Essayes* (1597), which offers his perspective on a number of topics, from love and marriage to studies and human values. An enlarged edition of the book appeared in 1612, and a final collection was published in 1625, numbering fifty-eight essays. Bacon's short, compact, and rather impersonal essays introduced a distinct version of the genre, one many writers have modeled their work after. In the following selection, taken from *Essayes*, Bacon muses on married life in relation to single life.

1    He that hath wife and children hath given hostages to fortune; for they are impediments to great enterprises, either of virtue or mischief. Certainly the best works and of greatest merit for the public have proceeded from the unmarried or childless men: which both in affection and means have married and endowed the public. Yet it were great reason that those that have children should have greatest care of future times unto which they know they must transmit their dearest pledges. Some there are, who though they lead a single life, yet their thoughts do end with themselves, and account future times impertinences. Nay, there are some other that account wife and children but as bills of charges. Nay, more, there are some foolish rich covetous men, that take a pride in having no children because they may be thought so much the richer. For perhaps they have heard some talk, Such a one is a great rich man; and another except to it, Yea, but he hath a great charge of children,—as if it were an abatement to his riches. But the most ordinary cause of a single life is liberty; especially in certain self-pleasing and humorous minds, which are so sensible of every restraint, as they will go near to think their girdles and garters to be bonds and shackles. Unmarried men are best friends, best masters, best servants, but not always best subjects; for they are light to run away: and almost all fugitives are of that condition. A single life doth well with churchmen: for charity will hardly water the ground, where it must first fill a pool. It is indifferent for judges and magistrates: for if they be facile and corrupt, you shall have a servant five times worse than a wife. For soldiers, I find the generals commonly, in their hortatives, put men in mind of their wives and children. And I think the despising of marriage amongst the Turks maketh the vulgar soldiers more base. Certainly, wife and children are a kind of discipline of humanity; and single men, though they be many times more charitable, because their means are less exhaust, yet, on the other side, they are more cruel and hardhearted, good to make severe inquisitors, because their tenderness is not so oft called upon. Grave natures, led by custom, and therefore constant, are commonly loving husbands; as was said of Ulysses, "*Vetulam suam prætulit immortalitati.*" Chaste women are often proud and froward, as presuming upon the merit of their chastity. It is one of the best bonds, both of chastity and obedience, in the wife, if she think her husband wise: which she will never do if she find him jealous. Wives are young men's mistresses; companions for middle

ages; and old men's nurses. So as a man may have a quarrel to marry when he will. But yet he was reputed one of the wise men, that made answer to the question, when a man should marry: "A young man not yet, an elder man not at all." It is often seen that bad husbands have very good wives; whether it be that it raiseth the price of their husbands' kindness when it comes, or that the wives take a pride in their patience. But this never fails if the bad husbands were of their own choosing, against their friends' consent; for then they will be sure to make good their own folly.

## Discussion Questions

1. Summarize Bacon's essay.
2. In small groups, discuss the following question: Of all the traits Bacon offers regarding unmarried men, which are most plausible and which most ludicrous?
3. What does Bacon mean when he states that "wife and children are a kind of discipline of humanity"?
4. Characterize Bacon based on his opinions regarding marriage and single life.
5. Bacon states, "Wives are young men's mistresses; companions for middle ages; and old men's nurses." Is this statement convincing and true? Explain.

## Writing Assignments

1. Write a companion piece to Bacon's in which you discuss unmarried *women* as opposed to unmarried men.
2. Write a paper that completes and supports the following sentence, "Unmarried men are best _____."
3. In an essay, identify how the roles of and demands placed on men and women have changed from your parents' generation to yours. Analyze whether these changes have been positive or negative.
4. Is the trend of young people waiting to get married good or bad? Write a paper in which you support your answer.

# On Marriage

## ROBERT LOUIS STEVENSON

Robert Louis Stevenson (1850–1894) was born in Edinburgh, Scotland. Although he studied law and passed the bar examinations, he never practiced law. In 1875, Stevenson began to write essays for various magazines. In 1880, he married Fanny Osbourne, an American, and they spent the next fourteen years searching for a climate that was suitable for his tuberculosis. In 1890, they moved to Samoa. Stevenson is most noted for his children's adventure novels, *Treasure Island* (1883) and *Kidnapped* (1886). He is also the author of the horror classic *The Strange Case of Dr. Jekyll and Mr. Hyde* (1886). His other publications include *Travels with a Donkey in the Cévennes* (1879), *A Child's Garden of Verses* (1885), and *The Black Arrow* (1888). An accomplished storyteller, Stevenson reveals another side of his talent in his essays. "On Marriage" is part of a collection of essays about love, sex, and marriage entitled *Virginibus Puerisque*. In this essay, Stevenson makes a case that "there is probably no other act in a man's life so hot-headed and foolhardy as this one of marriage."

1    Hope, they say, deserts us at no period of our existence. From first to last, and in the face of smarting disillusions, we continue to expect good fortune, better health, and better conduct; and that so confidently, that we judge it needless to deserve them. I think it

improbable that I shall ever write like Shakespeare, conduct an army like Hannibal, or distinguish myself like Marcus Aurelius in the paths of virtue; and yet I have my by-days, hope prompting, when I am very ready to believe that I shall combine all these various excellences in my own person, and go marching down to posterity with divine honors. There is nothing so monstrous but we can believe it of ourselves. About ourselves, about our aspirations and delinquencies, we have dwelt by choice in a delicious vagueness from our boyhood up. No one will have forgotten Tom Sawyer's aspiration: "Ah, if he could only die *temporarily!*" Or, perhaps, better still, the inward resolution of the two pirates, that "so long as they remained in that business, their piracies should not again be sullied with the crime of stealing." Here we recognize the thoughts of our boyhood; and our boyhood ceased—well, when?—not, I think, at twenty; nor, perhaps, altogether at twenty-five; nor yet at thirty; and possibly, to be quite frank, we are still in the thick of that Arcadian period. For as the race of man, after centuries of civilization, still keeps some traits of their barbarian fathers, so man the individual is not altogether quit of youth, when he is already old and honored, and Lord Chancellor of England. We advance in years somewhat in the manner of an invading army in a barren land; the age that we have reached, as the phrase goes, we but hold with an outpost, and still keep open our communications with the extreme rear and first beginnings of the march. There is our true base; that is not only the beginning, but the perennial spring of our faculties; and grandfather William can retire upon occasion into the green enchanted forest of his boyhood.

2    The unfading boyishness of hope and its vigorous irrationality are nowhere better displayed than in questions of conduct. There is a character in the *Pilgrim's Progress*, one Mr. *Linger-after-Lust*, with whom I fancy we are all on speaking terms; one famous among the famous for ingenuity of hope up to and beyond the moment of defeat; one who, after eighty years of contrary experience, will believe it possible to continue in the business of piracy and yet avoid the guilt of theft. Every sin is our last; every 1st of January a remarkable turning-point in our career. Any overt act, above all, is felt to be alchemic in its power to change. A drunkard takes the pledge; it will be strange if that does not help him. For how many years did Mr. Pepys continue to make and break his little vows? And yet I have not

heard that he was discouraged in the end. By such steps we think to fix a momentary resolution; as a timid fellow hies him to the dentist's while the tooth is stinging.

3     But, alas, by planting a stake at the top of flood, you can neither prevent nor delay the inevitable ebb. There is no hocus-pocus in morality; and even the "sanctimonious ceremony" of marriage leaves the man unchanged. This is a hard saying, and has an air of paradox. For there is something in marriage so natural and inviting, that the step has an air of great simplicity and ease; it offers to bury forever many aching preoccupations; it is to afford us unfailing and familiar company through life; it opens up a smiling prospect of the blest and passive kind of love, rather than the blessing and active; it is approached not only through the delights of courtship, but by a public performance and repeated legal signatures. A man naturally thinks it will go hard with him if he cannot be good and fortunate and happy within such august circumvallations.

4     And yet there is probably no other act in a man's life so hotheaded and foolhardy as this one of marriage. For years, let us suppose, you have been making the most indifferent business of your career. Your experience has not, we may dare to say, been more encouraging than Paul's or Horace's; like them, you have seen and desired the good that you were not able to accomplish; like them, you have done the evil that you loathed. You have waked at night in a hot or a cold sweat, according to your habit of body, remembering, with dismal surprise, your own unpardonable acts and sayings. You have been sometimes tempted to withdraw entirely from this game of life; as a man who makes nothing but misses withdraws from that less dangerous one of billiards. You have fallen back upon the thought that you yourself most sharply smarted for your misdemeanors, or, in the old, plaintive phrase, that you were nobody's enemy but your own. And then you have been made aware of what was beautiful and amiable, wise and kind, in the other part of your behavior; and it seemed as if nothing could reconcile the contradiction, as indeed nothing can. If you are a man, you have shut your mouth hard and said nothing; and if you are only a man in the making, you have recognized that yours was quite a special case, and you yourself not guilty of your own pestiferous career.

5     Granted, and with all my heart. Let us accept these apologies; let us agree that you are nobody's enemy but your own; let us agree

that you are a sort of moral cripple, impotent for good; and let us regard you with the unmingled pity due to such a fate. But there is one thing to which, on these terms, we can never agree:—we can never agree to have you marry. What! you have had one life to manage, and have failed so strangely, and now can see nothing wiser than to conjoin with it the management of some one else's? Because you have been unfaithful in a very little, you propose yourself to be a ruler over ten cities. You strip yourself by such a step of all remaining consolations and excuses. You are no longer content to be your own enemy; you must be your wife's also. You have been hitherto in a mere subaltern attitude; dealing cruel blows about you in life, yet only half responsible, since you came there by no choice or movement of your own. Now, it appears, you must take things on your own authority: God made you, but you marry yourself; and for all that your wife suffers, no one is responsible but you. A man must be very certain of his knowledge ere he undertake to guide a ticket-of-leave man through a dangerous pass; you have eternally missed your way in life, with consequences that you still deplore, and yet you masterfully seize your wife's hand, and, blindfold, drag her after you to ruin. And it is your wife, you observe, whom you select. She, whose happiness you most desire, you choose to be your victim. You would earnestly warn her from a tottering bridge or bad investment. If she were to marry some one else, how you would tremble for her fate! If she were only your sister, and you thought half as much of her, how doubtfully would you entrust her future to a man no better than yourself!

6    Times are changed with him who marries; there are no more by-path meadows, where you may innocently linger, but the road lies long and straight and dusty to the grave. Idleness, which is often becoming and even wise in the bachelor, begins to wear a different aspect when you have a wife to support. Suppose, after you are married, one of those little slips were to befall you. What happened last November might surely happen February next. They may have annoyed you at the time, because they were not what you had meant; but how will they annoy you in the future, and how will they shake the fabric of your wife's confidence and peace! A thousand things unpleasing went on in the *chiaroscuro* of a life that you shrank from too particularly realizing; you did not care, in those days, to make a fetish of your conscience; you would recognize your failures

with a nod, and so, good-day. But the time for these reserves is over. You have wilfully introduced a witness into your life, the scene of these defeats, and can no longer close the mind's eye upon uncomely passages, but must stand up straight and put a name upon your actions. And your witness is not only the judge, but the victim of your sins; not only can she condemn you to the sharpest penalties, but she must herself share feelingly in their endurance. And observe, once more, with what temerity you have chosen precisely *her* to be your spy, whose esteem you value highest, and whom you have already taught to think you better than you are. You may think you had a conscience, and believed in God; but what is a conscience to a wife? Wise men of yore erected statues of their deities, and consciously performed their part in life before those marble eyes. A god watched them at the board, and stood by their bedside in the morning when they woke; and all about their ancient cities, where they bought and sold, or where they piped and wrestled, there would stand some symbol of the things that are outside of man. These were lessons, delivered in the quiet dialect of art, which told their story faithfully, but gently. It is the same lesson, if you will—but how harrowingly taught!—when the woman you respect shall weep from your unkindness or blush with shame at your misconduct. Poor girls in Italy turn their painted Madonnas to the wall: you cannot set aside your wife. To marry is to domesticate the Recording Angel. Once you are married, there is nothing left for you, not even suicide, but to be good.

And goodness in marriage is a more intricate problem than mere single virtue; for in marriage there are two ideals to be realized. A girl, it is true, has always lived in a glass house among reproving relatives, whose word was law; she has been bred up to sacrifice her judgments and take the key submissively from dear papa; and it is wonderful how swiftly she can change her tune into the husband's. Her morality has been, too often, an affair of precept and conformity. But in the case of a bachelor who has enjoyed some measure both of privacy and freedom, his moral judgments have been passed in some accordance with his nature. His sins were always sins in his own sight; he could then only sin when he did some act against his clear conviction; the light that he walked by was obscure, but it was single. Now, when two people of any grit and spirit put their fortunes into one, there succeeds to this comparative certainty a huge welter of competing jurisdictions. It no longer matters so much how life appears to one; one must consult another: one, who may be strong, must not offend the other, who is weak. The only weak brother I am willing to consider is (to make a bull for once) my wife. For her, and for her only, I must waive my righteous judgments, and go crookedly about my life. How, then, in such an atmosphere of compromise, to keep honor bright and abstain from base capitulations? How are you to put aside love's pleadings? How are you, the apostle of laxity, to turn suddenly about into the rabbi of precision; and after these years of ragged practice, pose for a hero to the lackey who has found you out? In this temptation to mutual indulgence lies the particular peril to morality in married life. Daily they drop a little lower from the first ideal, and for awhile continue to accept these changelings with a gross complacency. At last Love wakes and looks about him; finds his hero sunk into a stout old brute, intent on brandy pawnee; finds his heroine divested of her angel brightness; and in the flash of that first disenchantment, flees forever.

8 Again, the husband, in these unions, is usually a man, and the wife commonly enough a woman; and when this is the case, although it makes the firmer marriage, a thick additional veil of misconception hangs above the doubtful business. Women, I believe, are somewhat rarer than men; but then, if I were a woman myself, I dare say I should hold the reverse; and at least we all enter more or less wholly into one or other of these camps. A man who delights women by his feminine perceptions will often scatter his admirers by a chance explosion of the under side of man; and the most masculine and direct of women will some day, to your dire surprise, draw out like a telescope into successive lengths of personation. Alas! for the man, knowing her to be at heart more candid than himself, who shall flounder, panting, through these mazes in the quest for truth. The proper qualities of each sex are, indeed, eternally surprising to the other. Between the Latin and the Teuton races there are similar divergences, not to be bridged by the most liberal sympathy. And in the good, plain, cut-and-dry explanations of this life, which pass current among us as the wisdom of the elders, this difficulty has been turned with the aid of pious lies. Thus, when a young lady has angelic features, eats nothing to speak of, plays all day long on the piano, and sings ravishingly in church, it requires a rough infidelity, falsely called cynicism, to believe that she may be a little devil after

all. Yet so it is: she may be a tale-bearer, a liar, and a thief; she may have a taste for brandy, and no heart. My compliments to George Eliot for her Rosamond Vincy; the ugly work of satire she has transmuted to the ends of art, by the companion figure of Lydgate; and the satire was much wanted for the education of young men. That doctrine of the excellence of women, however chivalrous, is cowardly as well as false. It is better to face the fact, and know, when you marry, that you take into your life a creature of equal, if of unlike, frailties; whose weak human heart beats no more tunefully than yours.

9     But it is the object of a liberal education not only to obscure the knowledge of one sex by another, but to magnify the natural differences between the two. Man is a creature who lives not upon bread alone, but principally by catchwords; and the little rift between the sexes is astonishingly widened by simply teaching one set of catchwords to the girls and another to the boys. To the first, there is shown but a very small field of experience, and taught a very trenchant principle for judgment and action; to the other, the world of life is more largely displayed, and their rule of conduct is proportionately widened. They are taught to follow different virtues, to hate different vices, to place their ideal, even for each other, in different achievements. What should be the result of such a course? When a horse has run away, and the two flustered people in the gig have each possessed themselves of a rein, we know the end of that conveyance will be in the ditch. So, when I see a raw youth and a green girl, fluted and fiddled in a dancing measure into that most serious contract, and setting out upon life's journey with ideas so monstrously divergent, I am not surprised that some make shipwreck, but that any come to port. What the boy does almost proudly, as a manly peccadillo, the girl will shudder at as a debasing vice; what is to her the mere common-sense of tactics, he will spit out of his mouth as shameful. Through such a sea of contrarieties must this green couple steer their way; and contrive to love each other; and to respect, forsooth; and be ready, when the time arrives, to educate the little men and women who shall succeed to their places and perplexities.

10     And yet, when all has been said, the man who should hold back from marriage is in the same case with him who runs away from battle. To avoid an occasion for our virtues is a worse degree of failure

than to push forward pluckily and make a fall. It is lawful to pray God that we be not led into temptation; but not lawful to skulk from those that come to us. The noblest passage in one of the noblest books of this century, is where the old pope glories in the trial, nay, in the partial fall and but imperfect triumph, of the younger hero. Without some such manly note, it were perhaps better to have no conscience at all. But there is a vast difference between teaching flight, and showing points of peril that a man may march the more warily. And the true conclusion of this paper is to turn our back on apprehensions, and embrace that shining and courageous virtue, Faith. Hope is the boy, a blind, headlong, pleasant fellow, good to chase swallows with the salt; Faith is the grave, experienced, yet smiling man. Hope lives on ignorance; open-eyed Faith is built upon a knowledge of our life, of the tyranny of circumstance and the frailty of human resolution. Hope looks for unqualified success; but Faith counts certainly on failure, and takes honorable defeat to be a form of victory. Hope is a kind old pagan; but Faith grew up in Christian days, and early learned humility. In the one temper, a man is indignant that he cannot spring up in a clap to heights of elegance and virtue; in the other, out of a sense of his infirmities, he is filled with confidence because a year has come and gone, and he has still preserved some rags of honor. In the first, he expects an angel for a wife; in the last, he knows that she is like himself—erring, thoughtless, and untrue; but like himself also, filled with a struggling radiancy of better things, and adorned with ineffective qualities. You may safely go to school with hope; but ere you marry, should have learned the mingled lesson of the world: that dolls are stuffed with sawdust, and yet are excellent playthings; that hope and love address themselves to a perfection never realized, and yet, firmly held, become the salt and staff of life; that you yourself are compacted of infirmities, perfect, you might say, in imperfection, and yet you have a something in you lovable and worth preserving; and that, while the mass of mankind lies under this scurvy condemnation, you will scarce find one but, by some generous reading, will become to you a lesson, a model, and a noble spouse through life. So thinking, you will constantly support your own unworthiness, and easily forgive the failings of your friend. Nay, you will be wisely glad that you retain the sense of blemishes; for the faults of married people continually spur up each of them, hour by hour, to do better and to meet and love upon a higher ground. And ever, between the failures, there will come glimpses of kind virtues to encourage and console.

# Discussion Questions

1. Do you agree with Stevenson's opening statement: "Hope, they say, deserts us at no period of our existence"? Why?
2. How does the essay's first paragraph on hope relate to the rest of the essay?
3. Summarize Stevenson's attitude toward marriage. Explain how you arrived at your answer.
4. Whom do you think Stevenson envisioned as his audience? Why?
5. In small groups, discuss whether you agree with Stevenson's opinion that "there is probably no other act in a man's life so hot-headed and foolhardy as this one of marriage" (paragraph 4). Would you agree or disagree if the word *man's* were substituted with the word *woman's*? Explain.
6. Stevenson cites various reasons to support his statement in paragraph 6 that "times are changed with him who marries." Do you find these reasons convincing?
7. In light of the rest of his essay, explain Stevenson's thinking in paragraph 10.

# Writing Assignments

1. Write an essay in defense of marriage, playing off Stevenson's ideas.
2. Using the female perspective, respond in a journal entry to the ideas Stevenson proposes in his essay.
3. In a paper, explore to what extent, if any, marriage is an outdated institution.

# Undesirable Husbands

## DANIEL DEFOE

Daniel Defoe (1660–1731) was born outside of London, England. Because his parents were Dissenters (Protestants who did not subscribe to the tenets of the church), Defoe was forced into attending the Dissenters' academy instead of Oxford or Cambridge University. A merchant by trade, Defoe was an ardent Whig and writer of political verse and pamphlets, for which he was thrice pilloried and finally jailed in 1703. Defoe is the author of *The Shortest Way with the Dissenters* (1702) and *A Journal of the Plague Year* (1722). His novels include *Robinson Crusoe* (1719), *Captain Singleton* (1720), *Moll Flanders* (1722), *Colonel Jacque* (1722), and *Roxana* (1724). The following selection first appeared in a 1707 issue of *The Review*, a newspaper that Defoe founded in 1704 and edited until 1713. In this essay, Defoe provides four answers to the question he raises of what the worst kind of husband is. Although this essay is almost three hundred years old, Defoe's description of undesirable husbands is remarkably accurate for contemporary times.

1    It is but seldom that I have taken up any part of this paper with answering questions, and that is now and then to divert you. But I think the following question, as it was most seriously proposed, so it

may be of very good service to abundance of good people to have it answered. As to the ladies who are concerned in it, if they are not pleased I am sorry for it. The question, in short, was not proposed in a letter, but in conversation, and is promised an answer in this paper for the good of others, viz.:

2      What is the worst sort of husband a sober woman can marry?

3      I confess this question has led me a long way about, into the great, great variety of bad husbands of the age, with which many a poor lady is intolerably plagued throughout, as the wise man calls it, the years of her pilgrimage under the sun, the best of which kinds are bad enough. As

4      1. There is the drunken husband, whose picture it would take up a whole volume to describe; his drunken passions, his drunken humours, his drunken smell, his drunken bed-fellowship, and above all, his drunken love. O! An amorous drunkard when he comes home fully gorged and staggers into bed to a modest, a nice, and a virtuous wife must needs have a great many charms in it such as my pen cannot bear the stench of relating.

5      2. There is the debauched husband who, having a sober, young, pleasant and beautiful wife, slights and abandons her to take up with an ugly, a tawdry, nasty, and noisome strumpet, and convinces the world that lust is blinder than love. This sort of wretch has but one act of kindness to his wife which distinguishes him from other brutes of his kind, and that is that coming home laden with vice and rottenness, he gives his honest wife an ill disease that lifts her out of the world, putting her out of his reach, and out of her torment all together.

6      3. There is the fighting husband. I confess this is a strange creature that, when anything has put him in a passion abroad, comes and vents his thunder and lightning at home; that having not a heart to fight with a man, for generally speaking such fellows are always cowards, must come home and fight with his wife. These are excellent sort of people, and ought all to come to the same preferment one lately did in these parts who, beating his wife a little too much the poor woman took it so ill that she killed him for it. That is, she died, and he was hanged for the murder, as he deserved.

7      4. The extravagant husband. This is the *ill husband*, properly so-called, or as the word is generally received. This is a blessed fellow too, and his way is that he spends his money in roaring, gam-

ing, and drinking, when the poor woman sits quietly at home, waking and sighing for his company. If he is poor, as 'tis a wonder he should be rich, he feasts himself and his gang at the taverns and ale houses while the unhappy wife wants bread at home for his children. If he is an artist, he won't work; if he has a shop, he won't mind it; if business, it runs at random; the sot dreams away his time, ruins himself, and starves his family. The end of this wretch is generally to run away from her into the army or navy, and so dies like a rake, or perhaps takes up his lodgings nearer home in a gaol.

8      Well, good people, here are four sorts of ill husbands, and take one of them where you will, the best of them is bad enough, and hard is that woman's case, especially if she be a woman of any merit, whose lot it is; but yet I think my first rate is behind still; there is yet a bad husband that is worse than all these, and a woman of sense had better take up with any of these than with him, and that's a *fool husband*. The drunkard, the debauched, the fighting, and the extravagant; these may all have something attendant which in the intervals of their excesses may serve to alleviate and make a little amends to the poor woman, and held her to carry through the afflicting part; but a fool has something always about him that makes him intolerable; he is ever contemptible and uninterruptedly ridiculous—it is like a handsome woman with some deformity about her that makes all the rest be rejected. If he is kind, it is so apish, so below the rate of manhood, so surfeiting, and so disagreeable, that like an ill smell, it makes the face wrinkle at it; if he be froward, he is so unsufferably insolent that there is no bearing it; his passions are all flashes, struck out of him like fire from a flint. If it be anger, 'tis sullen and senseless; if love, 'tis coarse and brutish. He is in good, wavering; in mischief, obstinate; in society, empty; in management, unthinking; in manners, sordid; in error, incorrigible; and in everything ridiculous.

9      Wherefore upon the whole, my answer is in short, that the worst thing a sober woman can be married to is a FOOL. Of whom whoever has the lot, Lord have mercy, and a cross should be set on the door as of a house infected with the plague.

# Discussion Questions

1. Does Defoe adequately describe the four types of bad husbands? Why or why not?
2. Did Defoe neglect to include any other type of bad husband? If so, what would it be and why?
3. In small groups, discuss what Defoe's attitude toward women is. What leads you to your response?
4. From Defoe's characterizations, how well do you think he understands his topic? Explain.
5. Which of the undesirable husbands that Defoe describes do you find the worst? Why?
6. Why, in paragraph 8, does Defoe offer a fifth and worst type of husband: the fool?

# Writing Assignments

1. Write a journal entry that defines what you consider to be an "undesirable" husband or wife.
2. Write a twentieth-century version of Defoe's essay in which you describe the worst types of husbands.
3. Write an essay that complements Defoe's; that is, draw a portrait of undesirable wives.
4. In a paper, detail the characteristics that make for a desirable spouse or partner. Support your description with examples.

# The Necessary Enemy

## KATHERINE ANNE PORTER

Katherine Anne Porter (1890–1980) was born in Indian Creek, Texas. After receiving her education in convent schools in Texas and Louisiana, she moved to New York where she lived until 1937. A journalist and fiction writer, Porter was a freelance writer for such publications as *The Nation, The New Republic*, and *Century Magazine*. She later wrote and published short stories and novels. *Flowering Judas* (1930) includes the often-anthologized story "The Jilting of Granny Weatherall." Porter's other works include *Noon Wine* (1937), *Pale Horse, Pale Rider* (1939), *The Leaning Tower* (1944), and *Ship of Fools* (1962). *The Collected Stories of Katherine Anne Porter* (1966) was awarded the National Book Award and the Pulitzer Prize for fiction in 1966. In her fiction, one of Porter's themes is the social outcast and family misfit. Illness and death are also pervasive themes in her writing. In the following essay, which first appeared as "Love and Hate" in *Mademoiselle* magazine, Porter examines the often elusive and always confusing emotion: love.

1    She is a frank, charming, fresh-hearted young woman who married for love. She and her husband are one of those gay, good-looking young pairs who ornament this modern scene rather more in

profusion perhaps than ever before in our history. They are handsome, with a talent for finding their way in their world, they work at things that interest them, their tastes agree and their hopes. They intend in all good faith to spend their lives together, to have children and do well by them and each other—to be happy, in fact, which for them is the whole point of their marriage. And all in stride, keeping their wits about them. Nothing romantic, mind you; their feet are on the ground.

2    Unless they were this sort of person, there would be not much point to what I wish to say; for they would seem to be an example of the high-spirited, right-minded young whom the critics are always invoking to come forth and do their duty and practice all those sterling old-fashioned virtues which in every generation seem to be falling into disrepair. As for virtues, these young people are more or less on their own, like most of their kind; they get very little moral or other aid from their society; but after three years of marriage this very contemporary young woman finds herself facing the oldest and ugliest dilemma of marriage.

3    She is dismayed, horrified, full of guilt and forebodings because she is finding out little by little that she is capable of hating her husband, whom she loves faithfully. She can hate him at times as fiercely and mysteriously, indeed in terribly much the same way, as often she hated her parents, her brothers and sisters, whom she loves, when she was a child. Even then it had seemed to her a kind of black treacherousness in her, her private wickedness that, just the same, gave her her only private life. That was one thing her parents never knew about her, never seemed to suspect. For it was never given a name. They did and said hateful things to her and to each other as if by right, as if in them it was a kind of virtue. But when they said to her, "Control your feelings," it was never when she was amiable and obedient, only in the black times of her hate. So it was her secret, a shameful one. When they punished her, sometimes for the strangest reasons, it was, they said, only because they loved her—it was for her good. She did not believe this, but she thought herself guilty of something worse than ever they had punished her for. None of this really frightened her: the real fright came when she discovered that at times her father and mother hated each other; this was like standing on the doorsill of a familiar room and seeing in a lightning flash that the floor was gone, you were on the edge of a bottomless pit.

Sometimes she felt that both of them hated her, but that passed, it was simply not a thing to be thought of, much less believed. She thought she had outgrown all this, but here it was again, an element in her own nature she could not control, or feared she could not. She would have to hide from her husband, if she could, the same spot in her feelings she had hidden from her parents, and for the same no doubt disreputable, selfish reason: she wants to keep his love.

4    Above all, she wants him to be absolutely confident that she loves him, for that is the real truth, no matter how unreasonable it sounds, and no matter how her own feelings betray them both at times. She depends recklessly on his love; yet while she is hating him, he might very well be hating her as much or even more, and it would serve her right. But she does not want to be served right, she wants to be loved and forgiven—that is, to be sure he would forgive her anything, if he had any notion of what she had done. But best of all she would like not to have anything in her love that should ask for forgiveness. She doesn't mean about their quarrels—they are not so bad. Her feelings are out of proportion, perhaps. She knows it is perfectly natural for people to disagree, have fits of temper, fight it out; they learn quite a lot about each other that way, and not all of it disappointing either. When it passes, her hatred seems quite unreal. It always did.

5    Love. We are early taught to say it. I love you. We are trained to the thought of it as if there were nothing else, or nothing else worth having without it, or nothing worth having which it could not bring with it. Love is taught, always by precept, sometimes by example. Then hate, which no one meant to teach us, comes of itself. It is true that if we say I love you, it may be received with doubt, for there are times when it is hard to believe. Say I hate you, and the one spoken to believes it instantly, once for all.

6    Say I love you a thousand times to that person afterward and mean it every time, and still it does not change the fact that once we said I hate you, and meant that too. It leaves a mark on that surface love had worn so smooth with its eternal caresses. Love must be learned, and learned again and again; there is no end to it. Hate needs no instruction, but waits only to be provoked . . . hate, the unspoken word, the unacknowledged presence in the house, that faint smell of brimstone among the roses, that invisible tongue-trip-per, that unkempt finger in every pie, that sudden oh-so-curiously

*chilling* look—could it be boredom?—on your dear one's features, making them quite ugly. Be careful: love, perfect love, is in danger.

7     If it is not perfect, it is not love, and if it is not love, it is bound to be hate sooner or later. This is perhaps a not too exaggerated statement of the extreme position of Romantic Love, more especially in America, where we are all brought up on it, whether we know it or not. Romantic Love is changeless, faithful, passionate, and its sole end is to render the two lovers happy. It has no obstacles save those provided by the hazards of fate (that is to say, society), and such sufferings as the lovers may cause each other are only another word for delight: exciting jealousies, thrilling uncertainties, the ritual dance of courtship within the charmed closed circle of their secret alliance; all *real* troubles come from without, they face them unitedly in perfect confidence. Marriage is not the end but only the beginning of true happiness, cloudless, changeless to the end. That the candidates for this blissful condition have never seen an example of it, nor ever knew anyone who had, makes no difference. That is the ideal and they will achieve it.

8     How did Romantic Love manage to get into marriage at last, where it was most certainly never intended to be? At its highest it was tragic; the love of Héloïse and Abélard. At its most graceful, it was the homage of the trouvère for his lady. In its most popular form, the adulterous strayings of solidly married couples who meant to stray for their own good reasons, but at the same time do nothing to upset the property settlements or the line of legitimacy; at its most trivial, the pretty trifling of shepherd and the shepherdess.

9     This was generally condemned by church and state and a word of fear to honest wives whose mortal enemy it was. Love within the sober, sacred realities of marriage was a matter of personal luck, but in any case, private feelings were strictly a private affair having, at least in theory, no bearing whatever on the fixed practice of the rules of an institution never intended as a recreation ground for either sex. If the couple discharged their religious and social obligations, furnished forth a copious progeny, kept their troubles to themselves, maintained public civility and died under the same roof, even if not always on speaking terms, it was rightly regarded as a successful marriage. Apparently this testing ground was too severe for all but the stoutest spirits; it too was based on an ideal, as impossible in its way as the ideal Romantic Love. One good thing to be said for it is that society

took responsibility for the conditions of marriage, and the sufferers within its bonds could always blame the system, not themselves. But Romantic Love crept into the marriage bed, very stealthily, by centuries, bringing its absurd notions about love as eternal springtime and marriage as a personal adventure meant to provide personal happiness. To a Western romantic such as I, though my views have been much modified by painful experience, it still seems to me a charming work of the human imagination, and it is a pity its central notion has been taken too literally and has hardened into a convention as cramping and enslaving as the older one. The refusal to acknowledge the evils in ourselves which therefore are implicit in any human situation is as extreme and unworkable a proposition as the doctrine of total depravity; but somewhere between them, or maybe beyond them, there does exist a possibility for reconciliation between our desires for impossible satisfactions and the simple unalterable fact that we also desire to be unhappy and that we create our own sufferings; and out of these sufferings we salvage our fragments of happiness.

10    Our young woman who has been taught that an important part of her human nature is not real because it makes trouble and interferes with her peace of mind and shakes her self-love, has been very badly taught; but she has arrived at a most important stage of her re-education. She is afraid her marriage is going to fail because she has not love enough to face its difficulties; and this because at times she feels a painful hostility toward her husband, and cannot admit its reality because such an admission would damage in her own eyes her view of what love should be, an absurd view, based on her vanity of power. Her hatred is real as her love is real, but her hatred has the advantage at present because it works on a blind instinctual level, it is lawless; and her love is subjected to a code of ideal conditions, impossible by their very nature of fulfillment, which prevents its free growth and deprives it of its right to recognize its human limitations and come to grips with them. Hatred is natural in a sense that love, as she conceives it, a young person brought up in the tradition of Romantic Love, is not natural at all. Yet it did not come by hazard, it is the very imperfect expression of the need of the human imagination to create beauty and harmony out of chaos, no matter how mistaken its notion of these things may be, nor how clumsy its methods. It has conjured love out of the air, and seeks to preserve it

by incantations; when she spoke a vow to love and honor her husband until death, she did a very reckless thing, for it is not possible
by an act of the will to fulfill such an engagement. But it was the
necessary act of faith performed in defense of a mode of feeling, the
statement of honorable intention to practice as well as she is able the
noble, acquired faculty of love, that very mysterious overtone to sex
which is the best thing in it. Her hatred is part of it, the necessary
enemy and ally.

# Discussion Questions

1. Who is the "necessary enemy"?
2. Is the title of Porter's essay an oxymoron? Explain.
3. What is Porter saying about storybook romances as they relate to
   real-life marriages? Explain your reasons for agreeing or disagreeing with her thinking.
4. In paragraph 4, Porter discusses the seeming dichotomy between
   love and hate. Are there any experiences in your own life that
   illustrate what Porter is saying?
5. In paragraph 5, Porter begins a discussion on love. Identify specific statements she makes with which you agree or disagree.
   Explain your thinking.
6. Discuss the organization of Porter's essay, especially the recurring
   role of the young woman. What does it contribute to the essay?
7. In small groups, discuss whether Porter was writing to men or
   women.

# Writing Assignments

1. Write a journal entry in which you examine the problems created
   by the concept of romantic love.
2. Write an essay that supports or refutes the idea that "love must
   be learned, and learned again and again; there is no end to it."
3. Is Porter's essay still relevant? Write a paper in which you address
   this question.

# CLASSIC ESSAYS ON

# Children

# Of the Affection of Fathers for Their Children

## MICHEL DE MONTAIGNE

Michel de Montaigne (1533–1592) was born in Périgord, France. The son of affluent parents, Montaigne studied law and worked as a civil servant, serving first as counsellor in the Parlement of Bordeaux and then as mayor of Bordeaux in 1551. In 1571, Montaigne retired to his estate in Dordogne to devote the rest of his life to reading and writing. Montaigne is most noted for being the originator of the essay. He is the author of two volumes of *Essais* (1580), which were later revised in 1588 along with a third volume. In 1595, a posthumous version of the three books was published. The essay, as envisioned and written by Montaigne, is an open genre, not restricted by form or content; rather, Montaigne's vision was what the word *essay* actually means: a trying out, an experiment in which the writer discovers meaning through the actual process of writing. An adaptable genre, the essay can be a narrative, a description, an autobiography, an informal argument, or a reflective musing on a topic. The essay, as Montaigne envisioned it, became a popular genre, and writers in the centuries to follow have experimented with and modified the form but never lost sight of Montaigne's original idea. The following selection from *Essais* is one of

Montaigne's longer pieces in which he explores fathers' love of their children.

## To Madame d'Estissac

1    Madame, if strangeness and novelty, which customarily give value to things, do not save me, I shall never get out of this stupid enterprise with honor; but it is so fantastic and appears so remote from common usage that that may enable it to pass. It was a melancholy humor, and consequently a humor very hostile to my natural disposition, produced by the gloom of the solitude into which I had cast myself some years ago, the first put into my head this daydream of meddling with writing. And then, finding myself entirely destitute and void of any other matter. I presented myself to myself for argument and subject. It is the only book in the world of its kind, a book with a wild and eccentric plan. And so there is nothing in this job worth noting but its bizarreness; for a subject so vain and mean could not have been fashioned by the best workman in the world into something worthy of notice.

2    Now, Madame, having here to portray myself to the life, I would have forgotten one important feature if I had not represented the honor that I have always paid to your merits. And I wanted to say this particularly at the head of this chapter, since among your other good qualities the love you have shown your children holds one of the first ranks. Anyone who knows at what age Monsieur d'Estissac, your husband, left you a widow; the great and honorable matches that have been offered you, as many as to any lady in France of your rank; the constancy and firmness with which you sustained, for so many years and through so many thorny difficulties, the burden and the conduct of their affairs, which have driven you through all corners of France and still keep you besieged; the happy direction you have given them solely by your prudence or good fortune—such a person will readily say with me that we have in our time no clearer example of maternal affection than yours.

3    I praise God, Madame, that it has been so well employed: for the good hopes that your son Monsieur d'Estissac gives of himself are

assurance enough that when he comes of age you will draw from him the obedience and gratitude of a very good son. But since, because of his youth, he could not notice the supreme services that he has received from you in such great number, I want him, if these writings happen to fall into his hands some day when I shall have neither mouth nor speech left that can say it, to receive from me in all truth this testimony, which will be attested to him even more vividly by the good results which, if it please God, he will feel: that there is not a gentleman in France who owes more to his mother than he does, and that he cannot in the future give any more certain proof of his goodness and virtue than by recognizing you for what you are.

4    If there is any truly natural law, that is to say, any instinct that is seen universally and permanently imprinted in both the animals and ourselves (which is not beyond dispute), I may say that in my opinion, after the care every animal has for its own preservation and the avoidance of what is harmful, the affection that the begetter has for his begotten ranks second. And because Nature seems to have recommended it to us with a view to extending and advancing the successive parts of this machine of hers, it is no wonder if, turning backward, the affection of children for their fathers is not so great.

5    Add to that this other Aristotelian consideration, that he who does good to someone loves him better than he is loved by him; and that he to whom something is owed loves better than he who owes; and that every workman loves his work better than he would be loved by it if the work had feeling. For being is something we hold dear, and being consists in movement and action. Wherefore each man in some sort exists in his work. He who does good performs a beautiful and honorable action; he who receives performs only a useful one. Now, the useful is much less lovable than is the honorable. The honorable is stable and permanent, furnishing the man who has done it with a constant gratification. The useful easily escapes and is lost, and the memory of it is neither so fresh nor so sweet. Those things are dear to us that have cost us most; and it is more difficult to give than to take.

6    Since it has pleased God to give us some capacity for reason so that we should not be, like the animals, slavishly subjected to the common laws, but should apply ourselves to them by judgment and voluntary liberty, we must indeed yield a little to the simple author-

ity of Nature, but not let ourselves be carried away tyrannically by her; reason alone must guide our inclinations.

7    I, for my part, have a taste strangely blunted to these properties that are produced in us without the command and mediation of our judgment. For example, on this subject that I am talking about, I cannot entertain that passion which makes people hug infants that are hardly born yet, having neither movement in the soul nor recognizable shape to the body by which they can make themselves lovable. And I have not willingly suffered them to be brought up near me.

8    A true and well-regulated affection should be born and increase with the knowledge children give us of themselves; and then, if they are worthy of it, the natural propensity going along with reason, we should cherish them with a truly paternal love; and we should likewise pass judgment on them if they are otherwise, always submitting to reason, notwithstanding the force of nature. It is very often the reverse; and most commonly we feel more excited over the stamping, the games, and the infantile tricks of our children than we do later over their grown-up actions, as if we had loved them for our pastime, like monkeys, not like men. And some supply toys very liberally for their childhood, who tighten up at the slightest expenditure they need when they are of age. Indeed, it seems that the jealousy we feel at seeing them appear in the world and enjoy it when we are about to leave it makes us more stingy and tight with them; it vexes us that they are treading on our heels, as if to solicit us to leave. And if we had that to fear, then since in the nature of things they cannot in truth either be or live except at the expense of our being and our life, we should not have meddled with being fathers.

9    As for me, I think it is cruelty and injustice not to receive them into a share and association in our goods, and as companions in the understanding of our domestic affairs, when they are capable of it, and not to cut down and restrict our own comforts in order to provide for theirs, since we have begotten them to that end. It is an injustice that an old, broken, half-dead father should enjoy alone, in a corner of his hearth, possessions that would suffice for the advancement and maintenance of many children, and let them meanwhile, for lack of means, lose their best years without making progress in public service and the knowledge of men. They are cast into the desperate plight of seeking by any means, however unjust, to provide for their need; as I have seen in my time several young

men of good family so addicted to stealing that no correction could turn them from it. I know one, well-connected, to whom, at the request of a brother of his, a very honorable and brave gentleman, I once spoke to this purpose. He answered me and confessed quite roundly that he had been set on this filthy path by the rigor and avarice of his father, but that now he was so accustomed to it that he could not keep out of it. And he had then just been caught stealing the rings of a lady at whose levee he had been present with many others. He made me remember the story I had heard of another gentleman, so formed and fashioned to this fine trade in the time of his youth that when he came later to be master of his estate and determined to abandon this traffic, nevertheless, if he passed by a shop where there was something he needed, he could not keep himself from stealing it, on pain of sending to pay for it later. And I have seen several so trained and schooled to this that even among their comrades they regularly stole things which they intended to return.

10    I am a Gascon, and yet there is no vice in which I am less expert than this. I hate it a little more by temperament than I condemn it by reason: even in desire, I take nothing away from anyone. This province is indeed a little more decried in this respect than the others of the French nation; yet we have seen in our day at various times men of good families from other provinces in the hands of justice, convicted of many horrible robberies. I fear that this depravity must be blamed to some extent on the avarice of fathers.

11    Someone may answer me as one lord of good understanding did one day. From hoarding his riches, he said, he expected to derive no other benefit and use than to make himself honored and sought after by his dependents, since when age had deprived him of all other powers, he would have only this way left to maintain his authority in his family and to avoid incurring everyone's scorn and disdain. In truth not old age alone, but every weakness, according to Aristotle, is a promoter of avarice. There is something to be said for this; but it is medicine for a disease whose birth we should have prevented.

12    A father is very miserable who holds his children's affection only by the need they have of his help—if that is to be called affection. He should make himself worthy of respect by his virtue and by his ability, and of love by his goodness and the kindness of his behavior. The very ashes of a rich material have their value; and we are accus-

tomed to hold in respect and reverence the bones and relics of persons of honor. No old age can be so decrepit and rancid in a person who has passed his life in honor as not to be venerable, especially to his children, whose souls he ought to have trained to their duty by reason, not by necessity and need nor by harshness and force:

> In my opinion he is wrong who thinks
> That an authority by power attained
> Is more secure than that by friendship gained.

TERENCE

13     I condemn all violence in the education of a tender soul which is being trained for honor and liberty. There is a sort of servility about rigor and constraint; and I hold that what cannot be done by reason, and by wisdom and tact, is never done by force. I was brought up that way. They say that in all my childhood I felt the rod only twice, and that very softly. I have owed the same to the children I have had; they all die on me at nurse; but Léonor, one single daughter who escaped that misfortune, is over six years old now, and has never been guided or punished for her childish faults—her mother's indulgence easily concurring—by anything but words, and very gentle ones. And even if my wishes should be frustrated, there are enough other causes on which to place the blame without reproaching my system, which I know to be just and natural. I should have been much more scrupulous still in this respect toward boys, who are less born to serve and of a freer condition: I should have loved to swell their hearts with ingenuousness and frankness. I have seen no other effect of whips except to make souls more cowardly or more maliciously obstinate.

14     Do we want to be loved by our children? Do we want to take away from them the occasion for desiring our death (though no occasion for so horrible a wish can be either just or excusable: *no crime is based on reason*)? Let us furnish their life reasonably with what is in our power. For that purpose, we should not marry so young that our age comes to be almost confounded with theirs. For this inconvenience casts us into many great difficulties. I am referring especially to the nobility, which is a leisure class and lives, as they say, only on its private income. For with other groups, where a

living must be earned, the plurality and company of children is an advantage to the household; they are so many new tools and instruments for getting rich.

15    I married at thirty-three, and approve the suggestion of thirty-five, which they say is Aristotle's. Plato does not want people to marry before thirty; but he is right to laugh at those who perform the works of marriage after fifty-five; and he condemns their offspring as unworthy of nourishment and life. Thales sets its truest limits. When young, he answered his mother, who was urging him to marry, that it was not yet time; and, when he was getting old, that it was no longer time. We must deny that there is any appropriate time for any inappropriate action.

16    The ancient Gauls considered it extremely reprehensible for a man under twenty to have had knowledge of a woman, and particularly recommended to the men who wanted to train for war to keep their virginity until well along in years, since courage is softened and diverted by intercourse with women.

Happy in children, wed to a young wife,
For exploits he had lost his predilection
Through fatherly and marital affection.

TASSO

17    Greek history observes of Iccus of Tarentum, of Chryson, of Astylus, of Diopompus and others, that to keep their bodies strong for the races in the Olympic games, for wrestling, and for other exercises, they denied themselves any sort of sexual act as long as their training lasted. Muley Hassan, king of Tunis, the one whom the Emperor Charles V restored to his estate, reproached the memory of his father for his frequentation of his wives, and called him slack, effeminate, maker of children. In a certain country of the Spanish Indies, they did not permit men to marry until after forty, and yet they permitted girls to do so at ten.

18    When a gentleman is thirty-five, it is not time for him to give place to his son who is twenty: he is himself in the midst of appearing on military expeditions and in the court of his prince; he needs his resources, and should certainly share them, but not so as to forget himself for others. And such a man may justifiably use the reply

that fathers have ordinarily in their mouths: "I do not want to strip myself before I go to bed."

19     But a father prostrated by years and infirmities, deprived by his weakness and lack of health of the common society of men, wrongs himself and his family by uselessly brooding over a great heap of riches. He is pretty well in shape, if he is wise, to want to strip himself for bed, not down to his shirt, but to a good warm nightshirt. The remaining pomps, for which he has no more use, he should willingly present to those to whom by the order of nature they should belong. It is right that he should leave the enjoyment of these things to them, since nature deprives him of it; if he does otherwise, there is malice and envy involved without a doubt.

20     The finest act of Emperor Charles V was this: that he was able to recognize, in imitation of certain ancients of his caliber, that reason commands us to strip ourselves when our robes become a burden and hindrance to us, and to go to bed when our legs fail us. He resigned his possessions, his greatness, and his power to his son when he felt himself failing in the firmness and strength to conduct affairs with the glory he had acquired in them.

> Set free the aging horse before it is too late,
> Lest he go stumbling broken-winded at the end.
>
>                    HORACE

21     This fault of not being able to recognize oneself early and not feeling the impotence and extreme alteration that age naturally brings to both body and soul, and in my opinion equally, unless the soul receives more than half of it, has ruined the reputation of most of the world's great men. I have seen in my time, and known intimately, persons of great authority who, it was easy to see, had declined marvelously from their former ability, which I knew of by the reputation they had acquired for it in their better years. I could readily, for their honor, have wished them retired, living at home at their ease and unburdened with public and warlike occupations that were no longer suited to their shoulders.

22     I was once an intimate in the house of a gentleman, a widower and very old, yet of a pretty green old age. He had several daughters to marry off and a son old enough to appear in the world. This bur-

dened his house with many expenses and visits of strangers, in which he took little pleasure, not only out of concern for economy, but even more because he had adopted, owing to his age, a mode of life far removed from ours. I told him one day a little boldly, as is my custom, that it would become him better to make room for us younger folk, to leave his principal house (for that was the only one he had that was well furnished and fitted out) to his son and retire to a neighboring estate of his where no one would trouble his repose, since he could not otherwise avoid being disturbed by us in view of the situation of his children. He took my advice later and was well off for it.

23     This is not to say that we should so obligate ourselves to our children that we can no longer retract what we give them. I, who am ready to play this role, would leave my children the enjoyment of my house and possessions, but with liberty to repent if they gave me occasion to. I would leave them the use of it because that would no longer be convenient to me; and of authority over affairs in general, I would reserve for myself as much as I pleased. For I have always judged that it must be a great contentment to an old father himself to give his children a start in managing his affairs, and during his lifetime to be able to oversee their conduct, furnishing them with instruction and advice according to the experience he has of them, directing their efforts to uphold the ancient honor and order of his house, and thereby finding firm ground for the hopes he may conceive of their future conduct.

24     And for this purpose I would not avoid their company; I would observe them close up, and enjoy their fun and festivities within the limitations of my age. If I did not live among them (as I could not without spoiling their gatherings by being fretful as old men are and a slave to my infirmities, and without also doing violence to the rules and ways of living that I should then have), I should at least want to live near them in a part of my house, not the most showy but the most comfortable. Not like a dean of the church of Saint Hilary at Poitiers whom I saw, some years ago, so cut off by his gloomy disagreeableness that when I entered his room it had been twenty-two years since he had gone one step out of it; and yet he was free and easy in all his functions, except for a cold that was going down into his stomach. Hardly once a week would he permit anyone to come in to see him; he kept himself always locked up in his chamber alone,

except that a servant, who only came in and went out, brought him something to eat once a day. His occupation was to walk around and read some book (for he had a certain knowledge of letters); moreover, he was obstinately set on dying in this routine, as he did soon after.

25 I would try by pleasant relations to foster in my children a lively and unfeigned affection and good will toward me, which is easily won in a wellborn nature; for if they are raging beasts, such as our time produces in profusion, we must hate and shun them as such.

26 I loathe the custom of forbidding children to use the name of father and enjoining upon them some strange address, as being more respectful; as if nature had not readily provided sufficiently for our authority. We call God Almighty father, and disdain to have our children call us that. It is also wrong and foolish to prohibit children who have come of age from being familiar with their fathers, and to prefer to maintain an austere and disdainful gravity toward them, hoping thereby to keep them in fear and obedience. For that is a very futile farce, which makes fathers annoying to their children and, what is worse, ridiculous. They have in their hands youth and vigor, and consequently the wind and favor of the world behind them; and they receive with mockery these fierce and tyrannical looks from men who have no blood left in either heart or veins—real scarecrows in a hemp field. Even if I could make myself feared, I would much rather make myself loved.

27 There are so many sorts of defects in old age, so much impotence, it is so liable to contempt, that the best acquisition it can make is the love and affection of our family: command and fear are no longer its weapons. I know one old man whose youth was very imperious. Now that age has come on, although he is as healthy as can be, he strikes, he bites, he swears: the most tempestuous master in France. He is eaten up by care and vigilance. All that is just a farce in which the family itself conspires: of the storeroom, the cellar, and even of his purse, others have the best share of the enjoyment, while he holds the keys in his pouch more dearly than if they were his eyes. While he is happy over the frugality and niggardliness of his table, everybody is living it up in various corners of his house, gaming, spending, and exchanging stories about his vain anger and foresight. Everyone is on guard against him. If, by chance, some wretched servant devotes himself to him, promptly he falls under his suspicion, a

trait on which old age is so prone to bite of its own accord. How many times has he boasted to me of the check he kept on his household and the strict obedience and reverence he received from them, and how clearly he saw into his own affairs!

> He alone is ignorant of all things.
>
> TERENCE

I know no man who can bring to bear more qualities, both natural and acquired, fit to preserve mastery, than he does; and yet he has fallen from authority like a child. Therefore I have chosen him from among several I know in that condition, as the best example.

28    It would be a matter for a scholastic dispute whether he is better off thus or otherwise. In his presence, all things yield to him. They allow his authority this vain course: they never resist him; they take his word, they fear him, they give him his bellyful of respect. Does he dismiss a servant? He packs his bundle, there he is gone—but only out of his presence. The steps of old age are so slow, the senses so blurred, that he will live and do his job in the same house for a year without being perceived. And when the time comes, they have letters arrive from far away, piteous, suppliant, full of promises to do better, whereby he is restored to grace. Does Monsieur take some step or send some dispatch that displeases? They suppress it, soon afterward forging causes enough to excuse the lack of execution or reply. No letters from outside are brought to him first; he sees only those that it seems convenient for him to know. If by accident he gets hold of one, the person on whom he relies to read his letters to him promptly finds in it whatever he chooses; and all the time they have someone asking his pardon who is really insulting him in this very letter. In fine, he sees his affairs only in an image arranged, designed, and made just as satisfactory as possible, so as not to rouse his bad humor and anger. I have seen, under different forms, plenty of long, constant domestic economies with exactly the same result.

29    Wives always have a proclivity for disagreeing with their husbands. They seize with both hands every pretext to go contrary to them; the first excuse serves them as plenary justification. I have known one who robbed her husband wholesale in order, so she told

her confessor, to give fatter alms. Just trust that pious almsgiving! No responsibility seems to them to have sufficient dignity if it comes by the husband's concession. They have to usurp it either by cunning or by insolence, and always unjustly, to give it grace and authority. As in the case I am speaking of, when they act against a poor old man and for the sake of children, then they seize this pretext and glory in making it serve their passion, and, as if they were slaves making a common cause, readily conspire against his domination and government. As for sons, grown and vigorous, they also promptly suborn, either by force or by favor, both steward and receiver and all the rest.

30    Those who have neither wife nor son fall into this misfortune less easily, but also more cruelly and shamefully. Cato the Elder used to say in his time: "So many servants, so many enemies." Consider whether, in keeping with the difference in purity between his age and ours, he did not mean to warn us that wife, son, and servant are so many enemies to us. It is well that our declining years bring with them the sweet benefits of imperceptiveness and ignorance, and a facility for letting ourselves be deceived. If we got stirred up over this, what would become of us, especially in this age in which the judges who have to decide our controversies are commonly partisans of the young, and interested parties?

31    In case this deception escapes my sight, at least it does not escape my sight that I am very deceivable. And will it ever be said enough how precious is a friend, and how different a thing from these civil bonds? Even the image of friendship that I see in the animals, so pure, how religiously I respect it!

32    If others deceive me, at least I do not deceive myself, either by thinking myself capable of guarding against their deception, or by wracking my brains to make myself capable. I escape from such betrayals in my own bosom not by a restless and tumultuous curiosity, but rather by diversion and resolution.

33    When I hear tell of someone's condition, I do not dwell on him; I promptly turn my eyes to myself to see how it is with me. Everything that affects him concerns me. His mishap warns me and rouses me in that direction. Every day and every hour we say things about another that we would more properly say about ourselves, if we knew how to turn our attention inward as well as extend it outward.

34    And many authors in this manner injure their cause, running rashly forward to meet the one they are attacking, and hurling shafts at their enemies that are suited to being hurled back at them.

35    After the later Marshal de Monluc lost his son—in truth a brave gentleman and one of great promise, who died on the island of Madeira—he used to stress greatly to me, among his other regrets, the sorrow and heartbreak he felt for never having opened up to him. He had lost, he said, by that habit of paternal gravity and stiffness, the comfort of appreciating his son and knowing him well, and also of declaring to him the extreme affection that he bore him and the high opinion he had of his virtue. "And that poor boy," he would say, "saw nothing of me but a scowling and disdainful countenance, and took with him the belief that I knew neither how to love him nor how to esteem him according to his merit. For whom was I keeping the revelation of that singular affection that I bore him in my soul? Wasn't he the one who should have had all the pleasure of it and all the gratitude? I constrained and tortured myself to maintain this vain mask, and thereby lost the pleasure of association with him, and of his good will along with it, for he could not be other than very cool toward me, having never had anything but harshness from me or experienced any but a tyrannical bearing." I think this lament was well taken and reasonable; for, as I know by too certain experience, there is no consolation so sweet in the loss of our friends as that which comes to us from the knowledge of not having forgotten to tell them anything and of having had perfect and entire communication with them.

36    I open myself to my family as much as I can, and very readily signify to them the state of my will and my judgment toward them, as toward everyone. I hasten to bring myself out and put myself forth; I do not want people to be mistaken about me, whether for better or for worse.

37    Among other peculiar customs of our ancient Gauls, from what Caesar says, was this one: that children did not appear before their fathers or dare to be found in their company in public until they were beginning to bear arms; as if they meant that only then was it time for the fathers to receive their sons into their familiarity and acquaintance.

38    I have observed still another sort of error of judgment in some fathers of my time, who are not content with depriving their chil-

dren during their long lifetime of the share they naturally ought to have had in their fortunes, but afterward also leave to their wives this same authority over all their possessions and the right to dispose of them according to their fancy. And I have known one lord, one of the first officers of our crown, a man with an income of more than fifty thousand crowns in prospect by right of succession, who died needy and overwhelmed with debts at over fifty years of age, while his mother in her extreme decrepitude was still enjoying all his property by the will of his father, who for his part had lived nearly eighty years. This does not seem at all reasonable to me.

39    However, I find it of little advantage for a man whose affairs are going well to go looking for a wife who will burden him with a big dowry; there is no outside debt that brings more ruin on houses. My predecessors have generally followed this counsel to good advantage, and so have I. But those who advise us against rich wives for fear they may be less tractable and grateful are wrong to make us lose some real profit for so frivolous a conjecture. It costs an unreasonable woman no more to override one reason than another. They love themselves best wherever they are most in the wrong. Unfairness allures them, as the honor of their virtuous actions allures good women; and the richer these are, the nicer they are, as they are the more willingly and proudly chaste because they are beautiful.

40    It is right to leave the administration of affairs to mothers while the children are not yet of legal age to take over on their own. But the father has brought them up very badly if he cannot hope that at that age they will have more wisdom and ability than his wife, seeing the ordinary weakness of the sex. However, in truth, it would be much more contrary to nature to make mothers dependent on the discretion of their children. They should be given plentiful means to maintain themselves according to the standing of their house and their age, since necessity and indigence are much more unbecoming and hard to bear for them than for men: this should be borne by the children rather than by the mother.

41    In general the soundest distribution of our estate when we die seems to me the one prescribed by the custom of the country. The laws have thought about this better than we; and it is better to let them err in their choice than rashly to run the risk of erring in ours. The estate is not properly ours, since by a civil ordinance and independently of us it is destined to certain successors. And although we

have some liberty beyond that, I hold that we need a very great and apparent cause to make us take away from anyone that which his fortune has won him and to which common justice entitles him; and that it is abusing this liberty unreasonably to make it serve our frivolous and private fancies. My lot has been gracious to me in not having offered me occasions that could tempt me and divert my affection from the common and legitimate arrangement.

42   I see some on whom it is wasted time to take long pains in doing good services: one word taken amiss wipes out the merit of ten years. Happy the man who is there on the spot to anoint their good will at this last passage. The nearest action carries the day; not the best and most frequent services, but the most recent and present, do the job. Such men play with their wills as with apples or rods, to gratify or chastise every action of those who claim an interest in them. A will is a thing of too great consequence and weight to be thus trotted out at every instant; wise men take their stand on it once for all, having regard to reason and public observances.

43   We take these male entails too much to heart. And we look forward to a ridiculous eternity for our names. We also weigh too heavily the vain conjectures about the future that we draw from childish minds. They might perhaps have done an injustice by displacing me from my rank for having been the most sluggish and leaden, the slowest and most reluctant, in my lesson, not only of all my brothers, but of all the boys of my province, whether the lesson was in mental or bodily exercise. It is folly to make extraordinary selections on the faith of these divinations in which we are so often deceived. If one may violate this rule and correct the destinies in the choice they have made of our heirs, it is somewhat more reasonable to do so on grounds of some remarkable and enormous physical deformity, a constant, irremediable defect, and, according to us who greatly esteem beauty, a very harmful one.

44   The amusing dialogue between Plato's lawgiver and his fellow citizens will do honor to this passage. "What," say they, feeling the end approaching, "may we not dispose of what is ours to whom we please? Ye gods, what cruelty that it should not be lawful for us, according as our people have served us in our illnesses, in our old age, in our affairs, to give them more or less according to our fancies!" To which the lawgiver replies in this manner: "My friends, who no doubt have soon to die, it is hard both for you to know

yourselves and for you to know what is yours, according to the Delphic inscription. I who make the laws hold that neither are you your own nor is what you enjoy your own. Both your goods and yourselves belong to your family, past as well as future. But even more do both your family and your goods belong to the public. Wherefore if some flatterer in your old age or in your illness, or some passion, solicits you at a bad time to make an unjust will, I will guard you against it. But, having regard to both the general interest of the city and that of your family, I shall establish laws and make it felt, as is reasonable, that the private interest must yield to the public interest. Go your way then peacefully and with good will where human necessity calls you. It is for me, who do not regard one thing more than the other, who, as much as I can, look after the general interest, to take care of what you leave."

45    To return to my subject, it seems to me, I know not why, that no kind of mastery is due to women over men except the maternal and natural, unless it is for the punishment of those who, by some feverish humor, have voluntarily submitted themselves to them. But that does not concern old women, of whom we are speaking here. It is the reasonableness of this consideration that has made us create and so readily give force to this law, which no one has ever seen, that deprives women of the succession to our crown; and there is hardly a sovereignty in the world where it is not alleged, as it is here, by some appearance of reason that gives it authority; but fortune has given it more credit in certain places than in others.

46    It is dangerous to leave the disposal of our succession to women's judgment, according to the choice they will make among the children which is at all times unfair and capricious. For that disordered appetite and sick taste that they have at the time of their pregnancies they have in their soul at all times. We commonly see them devote themselves to the weakest and most ill-favored, or to those, if they have any, who are still hanging about their necks. For, not having enough force of reason to choose and embrace what deserves it, they most readily let themselves be carried away where the impressions of nature stand most alone; like the animals, who have no knowledge of their young except while they cling to their dugs.

47    Moreover, it is easy to see by experience that this natural affection to which we give so much authority has very weak roots. Every day we take their own children out of the arms of mothers, and make

them take charge of ours, for a very slight profit. We make them abandon their own to some wretched nurse to whom we do not want to entrust our own, or to some goat; forbidding them not only to give them suck, whatever danger they may thereby incur, but even to take any care of them, that they may be entirely employed in the service of ours. And we see in most of them a bastard affection soon engendered by habit, more vehement than the natural, and a greater solicitude for the preservation of the borrowed children than for their own.

48    And what I said about goats I said because it is ordinary around where I live to see village women, when they cannot feed their children from their breasts, call goats to their aid; and I have at this moment two lackeys who never sucked woman's milk for more than a week. These goats are promptly trained to come and suckle these little children; they recognize their voices when they call out, and come running. If any other than their nursling is presented to them, they refuse it; and the child does the same with another goat. I saw one the other day whose goat they took away because his father had only borrowed her from a neighbor of his; he never could take to the other that they presented to him, and doubtless died of hunger. Animals alter and corrupt their natural affection as easily as we.

49    Herodotus relates of a certain district of Libya that intercourse with women is promiscuous, but that the child, when he has the strength to walk, finds to be his father the one toward whom, in the crowd, natural inclination bears his first steps. I believe that this must lead to frequent mistakes.

50    Now when we consider this simple reason for loving our children—that we begot them, wherefore we call them our other selves—it seems to me that there is indeed another production proceeding from us that is no less commendable. For what we engender by the soul, the children of our mind, of our heart and our ability, are produced by a nobler part than the body and are more our own. We are father and mother both in this generation. These cost us a lot more, and bring us more honor, if they have any good in them. For the worth of our other children is much more theirs than ours; the share we have in it is very slight; but of these all the beauty, all the grace and value, is ours. Thus they represent and report us much more to the life than the others. Plato adds that

these are immortal children who immortalize their fathers and even deify them, as with Lycurgus, Solon, and Minos.

51 Now, since the histories are full of examples of that common affection of fathers toward their children, it seemed to me not inappropriate to pick out also some of this other kind.

52 Heliodorus, that good bishop of Tricca, preferred to lose the dignity, the profit, and the piety of so venerable a prelacy rather than lose his daughter—a daughter who still lives on, very nice, but for all that perhaps a little too curiously and loosely tricked out, and in too amorous a fashion, for the daughter of a churchman and a priest.

53 There was one Labienus in Rome, a person of great worth and authority, and, among other qualities, excelling in every sort of literature. He was, I believe, the son of that great Labienus, the first of the captains who were under Caesar in the Gallic war, and who later, after throwing himself to the great Pompey's side, maintained himself there so valorously until Caesar defeated him in Spain. The virtue of this Labienus aroused many people's envy; and, as seems likely, the courtiers and favorites of the emperors of his time opposed him for his independence and for the feelings against tyranny which he had from his father, which he still retained, and with which we may believe he had colored his books and writings. His adversaries prosecuted him before the magistrate in Rome and succeeded in having several of his published works condemned to be burned. It was with him that this new sort of penalty began, which was later continued in Rome against many others, of punishing by death even writings and studies. There was not enough means and matter for cruelty unless we brought in things which nature has exempted from all feeling and all suffering, such as reputation and the inventions of our mind, and unless we communicated corporal punishments to the teachings and monuments of the muses.

54 Now Labienus could not endure this loss nor survive that dear progeny of his; he had himself taken and shut up alive in the tomb of his ancestors, where he contrived to kill and bury himself at the same time. It is hard to show any more vehement paternal affection than that. Cassius Severus, a very eloquent man and his intimate friend, seeing his books burning, cried out that by the same sentence they should have condemned him to be burned alive with them; for he carried and preserved in his memory what they contained.

55    A like fate befell Greuntius Cordus, accused of having praised
Brutus and Cassius in his books. That vile, servile, and corrupt
Senate worthy of a worse master than Tiberius, condemned his writings to the fire. He was content to keep them company in their
death, and killed himself by abstaining from food.

56    In the last moments of the good Lucan's life, after he was condemned by that scoundrel Nero, when most of his blood had
already flowed out through the veins of his arms, which he had had
his doctor cut open so as to die, and when the cold had seized on his
extremities and was beginning to approach his vital parts, the last
thing he had in his memory was some of the verses of his book on
the battle of Pharsalia, which he recited; and he died with those last
words in his mouth. What was that but a tender and paternal leave
he was taking of his children, representing the farewells and close
embraces that we give to ours when we die, and an effect of that natural inclination that recalls to our memory in this extremity the
things we have held dearest during our life?

57    Do you think that Epicurus, who (while dying in torment, as he
says, from the utmost pains of colic) had all his consolation in the
beauty of the doctrine he was leaving to the world, would have
received as much contentment from a number of wellborn and well-
brought-up children, if he had had any, as he did from the production of his rich writings? And that if he had had to choose between
leaving behind a deformed and ill-born child and leaving behind a
stupid and inept book, he would not rather have chosen, and not
only he but any man of like ability, to incur the former misfortune
than the other? It would perhaps be impiety in Saint Augustine, for
example—if it were proposed to him on the one hand to bury his
writings, from which our religion receives such great fruit, or else to
bury his children, in case he had any—if he did not prefer to bury
his children.

58    And I do not know whether I would not like much better to have
produced one perfectly formed child by intercourse with the muses
than by intercourse with my wife.

59    To this child, such as it is, what I give I give purely and irrevocably, as one gives to the children of one's body. The little good I have
done for it is no longer at my disposal. It may know a good many
things that no I longer know and hold from me what I have not

retained and what, just like a stranger, I should have to borrow from it if I came to need it. If I am wiser than it, it is richer than I.

60     There are few men devoted to poetry who would not be prouder to be the father of the *Aeneid* than of the handsomest boy in Rome, and who would not more easily suffer the loss of the one than of the other. For, according to Aristotle, of all craftsmen the poet in particular is the most in love with his own work.

61     It is hard to believe that Epaminondas, who boasted of leaving as his entire posterity daughters who would one day do their father honor (these were the two noble victories he had won over the Lacedaemonians), would willingly have consented to exchange these for the most gorgeous daughters of all Greece, or that Alexander and Caesar ever wanted to be deprived of the grandeur of their glorious deeds of war for the satisfaction of having children and heirs, however perfect and accomplished they might be.

62     Indeed I very much doubt that Phidias or any other excellent sculptor would be so pleased with the preservation and long life of his natural children as with that of an excellent statue that his long labor and study had brought to artistic perfection. And as for those vicious and frenzied passions which have sometimes inflamed fathers with love for their daughters, or mothers for their sons, the like even of these are found in this other sort of parenthood: witness what they tell of Pygmalion, who after building a statue of a woman of singular beauty, became so madly and frantically smitten with love of this work that the gods, for the sake of his passion, had to bring it to life for him:

> Its hardness gone, the ivory softens, yields
> Beneath his fingers.
>
>                                                    OVID

# Discussion Questions

1. What in Montaigne's essay gives you some clues as to what kind of a father he was? Explain your answer.
2. In small groups, discuss how contemporary and timely you find Montaigne's thinking.

3. What is Montaigne's view of wives in his essay? What leads you to your answer?
4. Summarize the key points Montaigne makes in his essay.
5. What effect does Montaigne create by quoting or referring to other writers in his essay?
6. Explain how Montaigne's essay fulfills the criteria of the genre he created in the sixteenth century.

# Writing Assignments

1. In a letter to Montaigne, discuss what ideas you agree and disagree with in his essay.
2. Write a paper that argues why Montaigne would be a good father.
3. Write a paper that examines the ways in which Montaigne offers a feminist perspective in his essay.
4. Write a late twentieth-century version of Montaigne's essay.

# Dream Children: A Reverie

## CHARLES LAMB

Charles Lamb (1775–1834) was born in London and at the age of seven began his schooling at Christ's Hospital School. Family poverty forced Lamb to quit school when he was fourteen years old. He worked as a clerk in the accounting department of the East India Company where he remained for thirty-three years. After his parents died, Lamb, at the age of twenty-two, cared for his sister, Mary, until her death. To supplement his East India Company salary, Lamb wrote essays, which were published in *Works* (1818), and a sentimental novel, *Rosamund Gray* (1820). His work was later published in *London Magazine*, and his essays were later republished in two volumes, *Essays of Elia* (1823) and *Last Essays of Elia* (1833). A friend of William Wordsworth and Samuel Taylor Coleridge, Lamb is considered one of the great English essayists, using such British Renaissance prose writers as Sir Thomas Browne, Robert Burton, and Sir William Temple as his models. In the following essay, taken from *Essays of Elia*, "John L——" is Lamb's brother, James Elia; the "great-grandmother Field" is Lamb's grandmother, Mary Field; "Alice W——n" is Ann Simmons, Lamb's boyhood love; and "Bridget" is Lamb's sister, Mary. In the selection, Lamb recounts a story about his family.

1  Children love to listen to stories about their elders, when *they* were children; to stretch their imagination to the conception of a traditionary great-uncle, or grandame, whom they never saw. It was in this spirit that my little ones crept about me the other evening to hear about their great-grandmother Field, who lived in a great house in Norfolk, (a hundred times bigger than that in which they and papa lived) which had been the scene—so at least it was generally believed in that part of the country—of the tragic incidents which they had lately become familiar with from the ballad of the Children in the Wood. Certain it is that the whole story of the children and their cruel uncle was to be seen fairly carved out in wood upon the chimney-piece of the great hall, the whole story down to the Robin Redbreasts, till a foolish rich person pulled it down to set up a marble one of modern invention in its stead, with no story upon it. Here Alice put out one of her dear mother's looks, too tender to be called upbraiding. Then I went on to say how religious and how good their great-grandmother Field was, how beloved and respected by everybody, though she was not indeed the mistress of this great house, but had only the charge of it (and yet in some respects she might be said to be the mistress of it too) committed to her by the owner, who preferred living in a newer and more fashionable mansion which he had purchased somewhere in the adjoining county; but still she lived in it in a manner as if it had been her own, and kept up the dignity of the great house in a sort while she lived, which afterwards, came to decay, and was nearly pulled down, and all its old ornaments stripped and carried away to the owner's other house, where they were set up, and looked as awkward as if some one were to carry away the old tombs they had seen lately at the Abbey, and stick them up in Lady C's tawdry gilt drawing-room. Here John smiled, as much as to say, "that would be foolish indeed." And then I told how, when she came to die, her funeral was attended by a concourse of all the poor, and some of the gentry too, of the neighbourhood for many miles round, to show their respect for her memory, because she had been such a good and religious woman; so good indeed that she knew all the Psaltery by heart, ay, and a great part of the Testament besides. Here little Alice spread her hands. Then I told what a tall, upright, graceful person their great-grandmother Field once was; and how in her youth she was esteemed the best dancer—here Alice's little right foot played an

involuntary movement, till, upon my looking grave, it desisted—the best dancer, I was saying, in the county, till a cruel disease, called a cancer, came, and bowed her down with pain; but it could never bend her good spirits, or make them stoop, but they were still upright, because she was so good and religious. Then I told how she was used to sleep by herself in a lone chamber of the great lone house; and how she believed that an apparition of two infants was to be seen at midnight gliding up and down the great staircase near where she slept, but she said "those innocents would do her no harm"; and how frightened I used to be, though in those days I had my maid to sleep with me, because I was never half so good or religious as she—and yet I never saw the infants. Here John expanded all his eyebrows and tried to look courageous. Then I told how good she was to all her grandchildren, having us to the great house in the holydays, where I in particular used to spend many hours by myself, in gazing upon the old busts of the twelve Cæsars, that had been Emperors of Rome, till the old marble heads would seem to live again, or I to be turned into marble with them; how I never could be tired with roaming about that huge mansion, with its vast empty rooms, with their worn-out hangings, fluttering tapestry, and carved oaken panels, with the gilding almost rubbed out—sometimes in the spacious old-fashioned gardens, which I had almost to myself, unless when now and then a solitary gardening man would cross me—and how the nectarines and peaches hung upon the walls, without my ever offering to pluck them, because they were forbidden fruit, unless now and then,—and because I had more pleasure in strolling about among the old melancholy-looking yew trees, or the firs, and picking up the red berries, and the fir-apples, which were good for nothing but to look at—or in lying about upon the fresh grass with all the fine garden smells around me—or basking in the orangery, till I could almost fancy myself ripening too along with the oranges and the limes in that grateful warmth—or in watching the dace that darted to and fro in the fish-pond, at the bottom of the garden, with here and there a great sulky pike hanging midway down the water in silent state, as if it mocked at their impertinent friskings,—I had more pleasure in these busy-idle diversions than in all the sweet flavours of peaches, nectarines, oranges, and such-like common baits of children. Here John slyly deposited back upon the plate a bunch of grapes, which, not unobserved by Alice, he had meditated dividing with her, and both seemed willing to relinquish them for the present as irrelevant. Then, in somewhat a more heightened tone, I told how, though their great-grandmother Field loved all her grandchildren, yet in an especial manner she might be said to love their uncle, John L——, because he was so handsome and spirited a youth, and a king to the rest of us; and, instead of moping about in solitary corners, like some of us, he would mount the most mettlesome horse he could get, when but an imp no bigger than themselves, and make it carry him half over the county in a morning, and join the hunters when there were any out—and yet he loved the old great house and gardens too, but had too much spirit to be always pent up within their boundaries—and how their uncle grew up to man's estate as brave as he was handsome, to the admiration of everybody, but of their great-grandmother Field most especially; and how he used to carry me upon his back when I was a lame-footed boy—for he was a good bit older than me—many a mile when I could not walk for pain;—and how in after life he became lame-footed too, and I did not always (I fear) make allowances enough for him when he was impatient and in pain, nor remember sufficiently how considerate he had been to me when I was lame-footed; and how when he died, though he had not been dead an hour, it seemed as if he had died a great while ago, such a distance there is betwixt life and death; and how I bore his death as I thought pretty well at first, but afterwards it haunted and haunted me; and though I did not cry or take it to heart as some do, and as I think he would have done if I had died, yet I missed him all day long, and knew not till then how much I had loved him. I missed his kindness, and I missed his crossness, and wished him to be alive again, to be quarreling with him (for we quarrelled sometimes), rather than not have him again, and was as uneasy without him, as he, their poor uncle, must have been when the doctor took off his limb. Here the children fell a-crying, and asked if their little mourning which they had on was not for Uncle John, and they looked up, and prayed me not to go on about their uncle, but to tell them some stories about their pretty dead mother. Then I told how for seven long years, in hope sometimes, sometimes in despair, yet persisting ever, I courted the fair Alice W——n; and as much as children could understand, I explained to them what coyness, and difficulty, and denial, meant in maidens—when suddenly turning to Alice, the soul

of the first Alice looked out at her eyes with such a reality of re-pre-
sentment, that I became in doubt which of them stood there before
me, or whose that bright hair was; and while I stood gazing, both
the children gradually grew fainter to my view, receding, and still
receding, till nothing at last but two mournful features were seen in
the uttermost distance, which, without speech, strangely impressed
upon me the effects of speech: "We are not of Alice, nor of thee, nor
are we children at all. The children of Alice call Bartrum father. We
are nothing; less than nothing, and dreams. We are only what might
have been, and must wait upon the tedious shores of Lethe millions
of ages before we have existence, and a name"—and immediately
awaking, I found myself quietly seated in my bachelor arm-chair,
where I had fallen asleep, with the faithful Bridget unchanged by my
side—but John L. (or James Elia) was gone for ever.

# Discussion Questions

1. In small groups, discuss the point of this essay and how Lamb
   reveals it.
2. Why did Lamb choose to use the framework of a story as the
   structure of his essay?
3. How is this essay a reverie?
4. Describe with examples the tone of this essay.
5. What may have been Lamb's rationale for making this essay one
   paragraph long?

# Writing Assignments

1. Write a journal entry examining your reactions to hearing stories
   your parents tell about their own childhoods. Explain why you
   feel the way you do and what you learn from such stories.
2. Write an essay that explores the importance of parents recounting stories about their childhoods. Cite specific examples from
   your own experiences hearing your parent's stories.
3. Write a story in which your relatives appear as characters.
4. In a paper, explain the role that tone plays in essay writing. Use
   essays from this collection as supporting examples.

# On the Passing of the First-Born

## W. E. B. DU BOIS

W. E. B. (William Edward Burghardt) Du Bois (1868–1963) was born in Massachusetts. The descendant of a French Huguenot and an African slave, Du Bois earned his Ph.D. from Harvard University in 1895. A Greek and Latin scholar, he taught history and economics at Atlanta University where he actively sought social justice for African Americans. In 1909, Du Bois helped to found the National Association for the Advancement of Colored People (NAACP). Du Bois was also the publisher and editor of *Moon Illustrated Weekly* and editor-in-chief of *Phylon*. He began his most important work in journalism in 1910 when he began his twenty-four-year editorship on *The Crisis*, the journal of the NAACP. His articles, many of which appeared in that journal, reflect Du Bois's training in history, his interest in social issues, and his literary style of writing. He often used autobiography as a way to address social and political issues in his writing. A voluminous writer, Du Bois is the author of *The Souls of Black Folk: Essays and Sketches* (1903); *John Brown* (1909); a novel entitled *The Quest of the Fleece* (1911); *The Negro* (1915); *The Gift of Black Folk: The Negroes in the Making of America* (1924); a novel entitled *Dark Princess: A Romance* (1928); *Black Reconstruction in America* (1935); *Black Folk, Then and Now: An Essay in the History and Sociology of the Negro Race* (1939); an autobiography entitled *Dusk at Dawn: An Essay toward an Autobiography of a Race Concept* (1940); *Color and Democracy: Colonies and Peace* (1945); *In Battle for Peace: The Story of My 83rd Birthday* (1952); *The Ordeal of*

*Mansart* (1957); *Worlds of Color* (1961); and *The Autobiography: A Soliloquy on Viewing My Life from the Last Decade of Its First Century* (posthumous, 1968). In 1958, Du Bois, a fervent and well-respected social activist, was awarded the prestigious Lenin International Peace Prize. In the following essay, from *The Souls of Black Folks,* Du Bois pays tribute to his son and laments his death.

*O sister, sister, thy first-begotten,*
*The hands that cling and the feet that follow,*
*The voice of the child's blood crying yet,*
Who hath remembered me? who hath forgotten?
*Thou hast forgotten, O summer swallow,*
*But the world shall end when I forget.*

—Swinburne

1     "Unto you a child is born," sang the bit of yellow paper that fluttered into my room one brown October morning. Then the fear of fatherhood mingled wildly with the joy of creation; I wondered how it looked and how it felt,—what were its eyes, and how its hair curled and crumpled itself. And I thought in awe of her,—she who had slept with Death to tear a man-child from underneath her heart, while I was unconsciously wandering. I fled to my wife and child, repeating the while to myself half wonderingly, "Wife and child? Wife and child?"—fled fast and faster than boat and steam-car, and yet must ever impatiently await them; away from the hard-voiced city, away from the flickering sea into my own Berkshire Hills that sit all sadly guarding the gates of Massachusetts.

2     Up the stairs I ran to the wan mother and whimpering babe, to the sanctuary on whose altar a life at my bidding had offered itself to win a life, and won. What is this tiny formless thing, this newborn wail from an unknown world,—all head and voice? I handle it curiously, and watch perplexed its winking, breathing, and sneezing. I did not love it then; it seemed a ludicrous thing to love; but her I loved, my girl-mother, she whom now I saw unfolding like

the glory of the morning—the transfigured woman. Through her I came to love the wee thing, as it grew strong; as its little soul unfolded itself in twitter and cry and half-formed word, and as its eyes caught the gleam and flash of life. How beautiful he was, with his olive-tinted flesh and dark gold ringlets, his eyes of mingled blue and brown, his perfect little limbs, and the soft voluptuous roll which the blood of Africa had moulded into his features! I held him in my arms, after we had sped far away to our Southern home,—held him, and glanced at the hot red soil of Georgia and the breathless city of a hundred hills, and felt a vague unrest. Why was his hair tinted with gold? An evil omen was golden hair in my life. Why had not the brown of his eyes crushed out and killed the blue?—for brown were his father's eyes, and his father's father's. And thus in the Land of the Color-line I saw, as it fell across my baby, the shadow of the Veil.

3     Within the Veil was he born, said I; and there within shall he live,—a Negro and a Negro's son. Holding in that little head—ah, bitterly!—the unbowed pride of a hunted race, clinging with that tiny dimpled hand—ah, wearily!—to a hope not hopeless but unhopeful, and seeing with those bright wondering eyes that peer into my soul a land whose freedom is to us a mockery and whose liberty a lie. I saw the shadow of the Veil as it passed over my baby, I saw the cold city towering above the blood-red land. I held my face beside his little cheek, showed him the star-children and the twinkling lights as they began to flash, and stilled with an evensong the unvoiced terror of my life.

4     So sturdy and masterful he grew, so filled with bubbling life, so tremulous with the unspoken wisdom of a life but eighteen months distant from the All-life—we were not far from worshipping this revelation of the divine, my wife and I. Her own life builded and moulded itself upon the child; he tinged her every dream and idealized her every effort. No hands but hers must touch and garnish those little limbs; no dress or frill must touch them that had not wearied her fingers; no voice but hers could coax him off to Dreamland, and she and he together spoke some soft and unknown tongue and in it held communion. I too mused above this little white bed; saw the strength of my own arm stretched onward through the ages through the newer strength of his; saw the dream of my black fathers stagger a step onward in the wild phantasm of

the world; heard in his baby voice the voice of the Prophet that was
to rise within the Veil.

5    And so we dreamed and loved and planned by fall and winter, and
the full flush of the long Southern spring, till the hot winds rolled
from the fetid Gulf, till the roses shivered and the still stern sun
quivered its awful light over the hills of Atlanta. And then one night
the little feet pattered wearily to the wee white bed, and the tiny
hands trembled; and a warm flushed face tossed on the pillow, and
we knew baby was sick. Ten days he lay there,—a swift week and
three endless days, wasting, wasting away. Cheerily the mother
nursed him the first days, and laughed into the little eyes that smiled
again. Tenderly then she hovered round him, till the smile fled away
and Fear crouched beside the little bed.

6    Then the day ended not, and night was a dreamless terror, and
joy and sleep slipped away. I hear now that Voice at midnight calling
me from dull and dreamless trance,—crying, "The Shadow of
Death! The Shadow of Death!" Out into the starlight I crept, to
rouse the gray physician,—the Shadow of Death, the Shadow of
Death. The hours trembled on; the night listened; the ghastly dawn
glided like a tired thing across the lamplight. Then we two alone
looked upon the child as he turned toward us with great eyes, and
stretched his stringlike hands,—the Shadow of Death! And we spoke
no word, and turned away.

7    He died at eventide, when the sun lay like a brooding sorrow
above the western hills, veiling its face; when the winds spoke not,
and the trees, the great green trees he loved, stood motionless. I saw
his breath beat quicker and quicker, pause, and then his little soul
leapt like a star that travels in the night and left a world of darkness
in its train. The day changed not; the same tall trees peeped in at the
windows, the same green grass glinted in the setting sun. Only in
the chamber of death writhed the world's most piteous thing—a
childless mother.

8    I shirk not. I long for work. I pant for a life full of striving. I am
no coward, to shrink before the rugged rush of the storm, nor even
quail before the awful shadow of the Veil. But hearken, O Death! Is
not this my life hard enough,—is not that dull land that stretches its
sneering web about me cold enough,—is not all the world beyond
these four little walls pitiless enough, but that thou must needs enter

here;—thou, O Death? About my head the thundering storm beat like a heartless voice, and the crazy forest pulsed with the curses of the weak; but what cared I, within my home beside my wife and baby boy? Wast thou so jealous of one little coign of happiness that thou must needs enter there,—thou, O Death?

9    A perfect life was his, all joy and love, with tears to make it brighter,—sweet as a summer's day beside the Housatonic. The world loved him; the women kissed his curls, the men looked gravely into his wonderful eyes, and the children hovered and fluttered about him. I can see him now, changing like the sky from sparkling laughter to darkening frowns, and then to wondering thoughtfulness as he watched the world. He knew no color-line, poor dear,—and the Veil, though it shadowed him, had not yet darkened half his sun. He loved the white matron, he loved his black nurse; and in his little world walked souls alone, uncolored and unclothed. I—yea, all men—are larger and purer by the infinite breadth of that one little life. She who in simple clearness of vision sees beyond the stars said when he had flown, "He will be happy There; he ever loved beautiful things." And I, far more ignorant, and blind by the web of mine own weaving, sit alone winding words and muttering, "If still he be, and he be There, and there be a There, let him be happy, O Fate!"

10    Blithe was the morning of his burial, with bird and song and sweet-smelling flowers. The trees whispered to the grass, but the children sat with hushed faces. And yet it seemed a ghostly unreal day,—the wraith of Life. We seemed to rumble down an unknown street behind a little white bundle of posies, with the shadow of a song in our ears. The busy city dinned about us; they did not say much, those pale-faced hurrying men and women; they did not say much,—they only glanced and said, "Niggers!"

11    We could not lay him in the ground there in Georgia, for the earth there is strangely red, so we bore him away to the northward, with his flowers and his little folded hands. In vain, in vain!—for where, O God! beneath thy broad blue sky shall my dark baby rest in peace,—where Reverence dwells, and Goodness, and a Freedom that is free?

12    All that day and all that night there sat an awful gladness in my heart,—nay, blame me not if I see the world thus darkly through the

Veil,—and my soul whispers ever to me, saying, "Not dead, not dead, but escaped; not bond, but free." No bitter meanness now shall sicken his baby heart till it die a living death, no taunt shall madden his happy boyhood. Fool that I was to think or wish that this little soul should grow choked and deformed within the Veil! I might have known that yonder deep unworldly look that ever and anon floated past his eyes was peering far beyond this narrow Now. In the poise of his little curl-crowned head did there not sit all that wild pride of being which his father had hardly crushed in his own heart? For what, forsooth, shall a Negro want with pride amid the studied humiliations of fifty million fellows? Well sped, my boy, before the world had dubbed your ambition insolence, had held your ideals unattainable, and taught you to cringe and bow. Better far this nameless void that stops my life than the sea of sorrow for you.

13   Idle words; he might have borne his burden more bravely than we,—aye, and found it lighter too, some day; for surely, surely this is not the end. Surely there shall yet dawn some mighty morning to lift the Veil and set the prisoned free. Not for me—I shall die in my bonds,—but for fresh young souls who have not known the night and waken to the morning; a morning when men ask of the work-man, not "Is he white?" but "Can he work?" When men ask artists, not "Are they black?" but "Do they know?" Some morning this may be, long, long years to come. But now there wails, on that dark shore within the Veil, the same deep voice, *Thou shalt forego!* And all have I foregone at that command, and with small complaint,—all save that fair young form that lies so coldly wed with death in the nest I had builded.

14   If one must have gone, why not I? Why may I not rest me from this restlessness and sleep from this wide waking? Was not the world's alembic, Time, in his young hands, and is not my time wan-ing? Are there so many workers in the vineyard that the fair promise of this little body could lightly be tossed away? The wretched of my race that line the alleys of the nation sit fatherless and unmothered; but Love sat beside his cradle, and in his ear Wisdom waited to speak. Perhaps now he knows the All-love, and needs not to be wise. Sleep, then, child,—sleep till I sleep and waken to a baby voice and the ceaseless patter of little feet—above the Veil.

# Discussion Questions

1. Describe the tone of the essay and discuss its appropriateness.
2. Identify some specific examples that characterize Du Bois and his wife's relationship with their child.
3. What stylistic techniques does Du Bois use in his essay? Evaluate their effectiveness.
4. In small groups, discuss why Du Bois capitalizes such words as *life, goodness, freedom,* and *veil.*
5. Explain Du Bois's reasons for asking four questions in a row in the last paragraph. Are there any answers to those questions? Why or why not?
6. What is Du Bois's attitude toward his son's death? Does it change anywhere in the essay? Identify specific passages in the text that influence your response.

# Writing Assignments

1. Write a journal entry that examines how you think Du Bois handled his son's death.
2. Writing about the death of a loved one, especially that of a child, poses special difficulties for the writer. How does Du Bois avoid becoming maudlin and sentimental in this essay? Write a paper that examines the essay's style.
3. Write an essay that describes the way your feelings changed about an important event in your life (for example, the birth of a sibling, the death of a relative or friend).

# The Forgiveness of Daughters

## BARBARA
## LAZEAR
## ASCHER

Barbara Lazear Ascher (b. 1946) was born in Virginia and attended
Bennington College. She earned her law degree from Cardoza
School of Law in 1979 and was a practicing attorney before becoming a full-time writer. She has read her essays for National Public
Radio's *Morning Edition*. Her essays have appeared in such publications as *The New York Times, Saturday Review, The Yale Review,
European Travel and Life,* and *Vogue.* Ascher is the author of two
collections of essays: *Playing After Dark* (1986) and *The Habit of
Loving* (1989), in which the following essay appears. In *Landscape
without Gravity: A Memoir of Grief* (1993), Ascher chronicles coming to terms with the death of her brother from AIDS. Ascher has
distinguished herself by writing lyrical, personal narratives in which
are embedded her understandings about classic themes. The following essay is one such example in which Ascher recounts her daughter's comments about Mary Cassatt's paintings as a way to
introduce her reflections on her own relationship with her daughter,
as well as the meaning of parent-child relationships.

1    She's been looking at Mary Cassatt's paintings of mothers and
children, and says, "You know, when I look at those children, I
don't experience envy. I experience familiarity."

2    When I look at those same paintings, I experience yearning, a painful reach of the heart towards those moments when one could comfort. Fleeting moments, unlike Cassatt's which, captured in pigment, endure. Ours were interrupted by phone calls, dinner preparations, a social life. In Cassatt's paintings there are no bills to be paid, no meetings to attend. The dog is not howling to go out. Cassatt painted remembered moments of childhood such as my daughter describes, moments which rise to the top of memory's well and shimmer there above the more mundane and painful facts of family life. Childless, she painted from the memory of being a daughter, which is why my own daughter and I view her work from different perspectives. I look, and see not the comfort I gave, but the comfort I wish I had given.

3    I do not see myself as a source of reassurance and protection from the pains of the world. After all, she's now bigger than I. More outspoken. Strong in body and soul. When we stand, I have to look up in order to meet her eye-to-eye.

4    And I know my own psychic history. I know the times I let her down, times that weakened trust, drew a disappointed and hurt child away from her mother. The times she made me angry enough to scream in a rage that never enters the world of Cassatt's pictures. When she was two and defiant and when her defiance became physical in the form of a swift kick to the shins, and I, stunned, wailed to my husband, "I'm not sure I like her anymore!"

5    I know of the two A.M. feeding when we were new to each other and my milk came so fast she would choke and throw up and cry, and I would try again, and fail—the milk squirting into her eyes, her nostrils, and finally down her throat, but with such force, she gasped for relief. We didn't have our rhythms yet. We were unfamiliar with our ability to comfort and be comforted. Both of us felt awash in the world. Alone, with our enemy, our beloved. One of those dark winter nights of pacing and feeding and burping and soothing, I stopped to look out over Manhattan for lit windows, for signs of others suffering alone in the night. Instead, I caught our own reflection and was shocked by my small size, by the fact that in my arms there was a human life for which I was totally responsible. I thought, I'm not ready for this. I thought of the responsibility that would last a lifetime, and burst into tears.

6    I know all this and yet she sees me, through the eyes of love, as a Cassatt mother. Through the heart of forgiveness, she speaks of my

ability to make her feel that the world and she are all right. Children's forgiveness of their parents is a perfect forgiveness, forged out of love and lacking self-consciousness. Unlike adults, children's forgiveness comes from the generosity of their hearts, not from overbearing consciences shorn up by community mores or church sermons. The most our consciences do is demand that we say "I'm sorry," demand that we put on a good show of it. But it is the rare adult who does not, when hurt, bear a grudge and wish ill upon the perpetrators. Children's forgiveness is another matter, it is natural, full-spirited and complete. So complete that it is accompanied by amnesia for the hurtful event.

7    One day recently, as my daughter and I strolled in Central Park reminiscing about her New York childhood and rainy days spent at double feature Fred Astaire movies in the Village, she said, "I'm so glad that I didn't have a working mom." Her mind had taken a flying leap from the darkened movie theater to the present, skimming across the top of painful memories. She does not hear her ancient outcry, experience her loneliness, or sense of betrayal and abandonment. That blank in her memory is filled in by my own remembrance. Mother's memories are not as kind. I think of a night during my first year of law school when the family was gathered for dinner and her tears began to fill the carefully constructed well in the center of her mashed potatoes. "When I grow up," she choked, "I'm not going to betray my husband and daughter by going to law school."

8    I don't remind her. Not now. I would rather bask in this forgiveness, accept it as a balm. I hear the old refrains of the dangers of repression and am tempted, for a moment, to say, "But you did have a working mom." But I don't. I am silent as I am now as she tells me of the Cassatt paintings. As she tells me of love.

9    There is a place for nostalgia. It helps us to forgive. Her memories, incomplete and flawed, colored by wish as well as reality, make it possible for her to grant me absolution. I do not indulge in a confessional. I do not beg forgiveness. It's given without asking. Now, of course, the job is mine.

# Discussion Questions

1. Explain what Ascher's main point is in this essay.
2. What does Ascher achieve by comparing her experience with the images captured in Mary Cassatt's paintings?
3. Characterize Ascher and her daughter from what you learn about them in this essay.
4. In small groups, discuss whether you agree in paragraph 6 with the distinction Ascher makes between a child's forgiveness and an adult's.
5. What do you make of Ascher's daughter not remembering her mother went to law school and Ascher not correcting her daughter's mistake?
6. Do you agree with Ascher when she states in paragraph 9, "There is a place for nostalgia. It helps us to forgive"? Can you recall any experiences from your own life that confirm Ascher's observation?
7. Explain the last sentence of the essay.

# Writing Assignments

1. Write an essay in which you define with examples what true forgiveness means to you.
2. Write a journal entry that reflects on a time in which you forgave your parents. What made the incident so important?
3. Write an essay that details a moment in which you and your mother or father shared a special moment.
4. Assume the persona of Ascher's daughter and write a complementary essay in which you describe Cassatt's painting and its effect on you.
5. Recall a time when looking at the work of an artist—for example, a painting or a statue—enabled you to understand better something about your own life. Describe the work and your newfound realizations.

# On Being Raised by a Daughter

## NANCY MAIRS

Nancy Mairs (b. 1943) was born in Long Beach, California, and grew up in Massachusetts and New Hampshire. She attended Wheaton College and worked as a technical editor at the Smithsonian Astrophysical Observatory, the MIT Press, and Harvard Law School. In 1972, she moved to Arizona and earned an M.F.A. and a Ph.D. in English from the University of Arizona where she currently teaches. She was awarded a William P. Sloan fellowship in 1984 and a Western States Book Award in the same year for her poetry collection *All the Rooms in the Yellow House* (1983). Her interest in autobiographical writing led to her experimenting with the genre, and the resulting essays have appeared in numerous publications such as *Triquarterly, The New York Times, The American Voice, Kaleidoscope,* and *Working Mother.* She is the author of six autobiographical essay collections and memoirs: *Plaintext: Deciphering a Woman's Life* (1986), *Remembering the Bone House: An Erotics of Place and Space* (1989), *Carnal Acts* (1990), *Ordinary Time: Cycles in Marriage, Faith, and Renewal* (1993), *Voice Lessons: On Becoming a (Woman) Writer* (1994), and *Waist-High in the World: A Life among the Nondisabled* (1996). These books chronicle Mairs's life as a woman, a mother, a wife, a writer, and a person with multiple sclerosis, a degenerative neurological disease. Mairs's essays are characterized by an unremitting and honest focus on the ways in which chronic disease has affected her life.

In the following selection taken from *Plaintext*, Mairs discusses role reversal in which her daughter cares for her because of the disabling effects of multiple sclerosis.

1   Mothering. I didn't know how to do it. Does anyone? If there really were a maternal instinct, as a good many otherwise quite responsible human beings have claimed, then would we need men like Dr. Alan Guttmacher and Dr. Benjamin Spock to teach us how to mother, and would we be forever scrambling to keep up with the shifts in their child-bearing and child-rearing theories? Would we turn, shaken by our sense of our female incapacity, to the reassuring instructive voices of the fathers, who increasingly come in both sexes, murmuring how much weight to gain or lose, how long to offer the breast, how soon to toilet train, to send to school? Does the salmon ask for a map to the spawning ground? Does the bee send to the Department of Agriculture for a manual on honeymaking?

2   No, I came with no motherly chromosomes to pattern my gestures comfortably. Not only did I not know how to do it, I'm not even sure now that I wanted to do it. These days people choose whether or not to have children. I am not so very old—my forty-first birthday falls this month—yet I can say with the verity of a wrinkled granny that we did things differently in my day. I no more chose to have children than I had chosen to get married. I simply did what I had been raised to do. Right on schedule (or actually a little ahead of schedule, since I hadn't yet finished college) I wrapped myself in yards of white taffeta and put orange blossoms in my hair and marched myself, in front of the fond, approving gaze of a couple of hundred people, into the arms of a boy in a morning coat who was doing what he had been raised to do. After a year or so, the fond, approving gaze shifted to my belly, which I made swell to magnificent proportions before expelling an unpromising scrap of human flesh on whom the gaze could turn. This was Anne, created in a heedless gesture as close to instinctual as any I would ever per-

form: satisfaction of the social expectation that I, young, vigorous, equipped with functioning uterus and ovaries and breasts, would sanctify my union with George by bringing forth a son. (I missed, though I had better luck next time.)

3    The birth of Anne was dreadful, and at the beginning I hated her, briefly, more fiercely than I had ever hated anyone. My doctor, a small round elderly GP who delivered whatever babies came along in Bath, Maine, told me that my protracted pelvis might necessitate a Caesarian section, but he never instructed me what to do during this birth by whatever means. I guess I was supposed not to do but to endure. I remember, hours into a lengthy and complicated labor that ended in Dr. Fichtner's extracting Anne with forceps like a six-pound thirteen-ounce wisdom tooth, twisting my fingers through my hair, yanking, raking my face with my nails, shrieking at the nurse beside me, "Get this thing out of me! I hate it!" Until then I had rather liked Anne, as she humped up bigger and bigger each night under the bedsheet, her wriggles and thumps giving a constant undertone of companionship to my often solitary daily activities. But now I was sure she was killing me. The nurse loosened my fingers and soothed, "You'll feel differently in a little while."

4    She was right. In a rather long while I did feel differently. I was no longer in pain. But I didn't feel motherly. In fact, Anne on the outside wasn't half so companionable as Anne on the inside, and I think I felt a little lonely. And frightened. I hadn't the faintest idea what I was doing with this mite with the crossed blue eyes and the whoosh of hair sticking straight up. And now, more than eighteen years later, I still have the frequent sense that I don't know what I'm doing, complicated now, of course, by the guilt that I don't know what I've done and the terror that I don't know what I'm going to do. How, I wonder, when a young woman comes into my room and speaks to me, her hair blown dry to casual elegance and her eyes uncrossed behind round brown frames, how did you get here? And where, when you turn and walk out of here, out of my house and out of the dailiness of my life, where will you go?

5    I have been mystified by motherhood largely because motherhood itself has been mystified. Perhaps before Freud I might have raised my children without knowing consciously my power to damage their spirits beyond human repair, but the signs have always been there: the Good Mother and the Terrible Mother, the dead

saint and the wicked stepmother waiting to offer disguised poisons, shoes of hellfire. The one is as alien as the other. If you live in a culture where all children are raised by mothers, Nancy Chodorow points out in *The Reproduction of Mothering*, and if half those children are males who must separate with some violence from the mother in order to establish their different gender, and if the males have the power to determine, through the creation of symbolic systems like language and art, what culture itself is, then you will get a cultural view of mothers as others, on whom are projected traits that even they (who speak some form of the language, who look at the pictures even if they don't paint them) come to assume are their own. We live in a culture of object-mothers. The subject-mothers, culturally silenced for millennia, are only just beginning to speak.

6      The voices of authority tell me I may harm, even ruin my daughter (in large measure by spoiling her for the pleasurable uses of men). At first they issue from the eminences of science, in measured tones like those of Carl Jung: "Thus, if the child of an over-anxious mother regularly dreams that she is a terrifying animal or a witch, these experiences point to a split in the child's psyche that predisposes it to a neurosis." I am the stuff of my daughter's nightmares. Gradually the pronouncements trickle down into the market place and are reformulated for popular consumption by voices like Nancy Friday's in that long whine of sexual anxiety *My Mother/My Self*, which was on the bestseller list some years back: "When mother's silent and threatening disapproval adds dark colors to the girl's emergent sexuality, this fear becomes eroticized in such strange forms as masochism, love of the brute, rape fantasies—the thrill of whatever is most forbidden." I make of my daughter's life a waking nightmare as well. A book like *My Mother/My Self*, in dealing with our earliest relationship, out of which our ability to form all other relationships grows, taps a rich subterranean vein of desire and disappointment, but it does so only to portray daughter as victim.

7      The real danger these voices pose lies not so much in what they say as in what they leave out about motherhood, whether through ignorance or through incapacity. Jung was not a woman at all, at least socially speaking (archetypally, of course, he had an anima, which doesn't seem to have caused him much trouble). And Friday refused to have children on the grounds that if she chanced to have a daughter, she'd ruin her child just as her mother had ruined her

(such an assumption suggests that her choice was a wise one). But neither these two nor the vast crowd of fellow motherhood-mystifiers between them takes into adequate account the persistence of human development, which keeps the personality malleable indefinitely, if it is allowed to, or the implacable power of six pounds thirteen ounces of human flesh from the moment it draws a breath and wails its spirit out into the world.

8    Among all the uncertainties I have experienced about myself as a mother, of one point I feel sure: that I am not today the woman I would have been had Anne not been born one September evening almost nineteen years ago. I cannot prove this hypothesis, there being no control in this experiment, no twenty-two-year-old Nancy Mairs that night who had a son instead, whose baby died, who had had a miscarriage, who had not been able to get pregnant at all, who never married and lives now in a small, well-appointed apartment on the Marina in San Francisco, walking her Burmese cats on leashes in Golden Gate Park. There is only this Nancy Mairs who, for nearly half her life, has in raising been raised by a daughter.

9    Anne can't have found her job an easy one. Raising a mother is difficult enough under the best of circumstances. But when you get one who's both crippled and neurotic—who doesn't do her fair share of the housework, who lurches around the house and crashes to the floor in front of your friends, whose spirits flag and crumple unpredictably, who gets attacks of anxiety in the middle of stores and has to be cajoled into finishing simple errands—then you have your work cut out for you. Of all the things Anne has taught me, perhaps the most important is that one can live under difficult circumstances with a remarkable amount of equanimity and good humor. It's a lesson I need daily.

10    My education began, no doubt, from the moment of her birth. Perhaps even before. Perhaps from the moment I perceived her presence in the absence of my period, or from the instant (Christmas Eve, I'm convinced) of her conception, or even from the time I began to dream her. But then she was anonymous. As soon as she appeared, she took me firmly in diminutive hand and trained me much as I've come to see that my cats have trained me, rewarding my good behavior (what difference a smile or a purr?) and punishing my bad (they've both tended to bite). But I don't think of my education as being under way till about nine months later when one

day she heaved herself up in her car-bed, raised one arm in a stiff wave, and called, "Hi there!" A baby who could talk with me was beyond my ken. After all, I was raised before the days when dolls had electronic voice-boxes in their tummies and quavered "Hi there!" when you pulled the string. And anyway, Anne didn't have a string. *She* chose to speak to *me*.

11    I've ever been the same.

12    Birth is, I think, an attenuated process, though we tend to use the word to describe only the physical separation of the baby from the mother. Fortunately, those first hours of birth were the worst, in terms of pain, or I don't think I'd have lasted. Each phase of the process involves separation, which may or may not be physical but always carries heavy psychic freight. For me, Anne's speech was a major step. It set her apart from me, over there, an entity with whom I could, literally, have a dialogue. It made her an other.

13    Feminist psychologists note that psychical birth, the process of differentiating self from other, is particularly problematic for female children. As Chodorow writes,

> Because they are the same gender as their daughters and have been girls, mothers of daughters tend not to experience these infant daughters as separate from them in the same way as do mothers of infant sons. . . . Primary identification and symbiosis with daughters tend to be stronger and cathexis of daughters is more likely to retain and emphasize narcissistic elements, that is, to be based on experiencing a daughter as an extension or double of a mother herself, with cathexis of the daughter as a sexual other usually remaining a weaker, less significant theme.

The consequence of this feeling of continuity between mother and daughter is that "separation and individuation remain particularly female developmental issues." But "problematic" doesn't mean "bad," a leap that Friday makes when she lifts "symbiosis" out of the psychoanalytic context in which Chodorow uses it and applies it to noninfantile relationships, giving it then not its full range of meaning but that portion of meaning which suits her program: symbiosis as a kind of perverse parasitism: a large but weak organism feeding on a smaller but strong host which, as it grows, weakens until the two are evenly matched in size and incapacity. According to Friday, the mother limits her daughter's autonomy and independence, extinguishes her sexuality, terrifies her witless of men, then packages her in Saran Wrap to keep her fresh and hands her over to some man who, if she's not careful, will get on her a daughter on whom she will perform the same hideous rites.

14    I'm not saying that no mother does such things. Apparently Nancy Friday's mother did, and I recognize any number of my own experiences in hers. Nor am I saying that, through some virtue or miracle, I have avoided doing them to Anne. Of course I would want to think so; but God and Anne alone know what horrors I've perpetrated. All I can be sure of is that if Anne handed me a list of grievances, most of them would probably surprise me. If they didn't, I'd be a monster, not a mother.

15    What I am saying is that such things are not intrinsic to the mother-daughter relationship. As Chodorow notes in her study "Family Structure and Female Personality," women in societies as various as those in Atjeh, Java, and East London, where their "kin role, and in particular the mother role, is central and positively valued," have experiences and develop self-images very different from those of Western middle-class women:

> There is another important aspect of the situation in these societies. The continuing structural and practical importance of the mother-daughter tie not only ensures that a daughter develops a positive personal and role identification with her mother, but also requires that the close psychological tie between mother and daughter become firmly grounded in real role expectations. These provide a certain constraint and limitation upon the relationship, as well as an avenue for its expression through common spheres of interest based in the external social world.

Thus, although the problem of differentiation exists wherever mothers mother daughters, its implications vary from one social setting to another. If a woman like Friday's mother teaches her daughter that sex is risky at best and in general downright nasty, she does so not because she is a mother but because she is the product of a patriarchal order that demands that its women be chaste and compliant so that men may be sure of their paternity. In fact, such a concern is extrinsic to the mother-daughter relationship, which exists in essence outside the sphere of men. As soon as one can identify it for what it is, the concern of a particular group of human beings for maintaining a particular kind of power, one is free to choose whether or not to perpetuate it.

16    Thus, Friday's rationale for refusing to bear children, that she would inevitably visit upon her daughter the same evils her mother visited upon her, is off the mark, rooted in a sense of powerlessness in the face of the existing social order which seems to stem from belief in a biologically predetermined parasitism. Mothers, inexorably, must eat out the hearts of their daughters alive. Neither a mother nor a daughter has the power to avoid the dreadful outcome. They are only helpless women. But if we step outside socially imposed injunctions, then Friday is wrong, and daughters and their mothers wield powers for one another's help as well as harm. They may even make of one another revolutionaries.

17    Symbiosis is a spacious word. It may encompass parasitism and helotism (though the *Shorter Oxford Dictionary* disallows this meaning by requiring that the entities involved be mutually supportive). But it also—even chiefly—means commensalism, mutualism, "the intimate living together," says *Webster's Third*, "of two dissimilar organisms in any of various mutually beneficial relationships." The crux is the livingwithness the word demands: We may live with one another well or badly. To live together reciprocally, each contributing to the other's support, in the figurative sense in which symbiosis represents human relationship, requires delicate balance, difficult to establish and to maintain. Both partners must give to it and take from it. Both must flourish under its influence, or it is no longer symbiotic. For these reasons, a symbiotic relationship between a mother and her growing daughter—or between any other two people, for that matter—may be rather rare. For these reasons, also, emotional symbiosis is not an ascribed characteristic of a relationship; rather, it is the outcome of the dynamics of some relationships between some people some of the time.

18      Symbiosis as I am now using the word—not like Chodorow to
represent the phase of total infantile dependence or like Friday to
suggest emotional vampirism but rather as a metaphor for the inter-
dependence characteristic of living together well—does not result in
identity. On the contrary, every definition I've found requires the
difference of the entities involved. Thus, after the demands of
infancy have been made and met, individuation is necessary if a true
symbiotic system is to be maintained. Otherwise you get something
else, some solid lump of psychic flesh whose name I do not know.

19      All the analyses I've read of mother-daughter relationships fail to
account for my experience of Anne's power in our mutual life. The
assumption seems to be that I'm the one in control, not just because
I'm older than she is and, until recently, bigger and stronger, but
because I have society's acknowledgment and support in the venture
and she doesn't. I'm engaged in the honorable occupation of child-
rearing, and if I can't figure the procedures out for myself, I can find
shelves of manuals in any bookstore or library. No one even notices
that Anne is engaged in mother-rearing, much less offers her any hot
tips; indeed, books like *My Mother/My Self* only reinforce her powerlessness, making her out a victim of maternal solicitude and sub-
merged rage, whose only recourse is more rage, rebellion, rejection:
not an actor but a reactor. Such lopsided accounts arise, I suppose,
from the premise—the consequence of a hierarchical view of human
development—that adulthood signifies completion. But the fluidity,
the pains and delights, the spurts of growth and sluggish spells of
childhood never cease, though we may cease to acknowledge them
in an effort to establish difference from, and hence authority over,
our children. Out of the new arrivals in our lives—the odd word
stumbled upon in a difficult text, the handsome black stranger who
bursts in one night through the cat door, the telephone call out of a
friend's silence of years, the sudden greeting from the girl-child—we
constantly make of ourselves our selves.

20      When Anne waved and called out to me, she made an other not
only of herself but of me. Language is the ultimate alienator. When
she spoke she created for herself a self so remote from me that it
could communicate with me only—imprecisely, imperfectly—
through words. Shortly thereafter she named me, and went on naming me, into place, a slowish process. When she was not quite two, I
left the world. I went into a state mental hospital and stayed there

six months. During that time Anne lived with my mother, another Anne, and the two of them built a life around a space that they both expected me to come back to and fill. One afternoon, sitting in a basket in the checkout line at the IGA, Anne struck up a conversation with the man behind her who, gesturing toward Mother, said something about her mummy. "That's not my Mummy," Anne informed him, drawing herself high and fixing him with one crossed eye. "It's my Grandma. My Mummy is in the hospital." When Mother told me this story, I heard the message as I've heard it ever since: I'm the Mummy, the only Mummy (though I've grown up to be Mom, that hearty jokey apple-pie name, for reasons known only to my children), and that's who I've got to be.

21    As Mummy I have emphatically never been permitted to be Anne. Whatever fantasies I may have had, at some subliminal level, of my new daughter as a waxen dolly that I could pinch and pat into my likeness, Anne scotched them early, probably when she first spat puréed liver into my face (not to mention when she became the only one in the family who today eats liver in any form), certainly by the time she shouted out "Hi there!" (not "Mama" or "Dada," no private communiqué, but a greeting to all the world). Nor can I ever make her me. She wouldn't let me. Hence the possibility for our symbiosis, a state that demands two creatures for its establishment and maintenance. Anne has schooled me in the art of living well together by letting go.

22    Like any daughter's, hers hasn't been a simple task, but I don't think that the kind of gritty spirit it's called up in her will stand her in bad stead. She has been hampered by my own terror of separation, brought on perhaps by my early separation from my mother because of illness or my somewhat later permanent separation from my father through death. She has been helped, I think, by my curiosity to see what she would do next and by the fact that I've worked at jobs I enjoy since she was nine months old and that I've remained married, in considerable contentment, to her father, for as Chodorow points out, when "women do meaningful productive work, have ongoing adult companionship while they are parenting, and have satisfying emotional relationships with other adults, they are less likely to overinvest in children." And at least I've always *wanted* to let go. I just haven't always known how or when. Anne, through her peculiar quiet stubborn self-determination, has time

after time peeled my white-knuckled fingers loose and shrugged away from my grasp.

23    Neither of us has had a whole lot of help from the world at large. We live in a society that still expects, even demands, that mothers control and manipulate their children's actions right into adulthood; that judges them according to the acceptability or unacceptability of their children's appearance and behavior; and that ensures their dependence on maternity for a sense, however diffuse, of self by giving them precious little else of interest to do. The mother who does let go, especially of a daughter, is still often considered irresponsible at best, unnatural at worst.

24    When Anne was sixteen, for instance, she decided to join a volunteer organization called Amigos de las Americas, training in Spanish and public health for several months and then going to Honduras to vaccinate pigs against hog cholera. United States policies in Central America hadn't yet created thoroughgoing chaos, and George and I thought this a wonderful way for her to begin inserting herself into the world. But George's parents, on a visit during her preparations, challenged me about Anne's plans. She ought not to be allowed to go, they said. It would be too much for her. The shock of entering a new culture would make her emotionally ill. "Ugh," Mum Mairs shuddered, "girls shouldn't have to dig latrines." (At that time, Anne hadn't yet received her assignment, but I presume that girls shouldn't have to slog around in pigshit either.) I was so startled by this attack, in terms I had not thought of before, that I doubt I said much to allay their fears, though I did ask Anne to tell them about her training in order to reassure them that she wasn't being thrust into the jungle naked and naive. Meanwhile, I thought about those terms, those feminine terms, forgotten at least momentarily by me, foreign as a source of motivation to Anne: nicety, physical and emotional frailty, passivity: all rolled into that statement that girls shouldn't have to dig latrines. (The logical extension of this attitude, I suppose, is that if a girl is all you've got, then you don't get a latrine. Ugh.)

25    Later, comparing notes with George, I learned that his parents had never mentioned the matter to him. I was at first hurt, angry, feeling picked on; later I came to understand that I was the natural target of their misgivings. George couldn't be counted on to know what girls should or shouldn't do, or to communicate his knowl-

edge if he did. But I could. I was Anne's mother. And in letting her go to Latin America to live, if only briefly, in poverty, perhaps in squalor, and to perform manual labor, I was derelict in my duty.

26    Thus challenged, I had to rethink this duty. To Mum and Dad Mairs, obviously, it entailed the same protection I received growing up: keeping Anne safe and comfortable, even keeping her pure, at bottom probably protecting her maidenhead, though this mission is buried so deep in our cultural unconscious that I think they would be shocked at the mention of it. I recognized a different duty, a harsher one: to promote Anne's intellectual and spiritual growth even if it meant her leaving me. I didn't think that safety and comfort tended to lead to growth. As for protecting her maidenhead, I figured that was her responsibility, since she was the one who had it, or didn't have it, as the case might be. My duty, I saw, might in fact *be* dereliction, in the form of releasing her into the flood of choice and chance that would be her life. I thought she could swim. More important, she thought she could swim. Nonetheless, while she was gone I ran around distracted and stricken with guilt, mumbling primitive prayers to Our Lady of Guadalupe to take up the watch I had left off. Then she came home, bearing rum and machetes wide-eyed right through customs, with a new taste for mangoes and a new delight in hot showers but without even the lice and dysentery and other gruesome manifestations of tropical fauna she had been promised.

27    She came back but never, of course, all the way back. Each departure contains an irrevocable element of private growth and self-sufficiency. For the most part I have thought her departures thrilling: the month she spent in New England with her grandparents when she was eight, flying back to Tucson alone; her first period; the first night she spent (quite chastely) with a boy, and later her first lover; her excellence at calculus; her choice to leave lover and family and lifelong friends to go to college on the other side of the country. As long as her new flights give her joy, I rejoice. Where I balk—and balk badly—is at those junctures where the growing hurts her.

28    One night a couple of winters ago, I woke from heavy early sleep to a young man standing in the dark by my bed: David, Anne's boyfriend. "Mrs. Mairs," he whispered, "I think you'd better come. Anne is drunk and she's really sick and I think you should take care of her." Clearly David wasn't drunk, hadn't been at the same party,

he explained, but had met up with Anne afterward. He'd taken her to a friend's house, and though Chris wasn't at home, his mother had kindly taken them in, given them some tea, let Anne throw up in her toilet. But it was getting late, and David had a deadline. He had to bring Anne home, but he didn't dare leave her alone.

29    I hauled myself out of bed and padded to the other end of the cold house, where Anne was in her bathroom washing her face. When she heard my voice, she hissed, "David. I'll kill you," then came out and burst into tears. I sent David along as I held and rocked her, listening to her wretched tale. She certainly was drunk. The fumes rising from my sodden lap were enough to make me tiddly. Gradually I got her quieted and tucked into bed. The next day she felt suitably miserable. To this day she prefers milk to alcohol.

30    The children were surprised that I wasn't angry about this episode. In a way I was surprised myself. After all, I had forbidden Anne to drink alcohol outside our house, and she had disobeyed me. Wasn't anger the appropriate response to a disobedient child? But though I specialize in appropriate responses, I did not feel angry. Instead, I felt overwhelmingly sad. For days I was stabbed to the heart by the thought of Anne reeling and stumbling along a darkened street, her emotions black and muddled, abandoned by the group of nasty little boys who had given her beer and vodka and then gone off to have some other fun.

31    By that one act she stripped me of whatever vestiges of magical thinking I was clinging to about mothers and daughters. Until then, I think, I had still believed that through my wisdom and love I could protect her from the pains I had endured as a child. Suddenly my shield was in tatters. It was a thing of gauze and tissue anyway. She has taught me the bitterest lesson in child-rearing I've yet had to learn: that she will have pain, must have it if she is to get to—and through—this place I am now and the places to which I have yet to go. For, as Juliet Mitchell writes, "pain and lack of satisfaction are the point, the triggers that evoke desire," that essential longing which marks our being in the world, both Anne's and mine, as human.

32    In teaching me to be her mother, Anne has, among all her other gifts, given me my own mother in ways that have often surprised me. For, as the French theorist Julia Kristeva writes in *Desire in Language*, "By giving birth, the woman enters into contact with her

mother; she becomes, she is her own mother, they are the same continuity differentiating itself." Old rebellions have softened, old resentments cooled, now that I see my mother stereoscopically, the lens of motherhood superimposed on that of daughterhood. Every child, I'm sure, takes stern and secret vows along these lines: "When I grow up, I'm never going to make my child clean her room every Saturday, wear orange hair ribbons, babysit her sister, eat pea soup . . ."; and every mother must experience those moments of startlement and sometimes horror when she opens her mouth and hears issue forth not her own voice but the voice of her mother. Surprisingly often, I have found, my mother's voice speaks something that I, as a mother, want to say. I can remember that, when I had accepted a date with Fred—squat, chubby, a little loud, a French kisser, the bane of my high-school love life—and then got a better offer, Mother told me I had only two choices, to go with Fred or to stay home. I vowed then that I would never interfere with my child's social life. But I have had occasion to issue the same injunction, not because I can't tell where my mother ends and I begin, nor because I want Anne to suffer the same horrors I endured in the course of becoming a woman, but because I believe that the habit of courtesy toward one's fellow creatures is more durable than a fabulous night at the prom. Mother may have thought so too.

33      I gave Mother more trouble throughout my years at home than Anne has given me because, through some psychic and/or biochemical aberration, I was a depressive, though neither she nor I knew so at the time. I recognized that my behavior was erratic and that she got very angry with me for it. What I didn't see, and maybe she didn't either, was that behind her anger lay the anxiety and frustration caused by her helplessness to protect me from my pain. When, finally, I cracked up sufficiently to be sent to a mental hospital, I sensed that she was blaming herself for my troubledness (and no wonder in the disastrous wake of Freud), and I felt impatient with her for believing such silliness. But she was only exhibiting that reflexive maternal guilt which emerges at the infant's first wail: "I'm sorry. I'm sorry. I'm sorry I pushed you from this warm womb into the arms of strangers, me among them. I'm sorry I can't keep you perfectly full, perfectly dry, perfectly free from gas and fear, perfectly, perfectly happy." Any mother knows that if she could do these things, her infant would die more surely than if she covered its face

with a rose-printed pillow. Still, part of her desire is to prevent the
replication of desire.

34      Because I knew I had so often infuriated and wearied her, when I
left for college I thought only of Mother's relief, never of the possibility that she might miss me. Why should she? The house was still
crammed without me, my sister Sally still there, and my stepfather and
the babies, and my grandmother too, not to mention an elderly Irish
setter and a marmalade cat. As soon as I'd gone, Mother bought a
dishwasher, and I figured that took care of any gap I'd left. Not until
Anne began the process of selecting a college, finding a summer job in
Wisconsin, packing away her mementoes, filling her suitcases did I
think that Mother's first-born daughter (and not just a pair of hands
in the dishpan) had once left her, and she must have grieved at the
separation too. I love to visit her now because I know at last that she
is delighted to have me there—not just glad of the company—but
warmed and entertained by *me*, one of the daughters who raised her.

35      I am aware, too, that she once raised a mother, Granna, who lived
with us for many years. And Granna raised a mother, Grandma
Virchow, with whom she and Mother lived for many years. And
Grandma must have raised a mother as well, left behind in Germany
in the 1890s, who must herself have raised a mother. "For we think
back through our mothers if we are women," writes Virginia Woolf
in *A Room of One's Own*. Anne has helped me in that backward
dreaming. When she tells me that she doesn't plan to have children,
I feel sad, but not because I won't have grandchildren. I mean, I'd
welcome them, but I have quite enough characters populating my
life to keep me entertained. Rather, I would like her to have this particular adventure, this becoming that a daughter forces.

36      Overall, I think Anne has done a pretty good job with me. Even
without encouragement, in a society that doesn't consider her task
authentic, she's done her share of leaning and hauling, shaping me
to her needs, forcing me to learn and practice a role I have often
found wearying and frightening. Maybe some women are mothers
by nature, needing only an infant in their arms to bloom. I'm not.
I've needed a lot of nurture. And still I hate it sometimes, especially
when she makes me into an authoritarian ogre rumbling disapproval
(just as I did to Mother, oh, how many times?). But she's firm and
often fair. She doesn't coddle me. Years ago, before I got my brace,
I used to have a lot of trouble putting on my left shoe and she would

help me with it; the right shoe she'd hand me, saying, "You can do this one yourself." But on my birthday she bakes me lemon bread and, when I ask her what I smell, tells me she's washing dishes in lemon-scented detergent. I believe her and so am surprised by my birthday party. She is tolerant when I stamp my feet (figuratively speaking—if I really stamped my feet I'd fall in a heap and then we'd both get the giggles) and refuse to let her take my peach-colored gauze shirt to Honduras. But she is severe about suicide attempts. She has no use for my short stories, in which she says nothing ever happens, but she likes my essays, especially the ones she appears in, and sometimes my poems. She admires my clothing (especially my peach-colored gauze shirt), my hair, my cooking, but not my taste in music or in men. When my black cat, Bête Noire, the beast of my heart, was killed, she let me weep, hunched over, my tears splashing on the linoleum, and she never said, "Don't cry."

37    Before long Anne will have to consider the job done. A daughter can't spend a lifetime raising her mother any more than a mother can spend a lifetime raising her daughter; they both have other work to get on with. I can remember the liberating moment when I recognized that it was no longer my task to educate my mother in the ways of the real world; she'd just have to make the best of what she'd learned and muddle along on her own. Mother muddles well. I like to think because I gave her a good start. Anne deserves such a moment.

38    And I deserve her having it. It's what we've come this way for. Last summer, when George was visiting his parents, his mother sighed, "Life is never so good after the children have gone." George is her only child, and he's been gone for twenty-five years. I can't imagine sustaining a quarter of a century of anticlimax. Anne and I both confront transformation into women with wholly new sets of adventures as we learn to live well apart. I feel pretty well prepared now for muddling along on my own.

# Discussion Questions

1. Describe Mairs's reactions to needing her daughter's help. Is she angry? Humiliated? Relieved? Pleased? Support your response.

2. What does Mairs think about the idea that motherhood is instinctive? Explain your reasons for agreeing or disagreeing with her.

3. Characterize Mairs from what she reveals in this essay.

4. Does Mairs's rejecting, in paragraphs 19–37, all of the reports on mother-daughter relationships increase or decrease her credibility? Explain.

5. Mairs intersperses her personal experiences with scholarly research on mother-daughter relationships, as well as with dictionary definitions and other sources. Discuss the effectiveness of this approach.

6. In small groups, discuss the following question: Who or what do you think this essay is principally about: Mairs? Anne? Their relationship? Someone or something else? Support your response.

## Writing Assignments

1. Imagine you are Mairs's daughter. From her perspective, write a response to the essay.

2. Is motherhood or fatherhood an instinctive or a learned behavior? Support your stance in an essay.

3. Role reversal has become more commonplace than ever because people are living longer. Research the topic of children caring for their parents and write a paper that examines this growing phenomenon.

# A Second
# Adoption

## MICHAEL
## DORRIS

Michael Dorris (1945–1997) earned his doctorate in anthropology from Yale University. He taught anthropology and Native American studies at Franconia College and Dartmouth College. A member of the Modoc tribe, Dorris was a novelist, a writer of short stories and children's books, and a essayist. He is the author of *Native Americans: Five Hundred Years After* (1975); *A Yellow Raft in Blue Water* (1987); *The Crown of Columbus* (1991) cowritten with his wife, Louise Erdrich; *Morning Girl* (1992); and *Working Men* (1993). Dorris is most noted for *The Broken Cord* (1987), an autobiographical account of his adopting a Native American baby when he was single and the ravages that fetal alcohol syndrome had on the baby. The book won the National Book Critics Circle Award and was made into a television movie. *Paper Trails* (1994) is a compilation of Dorris's essays, in which the following piece appears. His numerous essays on the experiences of and issues involving Native Americans have earned Dorris the reputation as one of the most important contemporary Native American writers. In the following essay, Dorris recounts his first moments with his second adopted son.

1    There is one feature of single parenthood that any man or woman solely responsible for a young child knows, no matter how the arrangement evolved: dating is next to impossible. By the time a baby-sitter is found, picked up, given instructions, checked upon by telephone, driven home, and paid, your partner for the evening had better have been True Love. If not, you wonder: was it worth it? Furthermore, you become a kind of package deal: like me, like my child. Or forget it.

2    In 1974, with a demanding job, a six-year-old adopted son with special needs, and no fiancée on the horizon, I realized the time had come to recontact my adoption agency. If I was going to spend the next twelve or thirteen years of my life unpartnered—a distinct possibility—I wanted to do so with a larger family.

3    Denis Daigle, Abel's caseworker, was not encouraging. There were so many couples waiting for placement, he said, that it was unlikely that any agency would approve a second child for a single male, especially since this time I requested an infant or toddler. He would submit the paperwork, but I should not count on anything, not get my hopes up.

4    Okay, I promised, and pasted yellow wallpaper with a small green-and-red teddy bear design in the spare bedroom of our house. I watched yard sales for cribs and bassinets, and found a used rocking horse in mint condition. I put my name on the waiting list for a child-care center and arranged for a lighter teaching load.

5    When Denis called, his voice incredulous, I was ready.

6    "You won't believe it," he said. "There's a little Lakota boy, just over a year old, who's available. They've approved your application."

7    "When does it happen?" I felt the stirrings of the male analog for labor.

8    "He's in South Dakota."

9    I did some geographic calculations. "I'm presenting a paper at a one-day conference in Omaha next Tuesday," I said.

10   "Could you be in Pierre on Wednesday?"

11   *Could* I? I had already chosen his name, Sava, after a Native Alaskan friend who had taken me on as a salmon fishing partner for two summers while I was doing anthropological fieldwork.

12   On Tuesday afternoon the Nebraska weather turned nasty, grounding all planes, so I rented a car, called the caseworker in

South Dakota to tell her the name of my motel in Pierre, and drove all night. I checked into my room exhausted, unbathed, and bleary-eyed at 9 A.M., but before I had a chance to unpack my suitcase there was a knock on the door. I opened it to a smiling young blond woman bundled in a green parka.

13 I'm Jeanine from SDDSS," she announced. "Are you all set to meet your son?"

14 "Can you wait a few minutes? I want to take a shower, change my clothes, maybe pick up a present for him somewhere."

15 An uneasy expression crossed her face.

16 "Not a good idea?" I asked.

17 "Well . . . *actually* he's waiting in my car right now." Jeanine glanced to her left and, following her look, I saw in the backseat a baby carrier and the top of a purple knitted cap. I didn't want to give the impression of the slightest hesitation, so I said, "Great! Bring him right in."

18 The instant she turned her back I dashed to the bathroom, splashed water on my face, and dabbed some aftershave on my neck. First impressions are important and at least I could smell good.

19 When I emerged, Jeanine was standing in the room holding a solid-looking baby whose dark, intelligent eyes regarded me with raw suspicion.

20 "He's very friendly," Jeanine assured me. "He's been so anxious to meet you."

21 I held out my arms, savoring the tender moment of first encounter. He was no lightweight. I cradled him in my arms and lowered my face close to his to get a good look. "Hello Sava," I whispered.

22 His eyes widened, then closed tightly. Simultaneously his jaws opened and opened and opened, revealing a space more like the Grand Canyon than a mouth. I felt him draw a long breath into his lungs, and when he released it in a howl, my mind pictured a car-toon image of pure sound, strong as a hurricane, blowing every-thing—furniture, hair, trees—in its wake.

23 Jeanine made a step toward us, but I shook my head and spoke more confidently than I felt.

24 "Give us an hour or so." I nodded encouragingly to underscore my words, and she reluctantly departed.

25    Sava's yells did not abate but he didn't struggle as I sat down on the bed, jiggled him on my lap. He was not in the slightest afraid but was simply registering a protest, a critique of my grinning face. I unsnapped his coat, removed it, spoke softly in what I hoped was a comforting tone, and after a few long minutes he opened one eye and gave me a second appraisal.

26    He was a beauty: feathery straight black hair, a sensuous mouth, a strong, broad nose, a clean, sweeping jaw. His torso was wide and his hands were square-shaped with thick, tapering fingers. He opened the other eye and, as abruptly as he had begun to cry, he stopped. We stared at each other, amazed in the sudden silence.

27    "Hello Sava," I tried again. This time, speculatively, he only blinked.

28    Late the next day we boarded a plane back to New Hampshire. By then, I knew Sava's favorite food—mashed green beans mixed with cream of mushroom soup and canned fried onions sprinkled on top—and that he hated to have his hair washed. I knew he was a sound sleeper, that he had a long attention span, and that he was ticklish—just below his rib cage on his right side. I knew that he and Abel were profoundly different in their personalities—Abel would leap headfirst into any strange lake, while Sava would always test the water—but I trusted that they would be compatible brothers. And I knew all over again, as if for the first time in human history, the experience of becoming a parent. Within twenty-four hours of meeting my son, I had already forgotten what it felt like not to be his father.

# Discussion Questions

1. What does Dorris cite as a problem that every single parent experiences? To what extent do you agree with his observation? Explain.

2. What compelled Dorris to adopt a second child? Explain why his reasons were justified.

3. Comment on the effectiveness of dialogue as the principal way in which Dorris advances his narrative.

4. From this essay, what do you know about Dorris's success as a father? What specifically leads you to your response?
5. In small groups, discuss whether Dorris would have reacted differently had his new son been biologically his.
6. Explain what Dorris means in the last paragraph when he muses, "And I knew all over again, as if for the first time in human history, the experience of becoming a parent. Within twenty-four hours of meeting my son, I had already forgotten what it felt like not to be his father."

# Writing Assignments

1. In an essay, discuss what the advantages and disadvantages are of being a single parent.
2. Is single parenthood easier for men or for women? Answer this question in a paper.
3. Do adopted babies pose any problems for parents that are different from those caused by their biological children? Examine this question in a paper.
4. Read current research on adoptions and find a recurrent issue or topic that interests you. In a paper based on your findings, discuss your position on the topic.

# "Foreword" from
# The Broken Cord

## LOUISE
## ERDRICH

Louise Erdrich (b. 1954) was born in Minnesota and earned her
B.A. from Dartmouth College and her M.A. from Johns Hopkins
University. The daughter of a Chippewa Indian mother and a
German-American father, Erdrich has worked as a beet weeder, wait-
ress, psychiatric aide, lifeguard, construction flag signaler, textbook
writer, and visiting poet and teacher for the North Dakota State Arts
Council. A full-time writer, Erdrich is the author of the novels *Love
Medicine* (1984) and an expanded version in 1993; *The Beet Queen*
(1986); *Tracks* (1988); *The Crown of Columbus* (1991) cowritten
with her spouse, Michael Dorris; and *Bingo Palace* (1994). Her
poetry collections are *Jacklight* (1984) and *Baptism of Desire* (1989).
*The Bluejay's Dance* (1995) is her memoir of childbirth. Erdrich's
poems, stories, and essays have appeared in such publications as *The
New Yorker, American Indian Quarterly, Atlantic, Kenyon Review,
North American Review, The New York Times Book Review, Ms.,* and
*New England Review.* Erdrich's honors include the National Book
Critics Circle Award for best work in fiction, the Virginia
McCormick Scully Prize for best book of the year in 1984, a
Guggenheim fellowship in 1985–86, and an O. Henry Award in
1987. In the following selection, which appears as the foreword to
Dorris's *The Broken Cord* (1987), Erdrich reflects on her experiences
as a stepmother to the child Michael Dorris adopted.

1      The snow fell deep today. February 4, 1988, two days before
Michael and I are to leave for our first trip abroad together, ten days
before Saint Valentine's holiday, which we will spend in Paris, fifteen
days after Adam's twentieth birthday. This is no special day, it marks
no breakthrough in Adam's life or in mine, it is a day held in sus-
pension by the depth of snow, the silence, school closing, our seclu-
sion in the country along a steep gravel road which no cars will dare
use until the town plow goes through.

2      It is just a day when Adam had a seizure. His grandmother called
and said that she could see, from out the window, Adam lying in the
snow, having a seizure. He had fallen while shoveling the mailbox
clear. Michael was at the door too, but I got out first because I had
on sneakers. Jumping into the snow I felt a moment of obscure gratitude to Michael for letting me go to Adam's rescue. Though unacknowledged between us, these are the times when it is easy to be a
parent to Adam. His seizures are increasingly grand mal now. And
yet, unless he hurts himself in the fall there is nothing to do but be
a comforting presence, make sure he's turned on his side, breathing.
I ran to Adam and I held him, spoke his name, told him I was there,
used my most soothing tone. When he came back to consciousness
I rose, propped him against me, and we stood to shake out his
sleeves and the neck of his jacket.

3      A lone snowmobiler passed, then circled to make sure we were all
right. I suppose we made a picture that could cause mild concern.
We stood, propped together, hugging and breathing hard. Adam is
taller than me, and usually much stronger. I held him around the
waist with both arms and looked past his shoulder. The snow was
still coming, drifting through the deep-branched pines. All around
us there was such purity, a wet and electric silence. The air was warm
and the snow already melting in my shoes.

4      It is easy to give the absolute, dramatic love that a definite physical problem requires, easy to stagger back, slipping, to take off
Adam's boots and make sure he gets the right amount of medicine
into his system.

5      It is easy to be the occasional, ministering angel. But it is not easy
to live day in and day out with a child disabled by Fetal Alcohol
Syndrome or Fetal Alcohol Effect. This set of preventable birth
defects is manifested in a variety of ways, but caused solely by alcohol in an unborn baby's developing body and brain. The U.S.

Surgeon General's report for 1988 warned about the hazards of drinking while pregnant, and many doctors now say that since no level of alcohol has been established as safe for the fetus, the best policy to follow for nine months, longer if a mother nurses, is complete abstinence. As you will read, every woman reacts differently to alcohol, depending on age, diet, and metabolism. However, drinking at the wrong time of development can cause facial and bodily abnormalities, as well as lower intelligence, and may also impair certain types of judgment, or alter behavior. Adam suffers all the symptoms that I've mentioned, to some degree. It's a lot of fate to play with for the sake of a moment's relaxation.

6     I never intended to be the mother of a child with problems. Who does? But when, after a year of marriage to their father I legally adopted Adam, Sava, and Madeline—the three children *he* had adopted, years before, as a single parent—it simply happened. I've got less than the ordinary amount of patience, and for that reason I save all my admiration for those like Ken Kramberg, Adam's teacher, and others like Faith and Bob Annis, who work day in and day out with disability. I save it for my husband, Michael, who spent months of his life teaching Adam to tie his shoes. Living with Adam touches on my occupation only in the most peripheral ways; this is the first time I've ever written about him. I've never disguised him as a fictional character or consciously drawn on our experience together. It is, in fact, painful for a writer of fiction to write about actual events in one's personal life.

7     I have seen Michael, an anthropologist and novelist, struggle with this manuscript for six years. The work was a journey from the world of professional objectivity to a confusing realm where boundaries could no longer be so easily drawn. It has been wrenching for Michael to relive this story, but in the end, I think he felt compelled to do so after realizing the scope of the problem, after receiving so many desperate and generous stories from other people, and, in the end, out of that most frail of human motives—hope. If one story of FAS could be made accessible and real, it might just stop someone, somewhere, from producing another alcohol-stunted child.

8     Adam does not read with great ease, but he has pressed himself to read this story. He has reacted to it with fascination, and he has agreed to its publication. Although he has no concern about us as professionals, neither pride nor the slightest trace of resentment,

Adam takes pleasure when, as a family, our pictures have occasionally appeared in the paper. He sees Michael and me primarily in the roles to which we've assigned ourselves around the house. Michael is the laundryman, I am the cook. And beyond that, most important, we are the people who respond to him. In that way, though an adult, he is at the stage of a very young child who sees the world only as an extension of his or her will. Adam is the world, at least his version of it, and he knows us only as who we are when we enter his purview.

9 Because of this, there are ways Adam knows us better than we know ourselves, though it would be difficult for him to describe this knowledge. He knows our limits, and I, at least, hide my limits from myself, especially when I go beyond them, especially when it comes to anger. Sometimes it seems to me that from the beginning, in living with Adam, anger has been inextricable from love, and I've been as helpless before the one as before the other.

10 We were married, Michael, his three children, and I, on a slightly overcast October day, in 1981. Adam was thirteen, and because he had not yet gone through puberty, he was small, about the size of a ten-year-old. He was not, and is not, a charming person, but he is generous, invariably kind-hearted, and therefore lovable. He had then, and still possesses, the gift—which is also a curse, given the realities of the world—of absolute, serene trust. He took our ceremony, in which we exchanged vows, literally. At the end of it we were pronounced husband, wife, and family by the same friend, a local judge, who would later formally petition for me to become the adoptive mother of Adam, Sava, and Madeline; then still later, as we painfully came to terms with certain truths, he helped us set up a lifelong provision for Adam in our wills. As Judge Daschbach pronounced the magic words, Adam turned to me with delight and said, "Mom!" not Louise. Now it was official. I melted. That trust was not to change a whit, until I changed it.

11 Ten months pass. We're at the dinner table. I've eaten, so have our other children. It's a good dinner, one of their favorites. Michael's gone. Adam eats a bite then puts down his fork and sits before his plate. When I ask him to finish, he says, "But, Mom, I don't like this food."

12 "Yes, you do," I tell him. I'm used to a test or two from Adam when Michael is away, and these challenges are wearying, sometimes

even maddening. But Adam has to know that I have the same rules as his father. He has to know, over and over and over. And Adam *does* like the food. I made it because he gobbled it down the week before and said he liked it, and I was happy.

13   "You have to eat or else you'll have a seizure in the morning," I tell him. This has proved to be true time and again. I am reasonable, firm, even patient at first, although I've said the same thing many times before. This is normal, Adam's way, just a test. I tell him again to finish.

14   "I don't like this food," he says again.

15   "Adam," I say, "you have to eat or you'll have a seizure."

16   He stares at me. Nothing.

17   Our younger children take their empty dishes to the sink. I wash them. Adam sits. Sava and Madeline go upstairs to play, and Adam sits. I check his forehead, think perhaps he's ill, but he is cool, and rather pleased with himself. He has now turned fourteen years old. But he still doesn't understand that, in addition to his medication, he must absorb so many calories every day or else he'll suffer an attack. The electricity in his brain will lash out, the impulses scattered and random.

18   "Eat up. I'm not kidding."

19   "I did," he says, the plate still full before him.

20   I simply point.

21   "I don't like this food," he says to me again.

22   I walk back to the cupboard. I slap a peanut butter sandwich together. He likes those. Maybe a concession on my part will satisfy him, maybe he'll eat, but when I put it on his plate he just looks at it.

23   I go into the next room. It is eight o'clock and I am in the middle of a book by Bruce Chatwin. There is more to life . . . but I'm responsible. I have to make him see that he's not just driving me crazy.

24   "Eat the sandwich . . ."

25   "I did." The sandwich is untouched.

26   "Eat the dinner . . ."

27   "I don't like this food."

28   "Okay then. Eat half."

29   He won't. He sits there. In his eyes there is an expression of stubborn triumph that boils me with the suddenness of frustration, dammed and suppressed, surfacing all at once.

30    "EAT!" I yell at him.

31    Histrionics, stamping feet, loud voices, usually impress him with
the serious nature of our feelings much more than the use of reason.
But not this time. There is no ordering, begging, or pleading that
will make him eat, even for his own good. And he is thin, so thin.
His face is gaunt, his ribs arch out of his sternum, his knees are big,
bony, and his calves and thighs straight as sticks. I don't want him to
fall, to seize, to hurt himself.

32    "Please . . . for me. Just do it."

33    He looks at me calmly.

34    "Just for me, okay?"

35    "I don't like this food."

36    The lid blows off. Nothing is left. If I can't help him to survive in
the simplest way, how can I be his mother?

37    "Don't eat then. And don't call me Mom!"

38    Then I walk away, shaken. I leave him sitting and he does not eat,
and the next morning he does have a seizure. He falls next to the
aquarium, manages to grasp the table, and as his head bobs and his
mouth twists, I hold him, wait it out. It's still two days before
Michael will arrive home and I don't believe that I can handle it and
I don't know how Michael has, but that is only a momentary surge
of panic. Adam finally rights himself. He changes his pants. He goes
on with his day. He does not connect the seizure with the lack of
food: he won't. But he does connect my words, I begin to notice. He
does remember. From that night on he starts calling me Louise, and
I don't care. I'm glad of it at first, and think it will blow over when
we forgive and grow close again. After all, he forgets most things.

39    But of all that I've told Adam, all the words of love, all the
encouragements, the orders that I gave, assurances, explanations,
and instructions, the only one he remembers with perfect, fixed,
comprehension, even when I try to contradict it, even after months,
is "Don't call me Mom."

40    Adam calls me "Mother" or "Mom" now, but it took years of
patience, of backsliding, and of self-control, it took Adam's father
explaining and me explaining and rewarding with hugs when he
made me feel good, to get back to mother and son again. It took a
long trip out west, just the two of us. It took a summer of side-by-
side work. We planted thirty-five trees and one whole garden and a

flower bed. We thinned the strawberries, pruned the lilacs and for-
sythia. We played tic-tac-toe, then Sorry. We lived together. And I
gave up making him eat, or distanced myself enough to put the
medicine in his hand and walk away, and realize I can't protect him.

41   That's why I say it takes a certain fiber I don't truly possess to live
and work with a person obstinate to the core, yet a victim. Constant,
nagging insults to good sense eventually wear on the steel of the
soul. Logic that flies in the face of logic can madden one. In the
years I've spent with Adam, I have learned more about my limits
than I ever wanted to know. And yet, in spite of the ridiculous argu-
ments, the life-and-death battles over medication and the puny and
wearying orders one must give every day, in spite of pulling gloves
onto the chapped, frost-bitten hands of a nearly grown man and
knowing he will shed them, once out of sight, in the minus-thirty
windchill of January, something mysterious has flourished between
us, a bond of absolute simplicity, love. That is, unquestionably, the
alpha and omega of our relationship, even now that Adam has graduated to a somewhat more independent life.

42   But as I said, that love is inextricable from anger, and in loving
Adam, the anger is mostly directed elsewhere, for it is impossible to
love the sweetness, the inner light, the qualities that I trust in Adam,
without hating the fact that he will always be kept from fully
expressing those aspects of himself because of his biological
mother's drinking. He is a Fetal Alcohol Effect victim. He'll always,
all his life, be a lonely person.

43   I drank hard in my twenties, and eventually got hepatitis. I was
lucky. Beyond an occasional glass of wine, I can't tolerate liquor anymore. But from those early days, I understand the urge for alcohol,
its physical pull. I had formed an emotional bond with a special con-
figuration of chemicals, and I realize to this day the attraction of the
relationship and the immense difficulty in abandoning it.

44   Adam's mother never did let go. She died of alcohol poisoning,
and I'd feel sorrier for her, if we didn't have Adam. As it is, I only
hope that she died before she had a chance to produce another child
with his problems. I can't help but wish, too, that during her pregnancy, if she couldn't be counseled or helped, she had been forced
to abstain for those crucial nine months. On some American Indian
reservations, due to Reagan-era slashing of alcohol and drug treatment and prenatal care programs, the situation has grown so des-

perate that a jail internment during pregnancy has been the only answer possible in some cases. Some people, whose views you will read in these pages, have taken more drastic stands and even called for the forced sterilization of women who, after having previously blunted the lives of several children like Adam, refuse to stop drinking while they're pregnant. This will outrage some women, and men, good people who believe that it is the right of individuals to put themselves in harm's way, that drinking is a choice we make, that a person's liberty to court either happiness or despair is sacrosanct. I believed this, too, and yet the poignancy and frustration of Adam's life has fed my doubts, has convinced me that some of my principles were smug, untested. After all, where is the measure of responsibility here? Where, exactly, is the demarcation between self-harm and child abuse? Gross negligence is nearly equal to intentional wrong, goes a legal maxim. Where do we draw the line?

45     The people who advocate forcing pregnant women to abstain from drinking come from within the communities dealing with a problem of nightmarish proportions. Everyone agrees that the best answer is not to lock up pregnant women, but to treat them. However, this problem is now generations in the making. Women who themselves suffer from Fetal Alcohol Syndrome or Effect are extremely difficult to counsel because one of the most damaging aspects of FAS is the inability to make cause–effect connections, or to "think ahead." In addition, many alcohol and drug treatment programs are closed to pregnant women and, therefore, also to unborn children—the most crucial patients of all. It is obvious that the much-ballyhooed war on drugs is not being won with guns, but requires the concerted efforts of a compassionate society. Alcohol rehabilitation programs should be as easy to get into as liquor stores, and they should be free, paid for by the revenues from state liquor stores in some areas, and liquor taxes in others.

46     Since we the people are the government, we are all in some way to blame for allowing a problem of this magnitude to occur. Still, it is to devalue the worth of the individual not to hold one person, in some measure, responsible for his or her behavior. Once a woman decides to carry a child to term, to produce another human being, has she also the right to inflict on that person Adam's life? And isn't it also a father's responsibility to support and try to ensure an alcohol-free pregnancy? Because his mother drank, Adam is one of the

earth's damaged. Did his mother have the right to take away Adam's curiosity, the right to take away the joy he could have felt at receiving a high math score, in reading a book, in wondering at the complexity and quirks of nature? Did she and his absent father have the right to make him an outcast among children, to make him friendless, to make of his sexuality a problem more than a pleasure, to slit his brain, to give him violent seizures?

47   It seems to me, in the end, that no one has the right to inflict such harm, even from the depth of ignorance. Roman Catholicism defines two kinds of ignorance, vincible and invincible. Invincible ignorance is that state in which a person is unexposed to certain forms of knowledge. The other type of ignorance, vincible, is willed. It is a conscious turning away from truth. In either case, I don't think Adam's mother had the right to harm her, and our, son.

48   Knowing what I know now, I am sure that even when I drank hard, I would rather have been incarcerated for nine months and produce a normal child than bear a human being who would, for the rest of his or her life, be imprisoned by what I had done. I would certainly go to jail for nine months now if it would make Adam whole. For those still outraged at this position, those so sure, so secure in opposition, I say the same thing I say to those who would not allow a poor woman a safe abortion and yet have not themselves gone to adoption agencies and taken in the unplaceable children, the troubled, the unwanted:

49   If you don't agree with me, then please, go and sit beside the alcohol-affected while they try to learn how to add. My mother, Rita Erdrich, who works with disabled children at the Wahpeton Indian School, does this every day. Dry their frustrated tears. Fight for them in the society they don't understand. Tell them every simple thing they must know for survival, one million, two million, three million times. Hold their heads when they have unnecessary seizures and wipe the blood from their bitten lips. Force them to take medicine. Keep the damaged of the earth safe. Love them. Watch them grow up to sink into the easy mud of alcoholism. Suffer a crime they won't understand committing. Try to understand lack of remorse. As taxpayers, you are already paying for their jail terms, and footing the bills for expensive treatment and education. Be a victim yourself, beat your head against a world of brick, fail constantly. Then go back to the mother, face to face, and say again: "*It was your right.*"

50     When I am angriest, I mentally tear into Adam's mother because, in the end, it was her hand that tilted the bottle. When I am saddest, I wish her, exhaustedly . . . but there is nowhere to wish her worse than the probable hell of her life and death. If I ever met her, I don't know what I'd do. Perhaps we'd both be resigned before this enormous lesson. It is almost impossible to hold another person responsible for so much hurt. Even though I know our son was half-starved, tied to the bars of his crib, removed by a welfare agency, I still think it must have been "society's fault." In public, when asked to comment on Native American issues, I am defensive. Yes, I say, there are terrible problems. It takes a long, long time to heal communities beaten by waves of conquest and disease. It takes a long time for people to heal themselves. Sometimes, it seems hopeless. Yet in places, it is happening. Tribal communities, most notably the Alkali Lake Band in Canada, are coming together, rejecting alcohol, reembracing their own humanity, their own culture. These are tough people and they teach a valuable lesson: to whatever extent we can, we must take charge of our lives.

51     Yet, in loving Adam, we bow to fate. Few of his problems can be solved or ultimately changed. So instead, Michael and I concentrate on only what we can control—our own reactions. If we can muster grace, joy, happiness in helping him confront and conquer the difficulties life presents . . . then we have received gifts. Adam has been deprived of giving so much else.

52     What I know my husband hopes for, in offering *The Broken Cord*, is a future in which this particular and preventable tragedy will not exist. I feel the same way. I would rather that FAS and FAE were eradicated through enlightenment, through education and a new commitment to treatment. That is the hope in which this book was written. But if that isn't possible, I would eliminate them any way I could.

53     Michael and I have a picture of our son. For some reason, in this photograph, taken on my grandfather's land in the Turtle Mountains of North Dakota, no defect is evident in Adam's stance or face. Although perhaps a knowing doctor could make the fetal alcohol diagnosis from his features, Adam's expression is intelligent and serene. He is smiling, his eyes are brilliant, and his brows are dark, sleek. There is no sign in this portrait that anything is lacking.

54     I look at this picture and think, "Here is the other Adam. The one our son would be if not for alcohol." Sometimes Michael and I

imagine that we greet him, that we look into his eyes, and he into ours, for a long time and in that gaze we not only understand our son, but he also understands us. He has grown up to be a colleague, a peer, not a person who needs pity, protection, or special breaks. By the old reservation cabin where my mother was born, in front of the swirled wheat fields and woods of ancestral land, Adam stands expectantly, the full-hearted man he was meant to be. The world opens before him—so many doors, so much light. In this picture, he is ready to go forward with his life.

## Discussion Questions

1. What do you make of Erdrich's citing an exact date, putting the date in the context of three family events, and then calling it "no special day"?
2. What is Erdrich's attitude toward Adam? Cite specific passages that lead you to your answer.
3. What is the tone of Erdrich's essay? Would the essay have imparted a different message had she used a different tone? Explain.
4. Characterize Erdrich as a mother, citing specific examples.
5. Explain what Erdrich means when she states that "love is inextricable from anger . . ." (paragraph 42).
6. What does Erdrich mean when she states, "Adam's mother never did let go" (paragraph 44)?
7. In small groups, discuss whether you find Erdrich's attitude toward Adam's birth mother appropriate.
8. Explain what Erdrich is intimating in the last paragraph.
9. Whom do you think Erdrich saw as her audience? Explain.

## Writing Assignments

1. Write a journal entry that explores the specific problems stepchildren are confronted with.

2. Interview some stepmothers and, in a paper, report on the particular problems they face in rearing their stepchildren.
3. What qualities should parents of disabled children possess? Write an essay that describes such an ideal parent.
4. Read current research on Fetal Alcohol Effect and, in a paper, report on the devastating effects that drinking has on infants. Explain why the measures to abolish the disease have been ineffective.

# CLASSIC ESSAYS ON

# *Grandparents and Ancestors*

# from *Years of My Youth*

## WILLIAM DEAN HOWELLS

William Dean Howells (1837–1920) was born in Martin's Ferry, Ohio, the son of a country printer and newspaper publisher. At age nine, Howells was setting type in his father's shop. Though Howells lacked a formal education, he was an insatiable reader. At the age of nineteen, he became a writer for newspapers in Cincinnati and Columbus before becoming the editor of the *Ohio State Journal*. At the age of twenty-nine, he became the assistant editor of the *Atlantic Monthly*, after which he spent four years abroad to travel and study. Howells's most famous book is *The Rise of Silas Lapham* (1885). He is also the author of *A Boy's Life* (1890), *My Year in a Log Cabin* (1893), *My Literary Passions* (1895), and *Literary Friends and Acquaintances* (1900). His travel books include *Venetian Life* (1866) and *Italian Journeys* (1867). After 1886, Howells began writing "The Editor's Study" column for *Harper's* magazine, and after 1890, he became the familiar essayist of "The Easy Chair" column. He wrote novels, too, including *Indian Summer* (1886), *A Hazard of New Fortunes* (1890), and *A Traveler from Altrurtia* (1894). Howells's writing is noted for its clearly and evocatively drawn characters. In the following selection, from his autobiography *Years of My Youth* (1916), Howells offers a profile of his ancestors.

1    It is hard to know the child's own earliest recollections from the things it has been told of itself by those with whom its life began. They remember for it the past which it afterward seems to remember for itself; the wavering outline of its nature is shadowed against the background of family, and from this it imagines an individual existence which has not yet begun. The events then have the quality of things dreamt, not lived, and they remain of that impalpable and elusive quality in all the after years.

# I

2    Of the facts which I must believe from the witness of others, is the fact that I was born on the 1st of March, 1837, at Martin's Ferry, Belmont County, Ohio. My father's name was William Cooper Howells, and my mother's was Mary Dean; they were married six years before my birth, and I was the second child in their family of eight. On my father's side my people were wholly Welsh, except his English grandmother, and on my mother's side wholly German, except her Irish father, of whom it is mainly known that he knew how to win my grandmother Elizabeth Dock away from her very loving family, where they dwelt in great Pennsylvania-German comfort and prosperity on their farm near Harrisburg, to share with him the hardships of the wild country over the westward mountains. She was the favorite of her brothers and sisters, and the best-beloved of her mother, perhaps because she was the youngest; there is a shadowy legend that she went one evening to milk the cows, and did not return from following after her husband; but I cannot associate this romantic story with the aging grandmother whom I tenderly loved when a child, and whom I still fondly remember. She spoke with a strong German accent, and she had her Luther Bible, for she never read English. Sometimes she came to visit my homesick mother after we went to live in southern Ohio; once I went with my mother to visit her in the little town where I was born, and of that visit I have the remembrance of her stopping me on the stairs, one morning when I had been out, and asking me in her German idiom and accent, "What fur a tay is it, child?"

3    I can reasonably suppose that it is because of the mixture of Welsh, German, and Irish in me that I feel myself so typically

American, and that I am of the imaginative temperament which has enabled me all the conscious years of my life to see reality more iridescent and beautiful, or more lurid and terrible than any make-believe about reality. Among my father's people the first who left Wales was his great-grandfather. He established himself in London as a clock and watch maker, and I like to believe that it is his name which my tall clock, paneled in the lovely *chinoiserie* of Queen Anne's time, bears graven on its dial. Two sons followed him, and wrought at the same art, then almost a fine art, and one of them married in London and took his English wife back with him to Wales. His people were, so far as my actual knowledge goes, middle-class Welsh, but the family is of such a remote antiquity as in its present dotage not to know what part of Wales it came from. As to our lineage a Welsh clergyman, a few years ago, noting the identity of name, invited me to the fond conjecture of descent from Hywel Dda, or Howel the Good, who became king of Wales about the time of Alfred the Great. He codified the laws or rather the customs of his realm, and produced one of the most interesting books I have read, and I have finally preferred him as an ancestor because he was the first literary man of our name. There was a time when I leaned toward the delightful James Howell, who wrote the *Familiar Letters* and many books in verse and prose, and was of several shades of politics in the difficult days of Charles and Oliver; but I was forced to relinquish him because he was never married. My father, for his part, when once questioned as to our origin, answered that so far as he could make out we derived from a blacksmith, whom he considered a good sort of ancestor, but he could not name him, and he must have been, whatever his merit, a person of extreme obscurity.

4    There is no record of the time when my great-grandfather with his brothers went to London and fixed there as watchmakers. My tall clock, which bears our name on its dial, has no date, and I can only imagine their London epoch to have begun about the middle of the eighteenth century. Being Welsh, they were no doubt musical, and I like to cherish the tradition of singing and playing women in our line, and a somehow cousinship with the famous Parepa. But this is very uncertain; what is certain is that when my great-grandfather went back to Wales he fixed himself in the little town of Hay, where he began the manufacture of Welsh flannels, a fabric still esteemed for its many virtues, and greatly prospered. When I visited

Hay in 1883 (my father always called it, after the old fashion, The Hay, which was the right version of its Norman name of La Haye), three of his mills were yet standing, and one of them was working, very modestly, on the sloping bank of the lovely river Wye. Another had sunk to be a stable, but the third, in the spirit of our New World lives, had become a bookstore and printing-office, a well-preserved stone edifice of four or five stories, such as there was not the like of, probably, in the whole of Wales when Hywel Dda was king. My great-grandfather was apparently an excellent business man, but I am afraid I must own (reluctantly, with my Celtic prejudice) that literature, or the love of it, came into our family with the English girl whom he married in London. She was, at least, a reader of the fiction of the day, if I may judge from the high-colored style of the now pathetically faded letter which she wrote to reproach a daughter who had made a runaway match and fled to America. So many people then used to make runaway matches; but when very late in the lives of these eloping lovers I once saw them, an old man and woman, at our house in Columbus, they hardly looked their youthful adventure, even to the fancy of a boy beginning to unrealize life. The reader may care to learn that they were the ancestors of Vaughan Kester, the very gifted young novelist, who came into popular recognition almost in the hour of his most untimely death, and of his brother Paul Kester, the playwright.

## II

My great-grandfather became "a Friend by Convincement," as the Quakers called the Friends not born in their Society; but I do not know whether it was before or after his convincement that he sailed to Philadelphia with a stock of his Welsh flannels, which he sold to such advantage that a dramatic family tradition represents him wheeling the proceeds in a barrel of silver down the street to the vessel which brought him and which took him away. That was in the time of Washington's second Presidency, and Washington strongly advised his staying in the country and setting up his manufacture here; but he was prospering in Wales, and why should he come to America even at the suggestion of Washington? It is another family tradition that he complied so far as to purchase a vast acreage of land on the Potomac, including the site of our present capital, as some of his descendants in each generation have believed, without the means of expropriating the nation from its unlawful holdings. This would have been the more difficult as he never took a deed of his land, and he certainly never came back to America; yet he seems always to have been haunted by the allurement of it which my grandfather felt so potently that after twice visiting the country he came over a third time and cast his lot here.

6    He was already married, when with his young wife and my father a year old he sailed from London in 1808. Perhaps because they were chased by a French privateer, they speedily arrived in Boston after a voyage of only twenty-one days. In the memoir which my father wrote for his family, and which was published after his death, he tells that my grandmother formed the highest opinion of Boston, mainly, he surmises, from the very intelligent behavior of the young ladies in making a pet of her baby at the boarding-house where she stayed while her husband began going about wherever people wished his skill in setting up woolen-mills. The young ladies taught her little one to walk; and many years afterward, say fifty, when I saw her for the last time in a village of northwestern Ohio, she said "the Bostonians were very nice people," so faithfully had she cherished, through a thousand vicissitudes, the kind memory of that first sojourn in America.

7    I do not think she quite realized the pitch of greatness at which I had arrived in writing for the *Atlantic Monthly*, the renowned periodical then recently founded in Boston, or the fame of the poets whom I had met there the year before. I suspect that she was never of the literary taste of my English great-grandmother; but her father had been a school-teacher, and she had been carefully educated by the uncle and aunt to whom she was left at her parents' early death. They were Friends, but she never formally joined the Society, though worshipping with them; she was, like her husband, middle-class Welsh, and as long as they lived they both misplaced their aspirates. If I add that her maiden name was Thomas, and that her father's name was John Thomas, I think I have sufficiently attested her pure Cymric origin. So far as I know there was no mixture of Saxon blood on her side; but her people, like most of the border Welsh, spoke the languages of both races; and very late in my father's life, he mentioned casually, as old people will mention inter-

esting things, that he remembered his father and mother speaking Welsh together. Of the two she remained the fonder of their native country, and in that last visit I paid her she said, after half a century of exile, "We do so and so at home, and you do so and so here." I can see her now, the gentlest of little Quaker ladies, with her white fichu crossed on her breast; and I hesitate attributing to her my immemorial knowledge that the Welsh were never conquered, but were tricked into union with the English by having one of their princes born, as it were surreptitiously, in Wales; it must have been my father who told me this and amused himself with my childish race-pride in the fact. She gave me an illustrated *Tours of Wales*, having among its steel-engravings the picture of a Norman castle where, by favor of a cousin who was the housekeeper, she had slept one night when a girl; but in America she had slept oftener in log-cabins, which my grandfather satisfied his devoted unworldliness in making his earthly tabernacles. She herself was not, I think, a devout person; she had her spiritual life in his, and followed his varying fortunes, from richer to poorer, with a tacit adherence to what he believed, whether the mild doctrine of Quakerism or the fervid Methodism for which he never quite relinquished it.

8    He seems to have come to America with money enough to lose a good deal in his removals from Boston to Poughkeepsie, from Poughkeepsie to New York City, from New York to Virginia, and from Virginia to eastern Ohio, where he ended in such adversity on his farm that he was glad to accept the charge of a woolen-mill in Steubenville. He knew the business thoroughly and he had set up mills for others in his various sojourns, following the line of least resistance among the Quaker settlements opened to him by the letters he had brought from Wales. He even went to the new capital, Washington, in a hope of manufacturing in Virginia held out to him by a nephew of President Madison, but it failed him to his heavy cost; and in Ohio, his farming experiments, which he renewed in a few years on giving up that mill at Steubenville, were alike disastrous. After more than enough of them he rested for a while in Wheeling, West Virginia, where my father met my mother, and they were married.

9    They then continued the family wanderings in his own search for the chance of earning a living in what seems to have been a very

grudging country, even to industry so willing as his. He had now become a printer, and not that only, but a publisher, for he had already begun and ended the issue of a monthly magazine called *The Gleaner*, made up, as its name implied, chiefly of selections; his sister helped him as editor, and some old bound volumes of its few numbers show their joint work to have been done with good taste in the preferences of their day. He married upon the expectation of affluence from the publication of a work on *The Rise, Progress and Downfall of Aristocracy*, which almost immediately preceded the ruin of the enthusiastic author and of my father with him, if he indeed could have experienced further loss in his entire want of money. He did not lose heart, and he was presently living contentedly on three hundred dollars a year as foreman of a newspaper office in St. Clairville, Ohio. But his health gave way, and a little later, for the sake of the outdoor employment, he took up the trade of house-painter; and he was working at this in Wheeling when my grandfather Dean suggested his buying a lot and building a house in Martin's Ferry, just across the Ohio River. The lot must have been bought on credit, and he built mainly with his own capable hands a small brick house of one story and two rooms with a lean-to. In this house I was born, and my father and mother were very happy there; they never owned another house until their children helped them work and pay for it a quarter of a century afterward, though throughout this long time they made us a home inexpressibly dear to me still.

10　　My father now began to read medicine, but during the course of a winter's lectures at Cincinnati (where he worked as a printer meanwhile), his health again gave way and he returned to Martin's Ferry. When I was three years old, my grandmother Dean's eldest brother, William Dock, came to visit her. He was the beloved patriarch of a family which I am glad to claim my kindred and was a best type of his Pennsylvania-German race. He had prospered on through a life of kindness and good deeds; he was so rich that he had driven in his own carriage from Harrisburg, over the mountains, and he now asked my father to drive with him across the state of Ohio. When they arrived in Dayton, my father went on by canal to Hamilton, where he found friends to help him buy the Whig newspaper which he had only just paid for when he sold it eight years later.

# III

11  Of the first three years of my life which preceded this removal there is very little that I can honestly claim to remember. The things that I seem to remember are seeing from the window of our little house, when I woke one morning, a peach-tree in bloom; and again seeing from the steamboat which was carrying our family to Cincinnati, a man drowning in the river. But these visions, both of them very distinct, might very well have been the effect of hearing the things spoken of by my elders, though I am surest of the peach-tree in bloom as an authentic memory.

12  This time, so happy for my father and mother, was scarcely less happy because of its uncertainties. My young aunts lived with their now widowed mother not far from us; as the latest comer, I was in much request among them, of course; and my father was hardly less in favor with the whole family from his acceptable habit of finding a joke in everything. He supplied the place of son to my grandmother in the absence of my young uncles, then away most of their time on the river which they followed from the humblest beginnings on keel-boats to the proudest endings as pilots and captains and owners of steamboats. In those early days when they returned from the river they brought their earnings to their mother in gold coins, which they called Yellow Boys, and which she kept in a bowl in the cupboard, where I seem so vividly to have seen them, that I cannot quite believe I did not. These good sons were all Democrats except the youngest, but they finally became of my father's antislavery Whig faith in politics, and I believe they were as glad to have their home in a free state as my father's family, who had now left Wheeling, and were settled in southwestern Ohio.

13  There were not many slaves in Wheeling, but it was a sort of entrepôt where the negroes were collected and embarked for the plantations down the river, in their doom to the death-in-life of the far South. My grandfather Howells had, in the antislavery tradition of his motherland, made himself so little desired among his Virginian fellow-citizens that I have heard his removal from Wheeling was distinctly favored by public sentiment; and afterward, on the farm he bought in Ohio, his fences and corn-cribs suffered

from the proslavery convictions of his neighbors. But he was dwelling in safety and prosperity among the drugs and books which were his merchandise in the store where I began to remember him in my earliest days at Hamilton. He seemed to me a very old man, and I noticed with the keen observance of a child how the muscles sagged at the sides of his chin and how his under lip, which I did not know I had inherited from him, projected. His clothes, which had long ceased to be drab in color, were of a Quaker formality in cut; his black hat followed this world's fashion in color, but was broad in the brim and very low-crowned, which added somehow in my young sense to the reproving sadness of his presence. He had black Welsh eyes and was of the low stature of his race; my grandmother was blue-eyed; she was little, too; but my aunt, their only surviving daughter, with his black eyes, was among their taller children. She was born several years after their settlement in America, but she loyally misused her aspirates as they did, and, never marrying, was of a life-long devotion to them. They first lived over the drug-store, after the fashion of shopkeepers in England; I am aware of my grandfather soon afterward having a pretty house and a large garden quite away from the store, but he always lived more simply than his means obliged. Amidst the rude experiences of their backwoods years, the family had continued gentle in their thoughts and tastes, though my grandfather shared with poetry his passion for religion, and in my later boyhood when I had begun to print my verses, he wrote me a letter solemnly praising them, but adjuring me to devote my gifts to the service of my Maker, which I had so little notion of doing in a selfish ideal of my own glory.

14 Most of his father's fortune had somehow gone to other sons, but, whether rich or poor, their generation seemed to be of a like religiosity. One of them lived in worldly state at Bristol before coming to America, and was probably of a piety not so insupportable as I found him in the memoir which he wrote of his second wife, when I came to read it the other day. Him I never saw, but from time to time there was one or other of his many sons employed in my grandfather's store, whom I remember blithe spirits, disposed to seize whatever chance of a joke life offered them, such as selling Young's *Night Thoughts* to a customer who had whispered his wish for an improper book. Some of my father's younger brothers were of a like

cheerfulness with these lively cousins, and of the same aptness for laughter. One was a physician, another a dentist, another in a neighboring town a druggist, another yet a speculative adventurer in the regions to the southward: he came back from his commercial forays once with so many half-dollars that when spread out they covered the whole surface of our dining-table; but I am quite unable to report what negotiation they were the spoil of. There was a far cousin who was a painter, and left (possibly as a pledge of indebtedness) with my dentist uncle after a sojourn among us a picture which I early prized as a masterpiece, and still remember as the charming head of a girl shadowed by the fan she held over it. I never saw the painter, but I recall, from my father's singing them, the lines of a "doleful ballad" which he left behind him as well as the picture:

> A thief will steal from you all that you havye,
> But an unfaithful lovyer will bring you to your grave.

The uncle who was a physician, when he left off the practice of medicine about his eightieth year, took up the art of sculpture; he may have always had a taste for it, and his knowledge of anatomy would have helped qualify him for it. He modeled from photographs a head of my father admirably like and full of character, the really extraordinary witness of a gift latent till then through a long life devoted to other things.

15      We children had our preference among these Howells uncles, but we did not care for any of them so much as for our Dean uncles, who now and then found their way up to Hamilton from Cincinnati when their steamboats lay there in their trips from Pittsburg. They were all very jovial; and one of the younger among them could play the violin, not less acceptably because he played by ear and not by art. Of the youngest and best-loved I am lastingly aware in his coming late one night and of my creeping down-stairs from my sleep to sit in his lap and hear his talk with my father and mother, while his bursts of laughter agreeably shook my small person. I dare say these uncles used to bring us gifts from that steamboating world of theirs which seemed to us of a splendor not less than what I should now call oriental when we sometimes visited them at Cincinnati, and

came away bulging in every pocket with the more portable of the dainties we had been feasting upon. In the most signal of these visits, as I once sat between my father and my Uncle William, for whom I was named, on the hurricane roof of his boat, he took a silver half-dollar from his pocket and put it warm in my hand, with a quizzical look into my eyes. The sight of such unexampled riches stopped my breath for the moment, but I made out to ask, "Is it for me?" and he nodded his head smilingly up and down; then, for my experience had hitherto been of fippenny-bits yielded by my father after long reasoning, I asked, "Is it good?" and remained puzzled to know why they laughed so together; it must have been years before I understood.

16     These uncles had grown up in a slave state, and they thought, without thinking, that slavery must be right; but once when an abolition lecturer was denied public hearing at Martin's Ferry, they said he should speak in their mother's house; and there, much unaware, I heard my first and last abolition lecture, barely escaping with my life, for one of the objections urged by the mob outside was a stone hurled through the window, where my mother sat with me in her arms. At my Uncle William's house in the years after the Civil War, my father and he began talking of old times, and he told how, when a boy on a keel-boat, tied up to a Mississippi shore, he had seen an overseer steal upon a black girl loitering at her work, and wind his blacksnake-whip round her body, naked except for the one cotton garment she wore. "When I heard that colored female screech," he said, and the old-fashioned word female, used for compassionate respectfulness, remains with me, "and saw her jump, I knew that there must be something wrong in slavery." Perhaps the sense of this had been in his mind when he determined with his brothers that the abolition lecturer should be heard in their mother's house.

17     She sometimes came to visit us in Hamilton, to break the homesick separations from her which my mother suffered through for so many years, and her visits were times of high holiday for us children. I should be interested now to know what she and my Welsh grandmother made of each other, but I believe they were good friends, though probably not mutually very intelligible. My mother's young sisters, who also came on welcome visits, were always joking with my father and helping my mother at her work; but I cannot suppose

that there was much common ground between them and my grandfather's family except in their common Methodism. For me, I adored them; and if the truth must be told, though I had every reason to love my Welsh grandmother, I had a peculiar tenderness for my Pennsylvania-Dutch grandmother, with her German accent and her caressing ways. My grandfather, indeed, could have recognized no difference among heirs of equal complicity in Adam's sin; and in the situation such as it was, I lived blissfully unborn to all things of life outside of my home. I can recur to the time only as a dream of love and loving, and though I came out of it no longer a little child, but a boy struggling tooth and nail for my place among other boys, I must still recur to the ten or eleven years passed in Hamilton as the gladdest of all my years. They may have been even gladder than they now seem, because the incidents which embody happiness had then the novelty which such incidents lose from their recurrence; while the facts of unhappiness, no matter how often they repeat themselves, seem throughout life an unprecedented experience and impress themselves as vividly the last time as the first. I recall some occasions of grief and shame in that far past with unfailing distinctness, but the long spaces of blissful living which they interrupted hold few or no records which I can allege in proof of my belief that I was then, above every other when,

Joyful and free from blame.

# Discussion Questions

1. In small groups, discuss why Howells begins his essay the way he does. How does it affect your reading of the rest of the essay?
2. Throughout the essay, Howells intersperses such phrases as "I can reasonably suppose . . . ," "I like to believe . . . ," and "I do not know whether it was. . . ." Do these utterances add or detract from the essay's credibility? Why?
3. What exactly does Howells remember about his ancestry?
4. Describe the organization of Howells's essay.
5. Which of Howells's relatives do you remember most? Why?
6. Why were Howells's ten or eleven years in Hamilton his "gladdest"?

# Writing Assignments

1. Can you recall an incident from your past that you believe happened, but which you "remember" only because family members have told you about it? Write a journal entry describing the event.

2. Write your own family history, drawing on your memories and the stories relatives have told you.

3. In a paper, discuss the problems writers face in writing about events that happened when they were very young. How do writers rectify those problems?

# Searching for Ancestors

## BARRY LOPEZ

Barry Lopez (b. 1945) was born in Port Chester, New York. He holds a B.A. *cum laude* from the University of Notre Dame and an M.A.T. from the University of Oregon. From 1968 to 1969 he continued his graduate studies at the University of Oregon. A novelist, essayist, and natural history writer, Lopez's novels include *Desert Notes: Reflections in the Eye of a Raven* (1976), *Giving Birth to Thunder* (1977), *Sleeping with His Daughter: Coyote Builds North America* (1977), *Winter Count* (1981), *Crow and Weasel* (1990), and *Field Notes: The Grace Note of the Canyon Wren* (1994). *Of Wolves and Men* (1978) earned him the John Burroughs Medal, a medal awarded for distinguished natural history writing. His essay collections are *Crossing Open Ground* (1988) and *The Rediscovery of North America* (1991). *Arctic Dreams: Imagination and Desire in a Northern Landscape* (1986) was nominated for the National Book Critics Circle Award and received an American Library Association notable book citation. Lopez has also received an Award in Literature from the American Academy and Institute of Arts and Letters, a Guggenheim fellowship, and the Pacific Northwest Booksellers Award for excellence in nonfiction. Lopez is a contributing editor to *Harper's* magazine and *The North American Review*, and his work has appeared in such periodicals as *National Geographic*, *Science*, and *Antaeus*. Lopez has resided in rural Oregon for the past twenty years. The following essay, which appears in *Crossing Open Ground* (1988), reflects Lopez's interest in natural history. A discussion of the Anasazi, a prehistoric group that lived in the United States's Southwest, the essay addresses their culture and the lessons he learned from these people about the importance of ancestry.

1      I am lying on my back in northern Arizona. The sky above, the familiar arrangement of stars at this particular latitude on a soft June evening, is comforting. I reach out from my sleeping bag, waiting for sleep, and slowly brush the Kaibab Plateau, a grit of limestone 230 million years old. A slight breeze, the settling air at dusk, carries the pungent odor of blooming cliffrose.

2      Three of us sleep in this clearing, on the west rim of Marble Canyon above the Colorado River. Two archaeologists and myself, out hunting for tangible remains of the culture called Anasazi. The Anasazi abandoned this particular area for good around A.D. 1150, because of drought, deteriorating trade alliances, social hostilities— hard to say now. But while they flourished, both here and farther to the east in the austere beauty of canyons called de Chelly and Chaco, they represented an apotheosis in North American culture, like the Hopewell of Ohio or the horse-mounted Lakota of the plains in the last century.

3      In recent years the Anasazi have come to signify prehistoric Indians in the same way the Lakota people have been made to stand for all historic Indians. Much has been made of the "mystery" of their disappearance. And perhaps because they seem "primitive," they are too easily thought of as an uncomplicated people with a comprehensible culture. It is not, and they are not. We know some things about them. From the start they were deft weavers, plaiting even the utensils they cooked with. Later they became expert potters and masons, strongly influencing cultures around them. They were clever floodwater farmers. And astronomers; not as sophisticated as the Maya, but knowledgeable enough to pinpoint the major celestial events, to plant and celebrate accordingly.

4       They were intimate with the landscape, a successful people.
Around A.D. 1300 they slipped through a historical crevice to
emerge (as well as we know) as the people now called Hopi and
Zuni, and the pueblo peoples of the Rio Grande Valley—Keres,
Tiwa, Tewa.

5       On a long, dry June day like this, hundreds of tourists wander in
fascination at Mesa Verde and Pueblo Bonito; and I am out here on
the land the Anasazi once walked—here with two people who squat
down to look closely at the land itself before they say anything about
its former inhabitants. Even then they are reticent. We are camped
here amid the indigenous light siennas and dark umbers, the wild
red of ripe prickly pear fruit, the dull silver of buffalo berry bushes,
the dark, luminous green of a field of snakegrass.

6       We inquire after the Anasazi. Because we respect the spiritual
legacy of their descendants, the Hopi. Because of the contemporary
allure of Taos. Because in our own age we are "killing the hidden
waters" of the Southwest, and these were a people who took swift,
resourceful advantage of whatever water they could find. Because of
the compelling architecture of their cliff dwellings, the stunning
placement of their homes in the stone walls of Betatakin, as if set in
the mouth of an enormous wave or at the bottom of a towering
cumulus cloud. We make the long automobile trip to Hovenweep or
the hike into Tsegi Canyon to gaze at Keet Seel. It is as though we
believed *here* is a good example, here are stories to get us through
the night.

7       Some eight thousand years ago, after the decline of the Folsom and
Clovis hunters, whose spearpoints are still found in the crumbling
arroyos of New Mexico, a culture we know very little about
emerged in the Great Basin. Archaeologists call it simply the Desert
Culture. Some two thousand years ago, while Rome was engaged in
the Macedonian wars, a distinct group of people emerged from this
complex. They were called Anasazi from the Navajo *anaasázi*,
meaning "someone's ancestors." Their culture first appeared in the
Four Corners country, where Utah, Arizona, New Mexico, and
Colorado meet. By this time (A.D. 1) they were already proficient
weavers and basketmakers, living a mixed agricultural hunter-gath-
erer life and dwelling in small groups in semisubterranean houses.
Archaeologists call this period, up to about A.D. 700, the Basket

Maker Period. It was followed by a Pueblo Period (A.D. 700–1598), during which time the Anasazi built the great cliff and pueblo dwellings by which most of us know them.

8  Archaeologists divide the Anasazi occupation geographically into three contemporary traditions—Kayenta, Chaco, and Mesa Verde. Here, where I have rolled my sleeping bag out this June evening, Kayenta Anasazi lived, in an area of about ten thousand square miles bounded by the Henry Mountains in Utah, the Little Colorado River to the south, Grand Canyon to the west, and Chinle Wash, near the New Mexico border, to the east. This part of the Anasazi country has long been of interest to Robert Euler, the research anthropologist at Grand Canyon National Park. He lies quietly now a few yards away from me, in the night shadow of a large juniper tree. From here, at the lip of Marble Canyon and the old edge of Anasazi territory, amid the very same plants the Anasazi took such perceptive advantage of—threads of the yucca leaf to be made into snares; the soft, shreddy bark of the cliffrose to absorb the flow of blood; delicate black seeds of rice grass to eat—from here, with the aid of an observer like Euler, it is possible to imagine who these people might have been, to make some cautious surmise about them and the meaning they may have for us, who wistfully regard them now as mysterious and vanished, like the Eskimo curlew.

9  We go toward sleep this evening—Euler, a colleague named Trinkle Jones, and myself—restless with the bright, looming memory of a granary we have located today, a small storage structure below a cliff edge that has been visited only by violet-green swallows and pack rats since its Anasazi owners walked away some eight hundred years ago. It is like a piece of quartz in the mind.

10  In a quiet corner of the national park's health clinic on the south rim of the Grand Canyon, an entire wall of Euler's modest office is covered by books. A small slip of paper there reads:

> These are not books, lumps of lifeless paper, but
> *minds* alive on the shelves. From each of them goes
> out its own voice, as inaudible as the streams of sound
> conveyed day and night by electric waves beyond the
> range of our physical hearing; and just as the touch of

a button on our set will fill the room with music, so by taking down one of these volumes and opening it, one can call into range the far distant voice in time and space, and hear it speaking to us, mind to mind, heart to heart.

Gilbert Highet

11    Highet was a classics scholar. The words reflect his respect for the ideas of other cultures, other generations, and for the careful deliberations of trained minds. Euler is in this mold; keen and careful, expert in his field, but intent on fresh insight. At fifty-seven, with an ironic wit, willing to listen attentively to the ideas of an amateur, graciously polite, he is the sort of man you wish had taught you in college.

12    Of the Anasazi he says: "It is relatively easy to see *what* they did, but why did they do these things? What were their values? What were the fundamental relationships between their institutions—their politics, economics, religion? All we can do is infer, from what we pick up on the ground."

13    To elucidate the Anasazi, Euler and his colleagues have taken several ingenious steps in recent years. In the 1920s a man named Andrew Douglass pioneered a system of dating called dendrochronology. By comparing borings from timbers used in Anasazi dwellings, Douglass and his successors eventually constructed a continuous record of tree-ring patterns going back more than two thousand years. The measurements are so precise that archaeologists can, for instance, tell that a room in a particular dwelling in Chaco Canyon was roofed over in the spring or summer of 1040 with timbers cut in the fall or winter of 1039.

14    Using dendrochronology as a parallel guide in time, archaeologists have been able to corroborate and assemble long sequences of pottery design. With the aid of radiocarbon dating, obsidian hydration dating, and a technique called thermoluminescence, they have pinned down dates for cooking fires and various tools. By determining kinds of fossil pollens and their ratios to each other, palynologists have reconstructed former plant communities, shedding light on human diets at the time and establishing a history of weather patterns.

15    With such a convergence of dates and esoteric information, archaeologists can figure out when a group of people were occupying a certain canyon, what sort of meals they were eating, what kind of animals and plants were present there, and how they were adapting their farming methods and living patterns to cope with, say, several years of heavy rainfall. With more prosaic techniques—simple excavation and observation—much more becomes clear: details and artifacts of personal adornment; locally traded items (beans and squash for tanned deerskin) and distant trade patterns (turquoise for abalone shell beads from California or copper bells from Mexico); and prevalent infirmities and diseases (arthritis, iron-deficiency anemia).

16    As much as one can learn, however—the Anasazi were a short people with straight black hair, who domesticated turkeys for a supply of feathers, which they carefully wrapped around string and wove together to make blankets—the information seems hollow when you are standing in the cool silence of one of the great kivas at Mesa Verde. Or staring at the stone that soars like a cathedral vault above White House Ruin in Canyon de Chelly. Or turning an Anasazi flute over in your hands. The analytic tools of science can obscure the fact that these were a people. They had an obvious and pervasive spiritual and aesthetic life, as well as clothing made of feathers and teeth worn down by the grit in their cornmeal. Their abandoned dwellings and ceremonial kivas would seem to make this clear. This belief by itself—that they were a people of great spiritual strength—makes us want to know them, to understand what they understood.

17    The day Euler and Jones discovered the intact granary, with its handful of tiny corncobs, I was making notes about the plants and animals we had encountered and trying to envision how water fell and flowed away over this parched land. Euler had told me the area we were traversing was comparable to what the Anasazi had known when they were here, though it was a little drier now. Here then was buffalo berry, which must have irritated their flesh with the white powder beneath its leaves, as it did mine. And apache plume, from whose stout twigs the Anasazi made arrows. And a species of sumac, from the fruits of which they made a sweet lemonade. Dogbane, from whose fibrous sterns they wove sandals, proof against scorpi-

ons, cactus spines, and the other sharp and pointed edges of this country.

18    One afternoon I came on the remains of a mule deer killed by a mountain lion and thought the Anasazi, eminently practical, must have availed themselves of such meat. And I considered the sheltered, well-stocked dwellings of the pack rat, who may have indicated to the newly arrived Anasazi the value of providence and storage.

19    Such wandering is like an interrogation of the landscape, trying by means of natural history and analog to pry loose from it a sense of a people who would be intimate with it—knowledgeable of the behavior of its ground and surface water, its seven-year cycle of piñon nut production, the various subtle euphonies of whirring insects, bumblebees, and hummingbirds on a June afternoon—a people reflective of its order.

20    Euler stood by me at one point when I asked about a particular plant—did they parch, very carefully, the tiny seeds of this desert plume in fiber baskets over their fires?—and said that their botany was so good they probably made use of everything they could digest.

21    They made mistakes, too, if you want to call them that: farmed one area too intensively and ruined the soil; cut down too many trees with their stone axes for housing and firewood and abetted erosion; overhunted. But they survived. They lived through long droughts and took advantage of years of wetness to secure their future. One of the great lessons of the Anasazi is one of the great lessons of all aboriginal peoples, of human ecology in general: Individuals die—of starvation, disease, and injury; but the population itself—resourceful, practical, determined—carries on through nearly everything. Their indomitable fierceness is as attractive as the power we imagine concentrated in their kivas.

22    With the Anasazi, however, you must always turn back and look at the earth—the earth they farmed and hunted and gathered fruits and nuts and seeds upon—and to the weather. The Anasazi responded resourcefully and decisively to the earth and the weather that together made their land. If they were sometimes victims of their environment through drought or epidemic disease, they were more often on excellent terms with it. Given a slight advantage, as they were about A.D. 600 and again about A.D. 1150, when food was

abundant at the peak of the Southwest's 550-year moisture cycle, their culture flourished. Around A.D. 600 they developed pottery, the cultivated bean, and the bow and arrow. In the bean was an important amino acid, lysine, not available in the corn they cultivated. Their diet improved dramatically. By 1150 the Anasazi were building pueblos with three-story, freestanding walls, and their crafts were resurgent during this "classic" period. We can only wonder what might have happened at the next climatic, in 1700—but by then the hostile Spanish were among them.

23    The rise and fall of Anasazi fortunes in time with the weather patterns of the region is clear to most historians. What is not clear is how much of a role weather played in the final retreat of the Anasazi in A.D. 1300 from areas they had long occupied—Mesa Verde, southern Black Mesa, Chaco Canyon. Toward the end, the Anasazi were building what seem to be defensive structures, but it is unclear against whom they were defending themselves. A good guess is that they were defending themselves against themselves, that this was a period of intense social feuding. The sudden alteration of trading relationships, social and political realignment in the communities, drought—whatever the reasons, the Anasazi departed. Their descendants took up residence along the Rio Grande, near springs on the Hopi mesas, and on tributaries of the Little Colorado where water was more dependable. Here, too, they developed farming techniques that were not so harmful to the land.

24    For many in the Southwest today the Anasazi are a vague and nebulous passage in the history of human life. For others, like Euler, they are an intense reflection of the land, a puzzle to be addressed the way a man might try to understand the now-departed curlew. For still others they are a spiritual repository, a mysterious source of strength born of their intimacy with the Colorado Plateau.

25    To wonder about the Anasazi today at a place like the Grand Canyon is to be humbled—by space and the breadth of time—to find the Anasazi neither remote nor primitive, but transcendent. The English novelist J. B. Priestley once said that if he were an American he would make the final test of whatever men chose to do in art and politics a comparison with this place. He believed that whatever was cheap and ephemeral would be revealed for what it was when stood up against it. Priestley was an intellectual, but he

had his finger on an abiding aboriginal truth: If something will not stand up in the land, then it doesn't belong there. It is right that it should die. Most of us are now so far removed from either a practical or an aesthetic intimacy with North America that the land is no longer an arbiter for us. And a haunting sense that this arrangement is somewhat dangerous brings us to stare into the Grand Canyon and to contemplate the utter honesty of the Anasazi's life here.

26    In 1906, with some inkling that North America was slowly being stripped of the evidence of its aboriginal life and that a knowledge of such life was valuable, Congress passed a protective Antiquities Act. The impulse in 1979 to pass a much stronger Archaeological Resources Act was different. Spurred on by escalating prices for Anasazi artifacts, thieves had been systematically looting sites for commercial gain. The trend continues. A second serious current threat to this human heritage is the small number of tourists who, sometimes innocently, continue to destroy structures, walk off with artifacts, and deface petroglyphs. More ominously, the national parks and monuments where most Anasazi sites are now found operate on such restricted budgets that they are unable to adequately inventory, let alone protect, these cultural resources.

27    Of the Grand Canyon's two thousand or more aboriginal sites only three have been both excavated and stabilized. Of its 1.2 million acres, 500,000 have never even been visited by an archaeologist or historian. In the summer of 1981 an unknown person or persons pushed in the wall of an Anasazi granary on the Colorado River at the mouth of Nankoweap Canyon, one of the most famous sites in the park.

28    The sites, which people come so far every year to visit, are more vulnerable every year.

29    On a helicopter reconnaissance in September 1981, part of a long-term project to locate and describe aboriginal sites in the park, Trinkle Jones found what she thought was a set of untouched ruins in the west rim of Marble Canyon. It was almost a year before she and Euler could get there to record them, on a trip on which I accompanied them.

30    Euler is glad to get out into the country, into the canyons that have been the focus of his work since 1960. He moves easily through the

juniper-piñion savannahs, around the face of a cliff and along narrow trails with a practiced stride, examining bits of stone and brush. His blue eyes often fill with wonder when he relates bits of Anasazi history, his right hand sometimes turning slowly in the air as he speaks, as if he were showing you a rare fruit. He tells me one night that he reveres the land, that he thinks about his own footprints impressed in the soil and on the plants, how long before there will be no trace.

31    Euler is a former college president, an author and editor, has been on several university faculties and a codirector of the Black Mesa Archaeological Project, working one step ahead of Peabody Coal's drag buckets. The Park Service, so severely hampered by its humiliating lack of funds, is fortunate, at least, to be able to retain such men.

32    The granaries Jones found prove, indeed, to be untouched. Over a period of several days we map and describe nine new ruins. The process is somewhat mechanical, but we each take pleasure in the simple tasks. As the Anasazi had a complicated culture, so have we. We are takers of notes, measurers of stone, examiners of fragments in the dust. We search for order in chaos wherever we go. We worry over what is lost. In our best moments we remember to ask ourselves what it is we are doing, whom we are benefiting by these acts. One of the great dreams of man must be to find some place between the extremes of nature and civilization where it is possible to live without regret.

33    I lie in my sleeping bag, staring up at the Big Dipper and other familiar stars. It is surprisingly cool. The moon has risen over the land of the Navajo nation to the east. Bats flutter overhead, swooping after moths. We are the only people, I reflect, who go to such lengths to record and preserve the past. In the case of the Anasazi it is not even our own past. Until recently Indians distrusted this process. When Andrew Douglass roamed the Southwest looking for house timbers to core to establish his dendrochronologies, he was required to trade bolts of velveteen for the privilege and to close off every drill hole with a piece of turquoise.

34    I roll on my side and stare out into the canyon's abyss. I think of the astonishing variety of insects and spiders I have seen today— stinkbugs inverted in cactus flowers, butterflies, tiny biting gnats and exotic red velvet ants, and on the ceiling of an Anasazi granary

a very poisonous brown recluse spider. For all the unrelieved tedium there might seem to be in the miles of juniper-piñion savannah, for all the cactus spines, sharp stones, strong light, and imagined strikes of rattlesnakes, the land is replete with creatures, and there is a soft and subtle beauty here. Turn an ash-white mule deer antler over, and its underside, where it has lain against the earth, is flushed rose. Yellow pollen clings to the backs of my hands. Wild grasses roll in the wind, like the manes of horses. It is important to remember that the Anasazi lived in a place, and that the place was very much like the place I lie in tonight.

35    The Anasazi are a reminder: Human life is fundamentally diverse and finally impenetrable. That we cannot do better than a crude reconstruction of their life on the Colorado Plateau a thousand years ago is probably to our advantage, for it steers us away from presumption and judgment.

36    I roll over again and look at the brightening stars. How fortunate we all are, I think, to have people like Euler among us, with their long-lived inquiries; to have these bits of the Anasazi Way to provoke our speculation, to humble us in this long and endless struggle to find ourselves in the world.

37    The slow inhalation of light that is the fall of dusk is now complete. The stars are very bright. I lie there recalling the land as if the Anasazi were something that had once bloomed in it.

## Discussion Questions

1. What is Lopez searching for and why does he search in the manner he describes?
2. Explain why Lopez intersperses personal narrative throughout his essay.
3. Lopez provides a great deal of history of the Anasazi. What does this information contribute to his essay? Explain.
4. In paragraph 6, Lopez lists four reasons for researching the Anasazi, all framed in sentence fragments beginning with the word *because*. Explain how effective you find this technique.
5. Explain what Lopez means in paragraph 25 when he claims, "Most of us are now so far removed from either a practical or an

aesthetic intimacy with North America that the land is no longer an arbiter for us." Do you agree with him? Why or why not?

6. In small groups, discuss what Lopez's thesis is. Explain your responses.

7. How appropriate and convincing is Lopez's conclusion in paragraph 35: "The Anasazi are a reminder: Human life is fundamentally diverse and finally impenetrable"?

# Writing Assignments

1. Write an essay outlining the importance of studying past civilizations—your own and others'.

2. In an essay, explore what you have learned from studying civilizations other than your own. What has this knowledge taught you about your own civilization?

3. Why, as Lopez asserts, are Americans reluctant to develop "a practical or an aesthetic intimacy" with the land? Respond to that question in a paper, discussing what they are missing.

# The World of Our Grandmothers

## CONNIE YOUNG YU

Connie Young Yu was born in Los Angeles in 1941 and moved to San Francisco when she was six years old. She is a 1959 graduate of Mills College. Yu is a Chinese historian, poet, fiction writer, and essayist. Her work on Chinese American history and Asian America has appeared in such publications as the *Civil Rights Digest*, *Amerasia*, and *Working It Out*, an anthology of women's writing. Yu is also the author of *Profiles in Excellence* (1986), a collection of biographies of Chinese Americans, and *Chinatown San Jose, U.S.A.* (1991). Yu's interest in social concerns includes domestic violence and immigration. The following essay, which appears in *Making Waves: An Anthology of Writings by and about Asian American Women* (1989), combines descriptions of Yu's family history with historical data of Chinese immigration.

1    In Asian America there are two kinds of history. The first is what is written about us in various old volumes on immigrants and echoed in textbooks, and the second is our own oral history, what we learn in the family chain of generations. We are writing this oral history ourselves. But as we research the factual background of our story, we face the dilemma of finding sources. Worse than burning

the books is not being included in the record at all, and in American history—traditionally viewed from the white male perspective—minority women have been virtually ignored. Certainly the accomplishments and struggles of early Chinese immigrants, men as well as women, have been obscured.

2    Yet for a period in the development of the West, Chinese immigration was a focus of prolonged political and social debate and a subject of daily news. When I first began searching into the background of my people, I read this nineteenth-century material with curious excitement, grateful for any information on Chinese immigration.

3    Looking for the history of Chinese pioneer women, I began with the first glimpses of Chinese in America—newspaper accounts found in bound volumes of the *Alta California* in the basement of a university library. For Chinese workers, survival in the hostile and chaotic world of Gum San, or Gold Mountain, as California was called by Chinese immigrants, was perilous and a constant struggle, leaving little time or inclination for reflection or diary writing. So for a look into the everyday life of early arrivals from China, we have only the impressions of white reporters on which to depend.

4    The newspapers told of the comings and goings of "Chinamen," their mining activities, new Chinese settlements, their murders by claim-jumpers, and assaults by whites in the city. An item from 17 August 1855, reported a "disgraceful outrage": Mr. Ho Alum was setting his watch under a street clock when a man called Thomas Field walked up and deliberately dashed the time-piece to the pavement. "Such unprovoked assaults upon unoffending Chinamen are not of rare occurrence. . . ." On the same day the paper also reported the suicide of a Chinese prostitute. In this item no name, details, or commentary were given, only a stark announcement. We can imagine the tragic story behind it: the short miserable life of a young girl sold into slavery by her impoverished parents and taken to Gum San to be a prostitute in a society of single men.

5    An early history of this period, *Lights and Shades in San Francisco* by B. E. Lloyd (1878), devoted ten chapters to the life of California Chinese, describing in detail "the subjects of the Celestial Kingdom." Chinese women, however, are relegated to a single paragraph:

Females are little better than slaves. They are looked
upon as merchantable property, and are bought and
sold like any other article of traffic, though their value
is not generally great. A Chinese woman never gains
any distinction until after death. . . . Considering the
humble position the women occupy in China, and the
hard life they therefore lead, it would perhaps be better (certainly more merciful) were they all slain in
infancy, and better still, were they never born.

6    Public opinion, inflamed by lurid stories of Chinese slave girls,
agreed with this odious commentary. The only Chinese women
whose existence American society acknowledged were the prostitutes who lived miserable and usually short lives. Senate hearings on
Chinese immigration in 1876 resounded with harangues about
prostitutes and slave girls corrupting the morals of young white
boys. "The Chinese race is debauched," claimed one lawyer arguing
for the passage of the Chinese Exclusion Law: "They bring no
decent women with them." This stigma on the Chinese immigrant
woman remained for many decades, causing unnecessary hardship
for countless wives, daughters, and slave girls.

7    Chinese American society finally established itself as families
appeared, just as they did in the white society of the forty-niners who
arrived from the East Coast without bringing "decent women" with
them. Despite American laws intended to prevent the "settlement"
of Chinese, Chinese women did make the journey and endured the
isolation and hostility, braving it for future generations here.

8    Even though Chinese working men were excluded from most
facets of American society and their lives were left unrecorded, their
labors bespoke their existence—completed railroads, reclaimed
lands, and a myriad of new industries. The evidence of women's lives
seems less tangible. Perhaps the record of their struggles to immi-
grate and overcome discriminatory barriers is their greatest legacy.
Tracing that record therefore becomes a means of recovering our
history.

9    Our grandmothers are our historical links. As a fourth-generation
Chinese American on my mother's side, and a third-generation on
my father's, I grew up hearing stories about ancestors coming from

China and going back and returning again. Both of my grandmothers, like so many others, spent a lot of time waiting in China.

10    My father's parents lived with us when I was growing up, and through them I absorbed a village culture and the heritage of my pioneer Chinese family. In the kitchen my grandmother told repeated stories of coming to America after waiting for her husband to send for her. (It took sixteen years before Grandfather could attain the status of merchant and only then arrange for her passage to this country.) She also told stories from the village about bandits, festivals, and incidents showing the tyranny of tradition. For example, Grandma was forbidden by her mother-in-law to return to her own village to visit her mother: A married woman belonged solely within the boundaries of her husband's world.

11    Sometimes I was too young to understand or didn't listen, so my mother—who knew all the stories by heart—told me those stories again later. We heard over and over how lucky Grandpa was to have come to America when he was eleven—just one year before the gate was shut by the exclusion law banning Chinese laborers. Grandpa told of his many jobs washing dishes, making bricks, and working on a strawberry farm. Once, while walking outside Chinatown, he was stoned by a group of whites and ran so fast he lost his cap. Grandma had this story to tell of her anger and frustration: "While I was waiting in the immigration shed, Grandpa sent in a box of *dim sum*. I was still waiting to be released. I would have jumped in the ocean if they decided to deport me." A woman in her position was quite helpless, but she still had her pride and was not easily pacified. "I threw the box of *dim sum* out the window."

12    Such was the kind of history I absorbed. I regret deeply that I was too young to have asked the questions about the past that I now want answered; all my grandparents are now gone. But I have another chance to recover some history from my mother's side. Family papers, photographs, old trunks that have traveled across the ocean several times filled with clothes, letters, and mementos provide a documentary on our immigration. My mother—and some of my grandmother's younger contemporaries—fill in the narrative.

13    A year before the Joint Special Committee of Congress to investigate Chinese immigration met in San Francisco in 1876, my great-grandmother, Chin Shee, arrived to join her husband, Lee Wong Sang, who had come to America a decade earlier to work on the

transcontinental railroad. Chin Shee arrived with two brides who had never seen their husbands. Like her own, their marriages had been arranged by their families. The voyage on the clipper ship was rough and long. Seasick for weeks, rolling back and forth as she lay in the bunk, Chin Shee lost most of her hair. The two other women laughed, "Some newlywed you'll make!" But the joke was on them as they mistakenly set off with the wrong husbands, the situation realized only when one man looked at his bride's normal-sized feet and exclaimed, "But the letter described my bride as having bound feet!" Chin Shee did not have her feet bound because she came from a peasant family. But her husband did not seem to care about that nor that the back of her head was practically bald. He felt himself fortunate just to be able to bring his wife to Gum San.

14    Chin Shee bore six children in San Francisco, where her husband assisted in the deliveries. They all lived in the rear of their grocery store, which also exported dried shrimp and seaweed to China. Great-Grandma seldom left home; she could count the number of times she went out. She and other Chinese wives did not appear in the streets even for holidays, lest they be looked upon as prostitutes. She took care of the children, made special cakes to sell on feast days, and helped with her husband's work. A photograph of her shows a middle-aged woman with a kindly, but careworn face, wearing a very regal brocade gown and a long, beaded necklace. As a respectable, well-to-do Chinese wife in America, married to a successful Chinatown merchant, with children who were by birthright American citizens, she was a rarity in her day. (In contrast, in 1884 Mrs. Jew Lim, the wife of a laborer, sued in federal court to be allowed to join her husband, but was denied and deported.)

15    In 1890 there were only 3,868 Chinese women among 103,620 Chinese males in America. Men such as Lee Yoke Suey, my mother's father, went to China to marry. He was one of Chin Shee's sons born in the rear of the grocery store, and he grew up learning the import and export trade. As a Gum San merchant, he had money and status and was able to build a fine house in Toishan. Not only did he acquire a wife but also two concubines. When his wife became very ill after giving birth to an infant who soon died, Yoke Suey was warned by his father that she was too weak to return to America with him. Reminding Yoke Suey of the harsh life in Gum San, he advised his son to get a new wife.

16    In the town of Foshan, not far from my grandfather's village, lived a girl who was recommended to him by his father's friend. Extremely capable, bright, and with some education, she was from a once prosperous family that had fallen on hard times. A plague had killed her two older brothers, and her heartbroken mother died soon afterwards. She was an excellent cook and took good care of her father, an herb doctor. Her name was Jeong Hing Tong, and she was pretty, with bound feet only three and a half inches long. Her father rejected the offer of the Lee family at first; he did not want his daughter to be a concubine, even to a wealthy Gum San merchant. But the elder Lee assured him this girl would be the wife, the one who would go to America with her husband.

17    So my maternal grandmother, bride of sixteen, went with my grandfather, then twenty-six, to live in America. Once in San Francisco, Grandmother lived a life of confinement, as did her mother-in-law before her. When she went out, even in Chinatown, she was ridiculed for her bound feet. People called out mockingly to her, "*Jhat!*" meaning bound. She tried to unbind her feet by soaking them every night and putting a heavy weight on each foot. But she was already a grown woman, and her feet were permanently stunted, the arches bent and the toes crippled. It was hard for her to stand for long periods of time, and she frequently had to sit on the floor to do her chores. My mother comments: "Tradition makes life so hard. My father traveled all over the world. There were stamps all over his passport—London, Paris—and stickers all over his suitcases, but his wife could not go into the street by herself."

18    Their first child was a girl, and on the morning of her month-old "red eggs and ginger party" the earth shook 8.3 on the Richter scale. Everyone in San Francisco, even Chinese women, poured out into the streets. My grandmother, babe in arms, managed to get a ride to Golden Gate Park on a horse-drawn wagon. Two other Chinese women who survived the earthquake recall the shock of suddenly being out in the street milling with thousands of people. The elderly goldsmith in a dimly lit Chinatown store had a twinkle in his eye when I asked him about the scene after the quake. "We all stared at the women because we so seldom saw them in the streets." The city was soon in flames. "We could feel the fire on our faces," recalls Lily Sung, who was seven at the time, "but my sister and I couldn't walk very fast because we had to escort this lady, our neigh-

bor, who had bound feet." The poor woman kept stumbling and falling on the rubble and debris during their long walk to the Oakland-bound ferry.

19    That devastating natural disaster forced some modernity on the San Francisco Chinese community. Women had to adjust to the emergency and makeshift living conditions and had to work right alongside the men. Life in America, my grandmother found, was indeed rugged and unpredictable.

20    As the city began to rebuild itself, she proceeded to raise a large family, bearing four more children. The only school in San Francisco admitting Chinese was the Oriental school in Chinatown. But her husband felt, as did most men of his class, that the only way his children could get a good education was for the family to return to China. So they lived in China and my grandfather traveled back and forth to the United States for his trade business. Then suddenly, at the age of forty-three, he died of an illness on board a ship returning to China. After a long and painful mourning, Grandmother decided to return to America with her brood of now seven children. That decision eventually affected immigration history.

21    At the Angel Island immigration station in San Francisco Bay, Grandmother went through a physical examination so thorough that even her teeth were checked to determine whether she was the age stated on her passport. The health inspector said she had filariasis, liver fluke, a common ailment of Asian immigrants which caused their deportation by countless numbers. The authorities thereby ordered Grandmother to be deported as well.

22    While her distraught children had to fend for themselves in San Francisco (my mother, then fifteen, and her older sister had found work in a sewing factory), a lawyer was hired to fight for Grandmother's release from the detention barracks. A letter addressed to her on Angel Island from her attorney, C. M. Fickert, dated 24 March 1924, reads: "Everything I can legitimately do will be done on your behalf. As you say, it seems most inhuman for you to be separated from your children who need your care. I am sorry that the immigration officers will not look at the human side of your case."

23    Times were tough for Chinese immigrants in 1924. Two years before, the federal government had passed the Cable Act, which provided that any woman born in the United States who married a man "ineligible for citizenship" (including the Chinese, whose naturaliza-

tion rights had been eliminated by the Chinese Exclusion Act) would lose her own citizenship. So, for example, when American-born Lily Sung, whom I also interviewed, married a Chinese citizen she forfeited her birthright. When she and her four daughters tried to reenter the United States after a stay in China, they were denied permission. The immigration inspector accused her of "smuggling little girls to sell." The Cable Act was not repealed until 1930.

24  The year my grandmother was detained on Angel Island, a law had just taken effect that forbade all aliens ineligible for citizenship from landing in America. This constituted a virtual ban on the immigration of all Chinese, including Chinese wives of U.S. citizens.

25  Waiting month after month in the bleak barracks, Grandmother heard many heart-rending stories from women awaiting deportation. They spoke of the suicides of several despondent women who hanged themselves in the shower stalls. Grandmother could see the calligraphy carved on the walls by other detained immigrants, eloquent poems expressing homesickness, sorrow, and a sense of injustice.

26  Meanwhile, Fickert was sending telegrams to Washington (a total of ten the bill stated) and building up a case for the circuit court. Mrs. Lee, after all, was the wife of a citizen who was a respected San Francisco merchant, and her children were American citizens. He also consulted a medical authority to see about a cure for liver fluke.

27  My mother took the ferry from San Francisco twice a week to visit Grandmother and take her Chinese dishes such as salted eggs and steamed pork because Grandmother could not eat the beef stew served in the mess hall. Mother and daughter could not help crying frequently during their short visits in the administration building. They were under close watch of both a guard and an interpreter.

28  After fifteen months the case was finally won. Grandmother was easily cured of filariasis and was allowed—with nine months probation—to join her children in San Francisco. The legal fees amounted to $782.50, a fortune in those days.

29  In 1927 Dr. Frederick Lam in Hawaii, moved by the plight of Chinese families deported from the islands because of the liver fluke disease, worked to convince federal health officials that the disease was noncommunicable. He used the case of Mrs. Lee Yoke Suey, my grandmother, as a precedent for allowing an immigrant to land with such an ailment and thus succeeded in breaking down a major barrier to Asian immigration.

30    My most vivid memory of Grandmother Lee is when she was in her seventies and studying for her citizenship. She had asked me to test her on the three branches of government and how to pronounce them correctly. I was a sophomore in high school and had entered the "What American Democracy Means To Me" speech contest of the Chinese American Citizens Alliance. When I said the words "judicial, executive, and legislative," I looked directly at my grandmother in the audience. She didn't smile, and afterwards, didn't comment much on my patriotic words. She had never told me about being on Angel Island or about her friends losing their citizenship. It wasn't in my textbooks either. I may have thought she wanted to be a citizen because her sons and sons-in-law had fought for this country, and we lived in a land of freedom and opportunity, but my guess now is that she wanted to avoid any possible confrontation—even at her age—with immigration authorities. The bad laws had been repealed, but she wasn't taking any chances.

31    I think a lot about my grandmother now and can understand why, despite her quiet, elegant dignity, an aura of sadness always surrounded her. She suffered from racism in the new country, as well as from traditional cruelties in the old. We, her grandchildren, remember walking very slowly with her, escorting her to a family banquet in Chinatown, hating the stares of tourists at her tiny feet. Did she, I wonder, ever feel like the victim of a terrible hoax, told as a small weeping girl that if she tried to untie the bandages tightly binding her feet she would grow up ugly, unwanted, and without the comforts and privileges of the wife of a wealthy man?

32    We seemed so huge and clumsy around her—a small, slim figure always dressed in black. She exclaimed once that the size of my growing feet were "like boats." But she lived to see some of her granddaughters graduate from college and pursue careers and feel that the world she once knew with its feudal customs had begun to crumble. I wonder what she would have said of my own daughter who is now attending a university on an athletic scholarship. Feet like boats travel far?

33    I keep looking at the artifacts of the past: the photograph of my grandmother when she was an innocent young bride and the sad face in the news photo taken on Angel Island. I visit the immigration barracks from time to time, a weather-beaten wooden building with its walls marked by calligraphy bespeaking the struggles of our

history. I see the view of sky and water from the window out of which my grandmother gazed. My mother told me how, after visiting hours, she would walk to the ferry and turn back to see her mother waving to her from this window. This image has been passed on to me like an heirloom of pain and of love. When I leave the building, emerging from the darkness into the glaring sunlight of the island, I too turn back to look at my grandmother's window.

# Discussion Questions

1. What "two kinds of history" does Yu mention at the beginning of her essay?
2. Of the two kinds of history, which do you find more important? Why?
3. Yu focuses on women's lives as "a means of recovering our history." What reasons does she give for this focus and are they convincing?
4. Why does Yu provide information about Chinese history as well as her own family history?
5. Do you think Yu's grandmother's sadness was warranted? Why?
6. Answer the question Yu poses in paragraph 32: What do you think her grandmother would have said about Yu's daughter attending a university on an athletic scholarship?
7. In small groups, discuss what you think Yu learned about her ancestry from having written this essay.

# Writing Assignments

1. In a journal entry, recount a time when you learned valuable information about your family heritage. Relate how you reacted to that information. Did you learn something about yourself? Explain.
2. In a paper, discuss why it is important for people to acquire information about their family heritage or ancestry.

# Ask Me No Questions

## MARY MCCARTHY

Mary McCarthy (1912–1989) was born in Seattle but moved to Minneapolis at the age of six when her parents died in the flu epidemic of 1918. She and her siblings were raised by cruel guardians until their grandfather rescued them in 1923. McCarthy then moved back to Seattle. McCarthy earned her B.A. from Vassar College and wrote novels, theater reviews, and memoirs. She is the author of novels heavily infused with autobiography, including *The Company She Keeps* (1942), *The Oasis* (1949), *The Groves of Academe* (1952), *A Charmed Life* (1955), *Birds of America* (1971), *Cannibals and Missionaries* (1979), and her most famous book *The Group* (1963), which details the lives of eight Vassar College graduates in the 1930s. Her art and social histories are *Venice Observed* (1956) and *The Stones of Florence* (1959). In *Memories of a Catholic Girlhood* (1957), McCarthy chronicles her harrowing experiences of being orphaned. Her other works include *How I Grew* (1987) and *Intellectual Memoirs: New York 1936–1938* (published posthumously in 1992). In 1984, McCarthy was awarded the National Medal for Literature. In the following essay, taken from *Memories of a Catholic Girlhood*, McCarthy recalls members of her family, in particular her grandmother, as a way to understand better her ancestry.

1    Much of my adolescent boredom and discontent sprang from the fact that I had absolutely nothing to do but read and play the Victrola. I was not allowed in the kitchen, except to fix a sandwich for my lunch, because of an historic mess I had made with a batch of marshmallows; as with the dawn-colored dress, I had been too ambitious for a beginner. All I know today of sewing I learned in boarding school and, earlier, from the nuns in the convent, and the only person who was willing to show me anything about cooking was the old gardener-chauffeur, who used to come in and make German-fried potatoes for his lunch. On the cook's day out, he would let me watch him and then try it myself. In our family now, we have a dish called, in his memory, chauffeur-fried potatoes; they are very good.

2    My grandmother herself did not eat lunch as a regular thing, and at twelve o'clock every day, and sometimes earlier, my audience was over. She would get up from her chair and retire to the bathroom, shutting the door behind her. In a minute, her bedroom door closed, the nursery door closed. From then on till a time that varied between two and three o'clock, she was invisible; no one was allowed to disturb her. She was getting ready to go downtown. This sortie was the climax of her day. Her bedroom door would open, revealing her in festive array—every outfit she wore, like every meal, was a surprise. The car would be waiting, in front of the old carriage block, and we would set off, sometimes stopping for Aunt Rosie. The next two or three hours would be spent in the stores, trying on, ransacking counters. My grandmother was not much interested in bargains, though we never missed a sale at Helen Igoe's or Magnin's; what she cared about was the "latest wrinkle" in dresses or furs or notions—news from the fashion front. During these hours, she reached her highest point of laconic animation and sparkle; she shopped like an epigrammatist at the peak of form, and the extravagance of her purchases matched her brilliant hair and bobbing feathers and turkey walk and pursy pink cheeks.

3    But at a quarter of five, wherever we were, my grandmother would look at her watch. It was time to pick up Grandpa, in front of his club, where he always played a rubber of bridge after leaving the office. At five o'clock, punctually, he would be on the sidewalk, anxiously surveying the traffic for us. The car would draw up; he would climb in and kiss my grandmother's cheek. "Have a good day?" he would ask. "All right," she would reply, sighing a little. We would

get home at five-thirty; dinner was at six, punctually. During the
meal, my young uncle would be queried as to how he had passed his
day, and he would answer with a few monosyllables. My grandmother would mention the names of any persons she had seen on
her shopping tour. My grandfather might praise the food. "Allee
samee Victor Hugo," he would say, referring to a restaurant in Los
Angeles. After dinner, my married uncle would drop in with his
wife, perhaps on their way out to a party. My other uncle, yawning,
would retire to his quarters. The doorbell might ring. I would run
to answer it, and two or three of his friends would tramp past me
upstairs to his rooms. The door on the landing would shut. In a little while, he would lope down the stairs, to say that he was going
out. He would kiss his mother and father, and my grandfather
would say to him, "Home by eleven, son." My grandfather and
grandmother, having finished the evening papers, would start playing double Canfield, at which my grandmother nearly always won.
"I'll have to hitch up my trousers with a safety pin," my grandfather
would say to me, jesting, as he paid her over her winnings; this
expression signified to him the depths of poverty.

4      Then he might go downtown to his club for a game of poker, or
he might stay in his deep chair, smoking a cigar and reading a book
that always seemed to be the same book: *The Life and Letters of
Walter Hines Page*. My grandmother would take up her library
book, I would take up mine, and silence would resume its way over
the household. The only sound would be the turning of a page or
the click of the door on the kitchen landing as the cook went
upstairs to bed. Rarely, the telephone would ring, and I would rush
to get it, but it was never anything interesting—someone for my
uncle or a girl for me, asking what I was doing. Or my grandmother
would glance over at me as I lay stretched out on the sofa with my
copy (disappointing) of *Mademoiselle de Maupin*: "Mary, pull your
dress down." At ten o'clock, she would close her book, sighing, and
start out to the front hall, on her way to bed. "Going up, Mama?"
my grandfather would say, if he were at home, raising his gray eyes
with an invariable air of surprise. "I think so, Harry," she would
reply, sighing again, from the stairs. The stairs creaked; her door
closed; the bathroom door closed. Soon my grandfather would put
down his book and his paper knife, offer his cheek to me for a kiss,
and follow her up the stairs. The nursery door would shut.

5      Occasionally, we would all go to the movies, or to the theater if a New York company was in town; my grandfather did not care for stock. We saw *The Student Prince* and *No! No! Nanette!* I remember, and *Strange Interlude*, which my grandmother pronounced "talky." On Thursday nights, we might go out to dinner at my grandfather's club. On Sundays, the cook left a supper prepared for us; my married uncle and his wife always came to this meal, no matter how many invitations they had to turn down, and sometimes Aunt Eva and Aunt Alice. These suppers usually ended with our going to the movies afterward; we were always home by eleven.

6      About once a year, or possibly every two years, my grandmother gave a tea and we had the caterer in. That was the only entertaining we did. Except for Aunt Alice and Aunt Eva (both widows), we never gave anyone dinner outside the immediate family. We never had Uncle Mose and Aunt Rosie or Uncle Clarence and Aunt Abbie (a vegetarian pair) or any of my cousins and their wives or my grandfather's partners and theirs. My grandmother's brother Elkan, whom she saw rarely but was not on bad terms with, was never, to my knowledge, in our house, nor were his wife and his numerous progeny. This leads me to wonder whether it was not the Jewish connection that had put the bar on entertaining. "If we have one in the house, we'll have them all," my grandfather may have said. But we did have Aunt Eva, frequently, and once, a great exception, her daughter from Portland to Sunday lunch. The only other exception that comes back to me was a dinner we gave for old Judge Gilman, of the Great Northern, and his wife, a stout lady who called herself Little Eva; I remember this because the men were served whisky before dinner, the only time this ever happened in our house. But why we had Judge and Mrs. Gilman I do not know; I think it puzzled me at the time by introducing into my head the question of why we did not have other people, since, on this occasion, a good time was had by all.

7      Up to then, it had never occurred to me that my family was remarkably inhospitable. I did not realize how strange it was that no social life was ever planned for me or my young uncle, that no young people were invited for us and no attempt made to secure invitations on our behalf. Indeed, I did not fully realize it until I was over thirty and long a mother myself. If I did not have an ordinary social set but

only stray, odd friends, I blamed this on myself, thinking there was something wrong with me, like a petticoat showing, that other people could see and I couldn't. The notion that a family had responsibility for launching the younger members was more unknown to me than the theorem of Pythagoras, and if anybody had told me of it, I think I would have shut my ears, for I loved my family and did not wish to believe them remiss in any of their obligations. The fact that they would not let me go out with boys was an entirely different case; I saw their side of it, even though I disagreed violently—they were doing it for my own good, as they conceived it.

8    And yet I knew there was something odd about my grandmother's attitude toward outsiders. She would never go up to Lake Crescent, in the Olympic Mountains, with my grandfather and my young uncle and me in the summertime, where, amid my grandfather's circle of friends and their descendants, we had the only regular social life I ever experienced in the West. Life in the mountain hotel was very gay, even for the old people—Judge and Mrs. Battle, Colonel Blethen, Mr. Edgar Battle, Mr. Claude Ramsay, Mr. and Mrs. Boole—in my grandfather's set. They had card games on the big veranda and forest walks up to the Marymere waterfall; they took motorboat expeditions and automobile expeditions; they watched the young people dance in the evening, and sent big tips to the chef in the kitchen. I could not understand why my grandmother preferred to stay in Seattle, pursuing her inflexible routine.

9    She was funny that way—that was the only explanation—just as she was funny about not letting my young uncle or me ever have a friend stay to dinner. In all the years I lived with my grandmother, as a child and a woman, I can only recall two occasions when this rule was ever broken. The second one was when she was bedridden and too feeble, morally, to override my determination to ask a poet who was teaching at the university to stay and have supper with me. I felt a little compunction, though the nurse and the cook assured me that it would be all right—she would forget about it the next minute. But her pretty voice, querulous, was heard from upstairs at about eight-thirty in the evening: "Mary, has that man gone home yet?" And all through the rest of my visit, she kept reverting crossly to the subject of "that man" who had stayed to supper; it was no good explaining to her that he had no means of getting home, that he lived in rooms way out at the University and took his meals in din-

ers and tearooms, that he was an old friend to whom some hospital-
ity was owing in my native city. Nor could I laugh her out of it.
"Why didn't he go home for his dinner?" she reiterated, and those
dark, suspicious words were very nearly the last I heard from her.

10 This ungraciousness of my grandmother's was a deeply confirmed
trait. It was not only that she resisted offering meals to anyone outside the immediate family; she resented a mere caller. There was a
silver tray for calling cards on the hall table, but most of the cards in
it were yellow with age; my grandmother was always downtown
shopping at the hour when calls were normally paid. If I had a girl
in for the evening, we could not really talk until my grandmother
had gone to bed, and often she would outstay the guest, sitting in a
corner with her book and glancing at us from time to time as we sat
on the sofa endeavoring to improvise a dialogue. We could tell she
was listening, but she did not talk herself. Suddenly, looking up, she
would make the gesture to me that meant "Pull your skirt down."

11 My uncle's situation was the same, but he had the advantage of
having his own sitting room, where his friends could congregate.
For the most part, my grandmother ignored their presence; she
would nod to them curtly if she chanced to meet them in the hall.
The girls he knew were never asked to the house; he could never
give a party.

12 Yet she was not an unkindly woman. She was good to her servants and their families, and on some occasions, if she were persuaded to unbend and tell an anecdote, she could be positively
cordial. Her house, with its big rooms and wide porches, had been
built, it would seem, with a hospitable *intention*. And in my
mother's day, so I was told, things had been very different; the
house had been full of young people. The silver and crystal and cut
glass had not always been put away in the cupboard; there had been
music and dancing, and my mother's school and college friends had
spent night after night on the sleeping porches (which served as
guest rooms) without even the necessity of a permission.

13 My mother had been my grandmother's darling. The fact that we
did not entertain, I was given to understand, was related to my
mother's death. My grandmother had resented her marriage to my
father; according to my Irish relations, she would not have a priest
in the house, and so the ceremony had been performed on the lawn.

I do not believe this story, which is contradicted by other accounts, but it is true that my grandmother resented the Catholic Church, to which my mother was eventually converted. Dr. Sharples, the family physician, had told my father, it seems, that my mother would die if she had another child, and my father went right ahead anyway, refusing to practice birth control. Actually, my mother's death had nothing to do with childbearing; she died of the flu, like so many young women of her age during the great epidemic. But this would not have deterred a woman like my grandmother from holding my father and the Church responsible. That was perhaps the reason she took no interest in my three brothers, who were still living with my father's people in Minneapolis; she sent them checks and gifts at birthdays and Christmas, and remembered them later in her will, but during the years I lived with her, the three little boys who had been born against her judgment were very remote from her thoughts. Possibly, I was enough of a handful for a woman of her age; nevertheless, it seems odd, unfeeling, that dry lack of concern, when she well knew that their lot was not happy. But happiness, like love, was a concept she had no real patience with.

14      As for the impassibility or aloofness she showed sometimes toward me, this may have been due to an absence of temperamental sympathy (could she have thought I had my father's traits?), or it may have been because I reminded her painfully of my mother, (I was always conscious of a resemblance that did not go far enough; everyone was always telling me how "good" my mother had been.)

15      For three years after my mother's death, one of her friends told me, my grandmother did not go out socially. Five years, said another. And this prolonged mourning was always offered as the official explanation of any oddities in our household. My grandmother, people said, lowering their voices, had never recovered from the shock of my mother's death. As a child, I could not quite believe this; it was impossible for me to imagine this contained, self-centered woman overcome by a passion of grief. Without being a psychologist, I felt somehow that her obdurate mourning was willful and selfish.

16      Children generally feel this about any adult emotion which is beyond their ken, but in this case I think I was on the track of something real. My grandmother's grief had taken a form peculiar to herself, stamped, as it were, with her monogram—the severe "AMP," in

scroll lettering, that figured on her silver, her brushes and combs, her automobile. Her grief had the character of an inveterate hostility. One of my mother's friends recently wrote me a letter describing how my grandmother had hurt her feelings by refusing to speak to her whenever they met in the stores for a year after my mother's death. "Your grandmother could not bear the sight of me," she sadly decided.

17    And that is how I see my grandmother, bearing her loss like an affront, stubborn and angry, refusing to speak not only to individual persons but to life itself, which had wounded her by taking her daughter away. Her grief was a kind of pique, one of those nurtured *grievances* in which she specialized and which were deeply related to her coquetry. If I had only her photographs to go on, I might doubt the legend of her beauty; what confirms it for me is her manner of grieving, her mistrust of words, her refusal to listen to explanations from life or any other guilty suitor. Life itself was obliged to court her—in vain, as it appeared, for she had been mortally offended, once, twice, three times.

18    What the first offense was, I do not know, but I imagine it had something to do with her Jewish pride and sensitiveness; some injury was dealt her early in her marriage, and it may have been a very small thing—a chance word, even—that caused her to draw back into an August silence on this topic, a silence that lasted until her death. The second one I know about. This was the tragic face lifting that took place, in 1916 or 1917, I imagine, when she was in her forties and my mother was still living. Perhaps she really did have a mastoid operation at some later period (I rather think she must have), but the pouchy disfiguring scars I have spoken of that started on her cheeks and went down into her neck were the work of a face-lifter, who, as I understand the story, had pumped her face full of hot wax.

19    Such accidents were common in the early days of face lifting, and the scars, by the time she was sixty, were not especially noticeable. It was only that her cheeks had a puffy, swollen appearance, which her make-up did not conceal—in fact, if anything, enhanced, for though she did not know it, she always looked better in the morning, before she put on the rouge and the powder that made her skin's surface conspicuous. But when the scars were new, they must have been rather horrifying, and that was surely the reason for the dotted veils

she wore, pulled tight across her face. The photographs break off at the time of the operation. That was when she stopped speaking to the camera, and, according to one informant, my grandmother left Seattle for a year after the tragedy.

20    "According to one informant"—the story of the face lifting was well known in Seattle, and yet in the family no mention was ever made of it, at least in my hearing, so that I learned of it from outsiders—my father's people, friends of my mother's, who naturally were unable to supply all the details. I was grown up when I learned it, and yet that same unnatural tact that kept me from ever using the word "Jewish" to my grandmother kept me from prying into the matter with the family. "Your grandmother's tragedy"—so I first heard the face lifting alluded to, if I remember rightly, by one of my friends, who had heard of it from her mother. And I will not query the appropriateness of the term according to the Aristotelian canon; in this case, common usage seems right. It was a tragedy, for her, for her husband and family, who, deprived of her beauty through an act of folly, came to live in silence, like a house accursed.

21    My grandmother's withdrawal from society must have dated, really, from this period, and not from the time of my mother's death, which came as the crowning blow. That was why we were so peculiar, so unsocial, so, I would add, slightly inhuman; we were all devoting ourselves, literally, to the cult of a relic, which was my grandmother's body, laved and freshened every day in the big bathroom, and then paraded before the public in the downtown stores.

22    I was living in New York when my grandfather died, from a stroke, one morning, when he was seventy-nine, in the big bathroom. My grandmother's ritual did not change. She still dressed and went downtown at the same hours, returning at the time when she would have picked him up at his club. She was cheerful when I saw her, a year or so after this; she went to the races and had a new interest—night baseball; we went to the ball park together. Once in a great while, she would lunch and play bridge with a group of women friends, with whom she had resumed connections after twenty years. But she did not, to my knowledge, ever have them to her house; they met at the Seattle Golf Club usually, the best (non-Jewish) country club.

23    Like many widows, she appeared to have taken a new lease on life; I had never seen her so chatty, and she was looking very hand-

some. I remember an afternoon at the races, to which she drove Aunt Rosie and me in her car, at a speed of seventy miles an hour; she herself was well over seventy. The two sisters, one a lively robin and the other a brilliant toucan, chaffed and bantered with the sporting set in the clubhouse. Conscious of their powers and their desirability, they were plainly holding court. Aunt Rosie did not bet but advised us; my grandmother, as usual, won, and I think I won, too. That night, or in the small hours of the morning, Aunt Rosie died.

24    It was something, Dr. Sharples thought, that she had eaten at the races; an attack of indigestion caused a heart block. He believed at first he could save her, and I had persuaded my grandmother to go to bed, confident that Aunt Rosie would be almost herself the next day. But in the middle of the night, the phone rang. I ran to get it; it was Uncle Mose. "Rosie just went." My grandmother understood before I could tell her, before I had set down the telephone. A terrible scream—an unearthly scream—came from behind the closed door of her bedroom; I have never heard such a sound, neither animal nor human, and it did not stop, It went on and on, like a fire siren on the moon. In a minute, the whole household was roused; everybody came running. I got there first. Flinging open her bedroom door (even then with a sense of trepidation, of being an unwarranted intruder), I saw her, on her bed, the covers pushed back; her legs were sprawled out, and her yellow batiste nightgown, trimmed with white lace, was pulled up, revealing her thighs. She was writhing on the bed; the cook and I could barely get hold of her. My uncle appeared in the doorway, and my first thought (and I think the cook's also) was to get that nightgown down. The spectacle was indecent, and yet of a strange boudoir beauty that contrasted in an eerie way with that awful noise she was making, more like a howl than a scream and bearing no resemblance to sorrow. She was trying, we saw, to pull herself to her feet, to go somewhere or other, and the cook helped her up. But then, all at once, she became heavy, like a sack full of stones. The screaming stopped, and there was dead silence.

25    Eventually, I forget how, but thanks chiefly to the cook, we got her calmed down to the point where she was crying normally. Perhaps the doctor came and administered a sedative. I sat up with her, embracing her and trying to console her, and there was some-

thing sweet about this process, for it was the first time we had ever been close to each other. But all at once she would remember Rosie and shriek out her name; no one could take Rosie's place, and we both knew it. I felt like an utter outsider. It seemed clear to me that night, as I sat stroking her hair, that she had never really cared for anyone but her sister; that was her secret. The intellectual part of my mind was aware that some sort of revelation had taken place—of the nature of Jewish family feeling, possibly. And I wondered whether that fearful insensate noise had been classic Jewish mourning, going back to the waters of Babylon. Of one thing I was certain: my grandmother was more different from the rest of us than I could ever have conceived.

26　　Uncle Mose was taking it well, I learned the next morning. It was only my grandmother, so unemotional normally, who had given way to this extravagant grief, and the family, I gathered, were slightly embarrassed by her conduct, as though they, too, felt that she had revealed something, which, as far as they were concerned, would have been better left in the dark. But what *had* she revealed, as they saw it? Her essential Jewishness? I could never find out, for I had to take the train east that very day, with my baby, and when I came back several years later, no one seemed to remember anything unusual about the occasion of Aunt Rosie's death.

27　　"That's my sister," my grandmother would exclaim, eagerly pointing when we came to a photograph of Aunt Rosie. "My sister," she would say of Aunt Eva, in a somewhat grander tone. She always brightened when one of her two sisters turned up in the photograph collection, like a child when it is shown its favorite stuffed animal. I think she was a little more excited at the sight of Aunt Rosie. By that time, I imagine, she had forgotten that her sisters were dead, or, rather, the concept, death, no longer had any meaning for her; they had "gone away," she probably believed, just as children believe that this is what happens to their dead relations. I used to stand ready to prompt her with the names, but she did not seem to need or want this; her sisters' relationship to her was what mattered, and she always got that straight. "Aunt Rosie," I would observe, showing her a picture of a small, smiling, dark woman in a big marabou hat. "My sister," her voice would override me proudly, as if she were emending my statement.

28     The clothes in the old photographs amused her; she had not lost her interest in dress, and was very critical of my appearance, urging me, with impatient gestures, to pull my hair forward on my cheeks and surveying me with pride when I had done so; it gave a "softer" look. If I did not get it right, she would pull her own black waves forward, to show me what she meant. Though she could no longer go downtown, she still kept to the same schedule. Every day at twelve o'clock, the nurse would close my grandmother's door and the doors to the nursery and the bathroom, reopening them between two and three, when the beauty preparations had been completed. "You can come in now. Your grandmother is all prettied up." One afternoon, responding to the summons, I found my grandmother frowning and preoccupied. There was something the matter, and I could not make out what it was. She wanted me to get her something, the "whatchamacallit" from her bureau. I tried nearly everything—brush, comb, handkerchief, perfume, pincushion, pocketbook, photograph of my mother. All of them were wrong, and she grew more and more impatient, as if I were behaving like an imbecile. "Not the *comb*, the whachamacallit!" Finally, for she was getting quite wrought up, I rang for the nurse. "She wants something," I said. "But I can't make out what it is." The nurse glanced at the bureau top and then went swiftly over to the chiffonier; she picked up the hand mirror that was lying there and passed it silently to my grandmother, who at once began to beam and nod. "She's forgotten the word for mirror," the nurse said, winking at me. At that moment, the fact that my grandmother was senile became real to me.

## Discussion Questions

1. From the incidents McCarthy recounts, characterize her grandmother.
2. What events changed McCarthy's grandmother's attitude?
3. What accounted for the family's inhospitality?
4. Was the grandmother's grief warranted? Why or why not?
5. Why did it take so long for McCarthy to realize her grandmother was senile?

# Writing Assignments

1. Write a journal entry describing your most vivid memory of a grandparent.
2. Imagine you are McCarthy's grandmother. Write a letter to McCarthy in which you explain your seemingly antisocial behavior.
3. As McCarthy does in this essay, write an essay that examines how a significant family event affected, positively or negatively, the attitude of a family member.

# CLASSIC ESSAYS ON

# Families

# *from* *Reveries over Childhood and Youth*

## WILLIAM
## BUTLER YEATS

William Butler Yeats (1865–1939) was born in Dublin, Ireland. From 1874 until 1883, the Yeatses lived in London. Yeats began his education at the School of Art in Dublin but turned to writing at the age of twenty-one. First writing plays, including *The Countess Cathleen* (1892) and *Cathleen ni Houlihan* (1902), Yeats is most known for his poetry. His first published poem appeared in the *Dublin University Review* in 1885, and, in 1891, he became one of the founders of the Pre-Raphaelite Rhymer's Club. His volumes of poetry include *In the Seven Woods* (1904), *The Green Helmet and Other Poems* (1910), *The Tower* (1928), and *The Winding Stair* (1929). *Essays* (1924) is Yeats's collection of non-fiction, and *Essays and Introductions* (1961) was published posthumously. In 1923, he was awarded the Nobel Prize in literature for his poetry. Yeats's experiments with rhyme, his use of symbols, and his diverse styles have made him one of the greatest twentieth-century poets of the English language. In the following selection taken from *The Autobiography of William Butler Yeats* (1927), Yeats recalls his forebears, especially his grandparents.

# I

1     My first memories are fragmentary and isolated and contemporaneous, as though one remembered some first moments of the Seven Days. It seems as if time had not yet been created, for all thoughts connected with emotion and place are without sequence.

2     I remember sitting upon somebody's knee, looking out of an Irish window at a wall covered with cracked and falling plaster, but what wall I do not remember, and being told that some relation once lived there. I am looking out of a window in London. It is at Fitzroy Road. Some boys are playing in the road and among them a boy in uniform, a telegraph boy perhaps. When I ask who the boy is, a servant tells me that he is going to blow the town up, and I go to sleep in terror.

3     After that come memories of Sligo, where I live with my grandparents. I am sitting on the ground looking at a mastless toy boat with the paint rubbed and scratched, and I say to myself in great melancholy, "It is further away than it used to be," and while I am saying it I am looking at a long scratch in the stern, for it is especially the scratch which is further away. Then one day at dinner my great-uncle William Middleton says, "We should not make light of the troubles of children. They are worse than ours, because we can see the end of our trouble and they can never see any end," and I feel grateful for I know that I am very unhappy and have often said to myself, "When you grow up, never talk as grown-up people do of the happiness of childhood." I may have already had the night of misery when, having prayed for several days that I might die, I began to be afraid that I was dying and prayed that I might live. There was no reason for my unhappiness. Nobody was unkind, and my grandmother has still after so many years my gratitude and my reverence. The house was so big that there was always a room to hide in, and I had a red pony and a garden where I could wander, and there were two dogs to follow at my heels, one white with some black spots on his head and the other with long black hair all over him. I used to think about God and fancy that I was very wicked, and one day when I threw a stone and hit a duck in the yard by mischance and broke its wing, I was full of wonder when I was told that the duck would be cooked for dinner and that I should not be punished.

4     Some of my misery was loneliness and some of it fear of old William Pollexfen my grandfather. He was never unkind, and I cannot remember that he ever spoke harshly to me, but it was the custom to fear and admire him. He had won the freedom of some Spanish city, for saving life perhaps, but was so silent that his wife never knew it till he was near eighty, and then from the chance visit of some old sailor. She asked him if it was true and he said it was true, but she knew him too well to question and his old shipmate had left the town. She too had the habit of fear. We knew that he had been in many parts of the world, for there was a great scar on his hand made by a whaling-hook, and in the dining-room was a cabinet with bits of coral in it and a jar of water from the Jordan for the baptizing of his children and Chinese pictures upon rice-paper and an ivory walking-stick from India that came to me after his death. He had great physical strength and had the reputation of never ordering a man to do anything he would not do himself. He owned many sailing ships and once, when a captain just come to anchor at Rosses Point reported something wrong with the rudder, had sent a messenger to say "Send a man down to find out what's wrong." "The crew all refuse" was the answer, and to that my grandfather answered, "Go down yourself," and not being obeyed, he dived from the main deck, all the neighbourhood lined along the pebbles of the shore. He came up with his skin torn but well informed about the rudder. He had a violent temper and kept a hatchet at his bedside for burglars and would knock a man down instead of going to law, and I once saw him hunt a party of men with a horsewhip. He had no relation for he was an only child and, being solitary and silent, he had few friends. He corresponded with Campbell of Islay who had befriended him and his crew after a shipwreck, and Captain Webb, the first man who had swum the Channel and who was drowned swimming the Niagara Rapids, had been a mate in his employ and a close friend. That is all the friends I can remember and yet he was so looked up to and admired that when he returned from taking the waters at Bath his men would light bonfires along the railway line for miles; while his partner William Middleton whose father after the great famine had attended the sick for weeks, and taken cholera from a man he carried in his arms into his own house and died of it, and was himself civil to everybody and a cleverer man than my grandfather, came and went without notice.

I think I confused my grandfather with God, for I remember in one of my attacks of melancholy praying that he might punish me for my sins, and I was shocked and astonished when a daring little girl—a cousin I think—having waited under a group of trees in the avenue, where she knew he would pass near four o'clock on the way to his dinner, said to him, "If I were you and you were a little girl, I would give you a doll."

5   Yet for all my admiration and alarm, neither I nor any one else thought it wrong to outwit his violence or his rigour; and his lack of suspicion and something helpless about him made that easy while it stirred our affection. When I must have been still a very little boy, seven or eight years old perhaps, an uncle called me out of bed one night, to ride the five or six miles to Rosses Point to borrow a railway-pass from a cousin. My grandfather had one, but thought it dishonest to let another use it, but the cousin was not so particular. I was let out through a gate that opened upon a little lane beside the garden away from earshot of the house, and rode delighted through the moonlight, and awoke my cousin in the small hours by tapping on his window with a whip. I was home again by two or three in the morning and found the coachman waiting in the little lane. My grandfather would not have thought such an adventure possible, for every night at eight he believed that the stable-yard was locked, and he knew that he was brought the key. Some servant had once got into trouble at night and so he had arranged that they should all be locked in. He never knew, what everybody else in the house knew, that for all the ceremonious bringing of the key the gate was never locked.

6   Even today when I read *King Lear* his image is always before me and I often wonder if the delight in passionate men in my plays and in my poetry is more than his memory. He must have been ignorant, though I could not judge him in my childhood, for he had ran away to sea when a boy, "gone to sea through the hawsehole" as he phrased it, and I can but remember him with two books—his Bible and Falconer's *Shipwreck*, a little green-covered book that lay always upon his table; he belonged to some younger branch of an old Cornish family. His father had been in the Army, had retired to become an owner of sailing ships, and an engraving of some old family place my grandfather thought should have been his hung next a painted coat of arms in the little back parlour. His mother had

been a Wexford woman, and there was a tradition that his family had been linked with Ireland for generations and once had their share in the old Spanish trade with Galway. He had a good deal of pride and disliked his neighbours, whereas his wife, a Middleton, was gentle and patient and did many charities in the little back parlour among frieze coats and shawled heads, and every night when she saw him asleep went the round of the house alone with a candle to make certain there was no burglar in danger of the hatchet. She was a true lover of her garden, and before the care of her house had grown upon her, would choose some favourite among her flowers and copy it upon rice-paper. I saw some of her handiwork the other day and I wondered at the delicacy of form and colour and at a handling that may have needed a magnifying glass it was so minute. I can remember no other pictures but the Chinese paintings, and some coloured prints of battles in the Crimea upon the wall of a passage, and the painting of a ship at the passage end darkened by time.

7      My grown-up uncles and aunts, my grandfather's many sons and daughters, came and went, and almost all they said or did has faded from my memory, except a few harsh words that convince me by a vividness out of proportion to their harshness that all were habitually kind and considerate. The youngest of my uncles was stout and humorous and had a tongue of leather over the keyhole of his door to keep the draught out, and another whose bedroom was at the end of a long stone passage had a model turret ship in a glass case. He was a clever man and had designed the Sligo quays, but was now going mad and inventing a vessel of war that could not be sunk, his pamphlet explained, because of a hull of solid wood. Only six months ago my sister awoke dreaming that she held a wingless sea bird in her arms and presently she heard that he had died in his madhouse, for a sea bird is the omen that announces the death or danger of a Pollexfen. An uncle, George Pollexfen, afterwards astrologer and mystic, and my dear friend, came but seldom from Ballina, once to a race meeting with two postillions dressed in green; and there was that younger uncle who had sent me for the railway-pass. He was my grandmother's favourite, and had, the servants told me, been sent away from school for taking a crowbar to a bully.

8      I can only remember my grandmother punishing me once. I was playing in the kitchen and a servant in horseplay pulled my shirt out of my trousers in front just as my grandmother came in and I,

accused of I knew not what childish indecency, was given my dinner
in a room by myself. But I was always afraid of my uncles and aunts,
and once the uncle who had taken the crowbar to the bully found
me eating lunch which my grandmother had given me and reproved
me for it and made me ashamed. We breakfasted at nine and dined
at four and it was considered self-indulgent to eat anything between
meals; and once an aunt told me that I had reined in my pony and
struck it at the same moment that I might show it off as I rode
through the town, and I, because I had been accused of what I
thought a very dark crime, had a night of misery. Indeed I remember little of childhood but its pain. I have grown happier with every
year of life as though gradually conquering something in myself, for
certainly my miseries were not made by others but were a part of my
own mind.

## 2

One day some one spoke to me of the voice of the conscience,
and as I brooded over the phrase I came to think that my soul,
because I did not hear an articulate voice, was lost. I had some
wretched days until being alone with one of my aunts I heard a
whisper in my ear, "What a tease you are!" At first I thought my
aunt must have spoken, but when I found she had not, I concluded
it was the voice of my conscience and was happy again. From that
day the voice has come to me at moments of crisis, but now it is a
voice in my head that is sudden and startling. It does not tell me
what to do, but often reproves me. It will say perhaps, "That is
unjust" of some thought; and once when I complained that a prayer
had not been heard, it said, "You have been helped." I had a little
flagstaff in front of the house and a red flag with the Union Jack in
the corner. Every night I pulled my flag down and folded it up and
laid it on a shelf in my bedroom, and one morning before breakfast
I found it, though I knew I had folded it up the night before, knot-
ted round the bottom of the flagstaff so that it was touching the
grass. I must have heard the servants talking of the faeries for I concluded at once that a faery had tied those four knots and from that
on believed that one had whispered in my ear. I have been told,

though I do not remember it myself, that I saw, whether once or many times I do not know, a supernatural bird in the corner of the room. Once too I was driving with my grandmother a little after dark close to the Channel that runs for some five miles from Sligo to the sea, and my grandmother showed me the red light of an out-ward-bound steamer and told me that my grandfather was on board, and that night in my sleep I screamed out and described the steamer's wreck. The next morning my grandfather arrived on a blind horse found for him by grateful passengers. He had, as I remember the story, been asleep when the captain aroused him to say they were going on the rocks. He said, "Have you tried sail on her?" and judging from some answer that the captain was demor-alised took over the command and, when the ship could not be saved, got the crew and passengers into the boats. His own boat was upset and he saved himself and some others by swimming; some women had drifted ashore, buoyed up by their crinolines. "I was not so much afraid of the sea as of that terrible man with his oar," was the comment of a schoolmaster who was among the survivors. Eight men were, however, drowned and my grandfather suffered from that memory at intervals all his life, and if asked to read family prayers never read anything but the shipwreck of St. Paul.

10    I remember the dogs more clearly than any one except my grand-father and grandmother. The black hairy one had no tail because it had been sliced off, if I was told the truth, by a railway train. I think I followed at their heels more than they did at mine, and that their journeys ended at a rabbit-warren behind the garden; and some-times they had savage fights, the black hairy dog, being well pro-tected by its hair, suffering least. I can remember one so savage that the white dog would not take his teeth out of the black dog's hair till the coachman hung them over the side of a water-butt, one out-side and one in the water. My grandmother once told the coachman to cut the hair like a lion's hair and, after a long consultation with the stable-boy, he cut it all over the head and shoulders and left it on the lower part of the body. The dog disappeared for a few days, and I did not doubt that its heart was broken.

11    There was a large garden behind the house full of apple trees, with flower-beds and grass-plots in the centre, and two figureheads of ships, one among the strawberry plants under a wall covered with fruit trees and one among the flowers. The one among the flowers

was a white lady in flowing robes, while the other, a stalwart man in uniform, had been taken from a three-masted ship of my grandfather's called *The Russia*, and there was a belief among the servants that the stalwart man represented the Tsar and had been presented by the Tsar himself. The avenue, or as they say in England the drive, that went from the hall door through a clump of big trees to an insignificant gate and a road bordered by broken and dirty cottages, was but two or three hundred yards, and I often thought it should have been made to wind more, for I judged people's social importance mainly by the length of their avenues. This idea may have come from the stable-boy, for he was my principal friend. He had a book of Orange rhymes, and the days when we read them together in the hay-loft gave me the pleasure of rhyme for the first time. Later on I can remember being told, when there was a rumour of a Fenian rising, that rifles had been served out to the Orangemen; and presently, when I had begun to dream of my future life, I thought I would like to die fighting the Fenians. I was to build a very fast and beautiful ship and to have under my command a company of young men who were always to be in training like athletes and so become as brave and handsome as the young men in the story-books, and there was to be a big battle on the seashore near Rosses and I was to be killed. I collected little pieces of wood and piled them up in a corner of the yard, and there was an old rotten log in a distant field I often went to look at because I thought it would go a long way in the making of the ship. All my dreams were of ships; and one day a sea captain who had come to dine with my grandfather put a hand on each side of my head and lifted me up to show me Africa, and another day a sea captain pointed to the smoke from the pern mill on the quays rising up beyond the trees of the lawn, as though it came from the mountain, and asked me if Ben Bulben was a burning mountain.

12    Once every few months I used to go to Rosses Point or Ballisodare to see another little boy, who had a piebald pony that had once been in a circus and sometimes forgot where it was and went round and round. He was George Middleton, son of my great-uncle William Middleton. Old Middleton had bought land, then believed a safe investment, at Ballisodare and at Rosses, and spent the winter at Ballisodare and the summer at Rosses. The Middleton and Pollexfen flour mills were at Ballisodare, and a great salmon

weir, rapids and a waterfall, but it was more often at Rosses that I saw my cousin. We rowed in the rivermouth or were taken sailing in a heavy slow schooner yacht or in a big ship's boat that had been rigged and decked. There were great cellars under the house, for it had been a smuggler's house a hundred years before, and sometimes three loud raps would come upon the drawing-room window at sun-down, setting all the dogs barking: some dead smuggler giving his accustomed signal. One night I heard them very distinctly and my cousins often heard them, and later on my sister. A pilot had told me that, after dreaming three times of a treasure bed in my uncle's garden, he had climbed the wall in the middle of the night and begun to dig but grew disheartened "because there was so much earth." I told somebody what he had said and was told that it was well he did not find it for it was guarded by a spirit that looked like a flat iron. At Ballisodare there was a cleft among the rocks that I passed with terror because I believed that a murderous monster lived there that made a buzzing sound like a bee.

13     It was through the Middletons perhaps that I got my interest in country stories, and certainly the first faery stories that I heard were in the cottages about their houses. The Middletons took the nearest for friends and were always in and out of the cottages of pilots and of tenants. They were practical, always doing something with their hands, making boats, feeding chickens, and without ambition. One of them had designed a steamer many years before my birth and, long after I had grown to manhood, one could hear it—it had some sort of obsolete engine—many miles off wheezing in the Channel like an asthmatic person. It had been built on the lake and dragged through the town by many horses, stopping before the windows where my mother was learning her lessons, and plunging the whole school into candlelight for five days, and was still patched and repatched mainly because it was believed to be a bringer of good luck. It had been called after the betrothed of its builder *Janet*, long corrupted into the more familiar *Jennet*, and the betrothed died in my youth having passed her eightieth year and been her husband's plague because of the violence of her temper. Another Middleton who was but a year or two older than myself used to shock me by running after hens to know by their feel if they were on the point of dropping an egg. They let their houses decay and the glass fall from the windows of their greenhouses, but one among them at any rate

had the second sight. They were liked but had not the pride and reserve, the sense of decorum and order, the instinctive playing before themselves that belongs to those who strike the popular imagination.

14 Sometimes my grandmother would bring me to see some old Sligo gentlewoman whose garden ran down to the river, ending there in a low wall full of wallflowers, and I would sit up upon my chair, very bored, while my elders ate their seed-cake and drank their sherry. My walks with the servants were more interesting; sometimes we would pass a little fat girl and a servant persuaded me to write her a love letter, and the next time she passed she put her tongue out. But it was the servants' stories that interested me. At such and such a corner a man had got a shilling from a drill sergeant by standing in a barrel and had then rolled out of it and shown his crippled legs. And in such and such a house an old woman had hid herself under the bed of her guests, an officer and his wife, and on hearing them abuse her beaten them with a broomstick. All the well-known families had their grotesque or tragic or romantic legends, and I often said to myself how terrible it would be to go away and die where nobody would know my story. Years afterwards, when I was ten or twelve years old and in London, I would remember Sligo with tears, and when I began to write, it was there I hoped to find my audience. Next to Merville where I lived, was another tree-surrounded house where I sometimes went to see a little boy who stayed there occasionally with his grandmother, whose name I forget and who seemed to me kind and friendly, though when I went to see her in my thirteenth or fourteenth year I discovered that she only cared for very little boys. When the visitors called I hid in the hay-loft and lay hidden behind the great heap of hay while a servant was calling my name in the yard.

15 I do not know how old I was (for all these events seem at the same distance) when I was made drunk. I had been out yachting with an uncle and my cousins and it had come on very rough. I had lain on deck between the mast and the bowsprit and a wave had burst over me and I had seen green water over my head. I was very proud and very wet. When we got into Rosses again, I was dressed up in an older boy's clothes so that the trousers came down below my boots and a pilot gave me a little raw whiskey. I drove home on an outside car and was so pleased with the strange state in which I

found myself that for all my uncle could do, I cried to every passer-by that I was drunk, and went on crying it through the town and everywhere until I was put to bed by my grandmother and given something to drink that tasted of black currants and so fell asleep.

## Discussion Questions

1. Explain why, in the first sentence, Yeats makes the following admission: "My first memories are fragmentary and isolated and contemporaneous . . ." How does it affect your reading of the essay?
2. What accounted for Yeats's misery as a child: was his unhappiness unique, or was it the kind of unhappiness that befalls many children? Explain your answer.
3. How typical do you think it is for children to "fear and admire" their elders? Explain.
4. Why do you think Yeats "confused my [his] grandfather with God"?
5. In small groups, discuss who of all the relatives Yeats describes you find most memorable. Explain.
6. From what Yeats has described, characterize his childhood. Identify specific passages that support your response.

## Writing Assignments

1. In a journal entry, write a few "fragmentary and isolated" memories from your childhood.
2. Write an essay that describes an older relative you both feared and admired.
3. Write an essay that recounts an incident in which you outwitted an adult. Describe the circumstances of the event and your feelings about it then and now.

# On Going Home

## JOAN DIDION

Joan Didion (b. 1934), born in Sacramento, California, graduated from the University of California at Berkeley and began her writing career in 1956 at *Vogue* magazine. A prolific writer, Didion is the author of many novels, including *River Run* (1963), *Play It As It Lays* (1970), *A Book of Common Prayer* (1977), *Democracy* (1984), *Sentimental Journeys* (1993), and *Run River* (1994). Her collections of classic essays, *Slouching towards Bethlehem* (1968) and *The White Album* (1979), examine the deterioration of the American spirit since the 1960s. *Salvador* (1983) and *Miami* (1987) are journalistic accounts of two places that experienced social upheaval in the 1980s. *After Henry* (1992) reports on current events, from the 1988 presidential campaign to the case of a New York investment banker who was raped and beaten nearly to death as she jogged in Central Park. With her spouse, John Gregory Dunne, Didion wrote the screenplay for the popular movie *Up Close and Personal*. Didion's most recent publication is a novel, *The Last Thing He Wanted* (1996). Combining her journalistic skills with her interest in social commentary, Didion has earned the reputation as one of the foremost contemporary American essayists. The following essay from *Slouching towards Bethlehem* presents Didion's observations and thoughts as she returns to her childhood home to celebrate her daughter's birthday.

1    I am home for my daughter's first birthday. By "home" I do not mean the house in Los Angeles where my husband and I and the baby live, but the place where my family is, in the Central Valley of California. It is a vital although troublesome distinction. My husband likes my family but is uneasy in their house, because once there I fall into their ways, which are difficult, oblique, deliberately inarticulate, not my husband's ways. We live in dusty houses ("D-U-S-T," he once wrote with his finger on surfaces all over the house, but no one noticed it) filled with mementos quite without value to him (what could the Canton dessert plates mean to him? how could he have known about the assay scales, why should he care if he did know?), and we appear to talk exclusively about people we know who have been committed to mental hospitals, about people we know who have been booked on drunk-driving charges, and about property, particularly about property, land, price per acre and C-2 zoning and assessments and freeway access. My brother does not understand my husband's inability to perceive the advantage in the rather common real-estate transaction known as "sale-leaseback," and my husband in turn does not understand why so many of the people he hears about in my father's house have recently been committed to mental hospitals or booked on drunk-driving charges. Nor does he understand that when we talk about sale-leasebacks and right-of-way condemnations we are talking in code about the things we like best, the yellow fields and the cottonwoods and the rivers rising and falling and the mountain roads closing when the heavy snow comes in. We miss each other's points, have another drink and regard the fire. My brother refers to my husband, in his presence, as "Joan's husband." Marriage is the classic betrayal.

2    Or perhaps it is not any more. Sometimes I think that those of us who are now in our thirties were born into the last generation to carry the burden of "home," to find in family life the source of all tension and drama. I had by all objective accounts a "normal" and a "happy" family situation, and yet I was almost thirty years old before I could talk to my family on the telephone without crying after I had hung up. We did not fight. Nothing was wrong. And yet some nameless anxiety colored the emotional charges between me and the place that I came from. The question of whether or not you could go home again was a very real part of the sentimental and largely literary baggage with which we left home in the fifties; I sus-

pect that it is irrelevant to the children born of the fragmentation after World War II. A few weeks ago in a San Francisco bar I saw a pretty young girl on crystal take off her clothes and dance for the cash prize in an "amateur-topless" contest. There was no particular sense of moment about this, none of the effect of romantic degradation, of "dark journey," for which my generation strived so assiduously. What sense could that girl possibly make of, say, *Long Day's Journey into Night*? Who is beside the point?

3    That I am trapped in this particular irrelevancy is never more apparent to me than when I am home. Paralyzed by the neurotic lassitude engendered by meeting one's past at every turn, around every corner, inside every cupboard, I go aimlessly from room to room. I decide to meet it head-on and clean out a drawer, and I spread the contents on the bed. A bathing suit I wore the summer I was seventeen. A letter of rejection from *The Nation*, an aerial photograph of the site for a shopping center my father did not build in 1954. Three teacups hand-painted with cabbage roses and signed "E.M.," my grandmother's initials. There is no final solution for letters of rejection from *The Nation* and teacups hand-painted in 1900. Nor is there any answer to snapshots of one's grandfather as a young man on skis, surveying around Donner Pass in the year 1910. I smooth out the snapshot and look into his face, and do not see my own. I close the drawer, and have another cup of coffee with my mother. We get along very well, veterans of a guerrilla war we never understood.

4    Days pass. I see no one. I come to dread my husband's evening call, not only because he is full of news of what by now seems to me our remote life in Los Angeles, people he has seen, letters which require attention, but because he asks what I have been doing, suggests uneasily that I get out, drive to San Francisco or Berkeley. Instead I drive across the river to a family graveyard. It has been vandalized since my last visit and the monuments are broken, overturned in the dry grass. Because I once saw a rattlesnake in the grass I stay in the car and listen to a country-and-Western station. Later I drive with my father to a ranch he has in the foothills. The man who runs his cattle on it asks us to the roundup, a week from Sunday, and although I know that I will be in Los Angeles I say, in the oblique way my family talks, that I will come. Once home I mention the broken monuments in the graveyard. My mother shrugs.

5    I go to visit my great-aunts. A few of them think now that I am my cousin, or their daughter who died young. We recall an anecdote about a relative last seen in 1948, and they ask if I still like living in New York City. I have lived in Los Angeles for three years, but I say that I do. The baby is offered a horehound drop, and I am slipped a dollar bill "to buy a treat." Questions trail off, answers are abandoned, the baby plays with the dust motes in a shaft of afternoon sun.

6    It is time for the baby's birthday party: a white cake, strawberry-marshmallow ice cream, a bottle of champagne saved from another party. In the evening, after she has gone to sleep, I kneel beside the crib and touch her face, where it is pressed against the slats, with mine. She is an open and trusting child, unprepared for and unaccustomed to the ambushes of family life, and perhaps it is just as well that I can offer her little of that life. I would like to give her more. I would like to promise her that she will grow up with a sense of her cousins and of rivers and of her great-grandmother's teacups, would like to pledge her a picnic on a river with fried chicken and her hair uncombed, would like to give her *home* for her birthday, but we live differently now and I can promise her nothing like that. I give her a xylophone and a sundress from Madeira, and promise to tell her a funny story.

# Discussion Questions

1. Why does Didion call the distinction she makes regarding the word *home* "vital although troublesome"?
2. Characterize Didion from her observations and reflections on returning to the home where she grew up.
3. Why do you think Didion was almost thirty before she could telephone her family without crying?
4. Why is Didion unable to promise her daughter those things she lists in the last paragraph?
5. What would Didion's family say about Didion's observations?
6. What does Didion mean in paragraph 6 when she states, ". . . we live differently now"?
7. In small groups, discuss whether the homecoming Didion describes is typical of most families.

# Writing Assignments

1. Write a journal entry in which you define *home*. Explain how you arrived at the definition.
2. Write an essay exploring the reasons people have difficulties returning to their childhood homes.
3. Support or refute the idea reflected in the title of Thomas Wolfe's famous novel *You Can't Go Home Again*.

# For My American Family

## JUNE JORDAN

June Jordan (b. 1936) was born in Harlem and raised in the Bedford-Stuyvesant area of Brooklyn. Educated in largely white public and private schools, Jordan was trained as a city planner. Having taught at many universities, she is currently a professor of Afro-American studies and women's studies at the University of California at Berkeley. A poet, biographer, playwright, essayist, and political activist, Jordan writes a regular column for *The Progressive*. She is the author of *Who Look at Me* (1969), *Some Changes* (1971), *His Own Where* (1971), *New Days: Poems of Exile and Return* (1974), *New Life: New Room* (1975), *Passion: New Poems 1977–1980* (1980), *Civil Wars* (1981), *Living Room* (1985), *On Call* (1985), *Naming Our Destiny* (1989), and *Technical Difficulties* (1992). Jordan is the recipient of numerous awards, including a Rockefeller grant in creative writing, a Prix de Rome in environmental design, a Creative Artist in Public Service grant in creative writing, and an NEA fellowship. Jordan's work reflects her interest in issues involving women and African Americans. The following essay originally appeared in the July 6, 1986 issue of the New York newspaper *Newsday* and is also included in *Technical Difficulties*. The selection is, as the title claims, a tribute to her family, in which Jordan thanks them and the United States for her becoming all that she currently is.

1     I would love to see pictures of the Statue of Liberty taken by my father. They would tell me so much about him that I wish I knew. He couldn't very well ask that lady to "hold that smile" or "put on a little something with red to brighten it up." He'd have to take her "as is," using a choice of angles or focus or distance as a means to his statement. And I imagine that my father would choose a long-shot, soft-focus, wide-angle lens: that would place Miss Liberty in her full formal setting, and yet suggest the tears that easily spilled from his eyes whenever he spoke about "this great country of ours: America."

2     A camera buff, not averse to wandering around the city with both a Rolleiflex and a Rolleicord at the ready, my father thought nothing of a two or three hours' "setup" for a couple of shots of anything he found beautiful. I remember one Saturday, late morning, when I watched my father push the "best" table in the house under the dining-room windows, fidget the venetian blinds in order to gain the most interesting, slatted light, and then bring the antique Chinese vase downstairs from the parlor, fill that with fresh roses from the backyard, and then run out to the corner store for several pieces of fruit to complete his still-life composition.

3     All of this took place in the 1940s. We lived in the Bedford-Stuyvesant neighborhood of Brooklyn, one of the largest urban Black communities in the world. Besides the fruit and the flowers of my father's aesthetic preoccupation, and just beyond those narrow brownstone dining-room windows, there was a burly mix of unpredictable street life that he could not control, despite incessant telephone calls, for example, to the Department of Sanitation: "Hello. This is a man by the name of Granville Ivanhoe Jordan, and I'm calling about garbage collection. What happened? Did you forget?!"

4     The unlikely elements of my father's name may summarize his history and character rather well. Jordan is a fairly common surname on the island of Jamaica where he was born, one of perhaps twelve or thirteen children who foraged for food, and who never forgot, or forgave, the ridicule his ragged clothing provoked in school. Leaving the classroom long before the normal conclusion to an elementary education, my father later taught himself to read and, after that, he never stopped reading and reading everything he could find, from Burpee seed catalogues to Shakespeare to the *National Geographic* magazines to "Negro" poetry to liner notes for the record albums of classical music that he devoured. But he was also

"the little bull"—someone who loved a good rough fight and who even volunteered to teach boxing to other young "Negroes" at the Harlem YMCA, where he frequently participated in political and militant "uplifting-the-race" meetings, on West 135th Street.

5     Except for weekends, my father pursued all of his studies in the long early hours of the night, 3 or 4 a.m., after eight hours' standing up at the post office where he speed-sorted mail quite without the assistance of computers and zip codes which, of course, had yet to be invented. Exceptionally handsome and exceptionally vain, Mr. G. I. Jordan, immaculate in one of his innumerable, rooster-elegant suits, would readily hack open a coconut with a machete, or slice a grapefruit in half, throw his head back, and squeeze the juice into his mouth—carefully held a tricky foot away—all to my mother's headshaking dismay: "Why now you have to act up like a monkey chaser, eh?"

6     It is a sad thing to consider that this country has given its least to those who have loved it the most. I am the daughter of West Indian immigrants. And perhaps there are other Americans as believing and as grateful and as loyal, but I doubt it. In general, the very word *immigrant* connotes somebody white, while *alien* denotes everybody else. But hundreds and hundreds of thousands of Americans are hardworking, naturalized Black citizens whose trust in the democratic promise of the mainland has never been reckoned with, fully, or truly reciprocated. For instance, I know that my parents would have wanted to say, "Thanks, America!" if only there had been some way, some public recognition and welcome of their presence, here, and then some really big shot to whom their gratitude might matter.

7     I have seen family snapshots of my mother pushing me in a baby carriage decorated with the single decal F.D.R., and I have listened to endless tall stories about what I did or didn't do when my father placed me in the lap of New York's mayor, Fiorello La Guardia, and, on top of the ornate wallpaper of our parlor floor there was a large color photograph of the archbishop of the Episcopal diocese of Long Island; my parents lived in America, full of faith.

8     When I visited the birthplace of my mother, twelve years ago, I was embarrassed by the shiny rented car that brought me there: even in 1974, there were no paved roads in Clonmel, a delicate dot of a mountain village in Jamaica. And despite the breathtaking altitude, you could not poke or peer yourself into a decent position for "a

view": the vegetation was that dense, that lush, and that chaotic. On or close to the site of my mother's childhood home, I found a neat wood cabin, still without windowpanes or screens, a dirt floor, and a barefoot family of seven, quietly bustling about.

9  I was stunned. There was neither electricity nor running water. How did my parents even hear about America, more than a half century ago? In the middle of the Roaring Twenties, these eager Black immigrants came, by boat. Did they have to borrow shoes for the journey?

10  I know that my aunt and my mother buckled into domestic work, once they arrived, barely into their teens. I'm not sure how my father managed to feed himself before that fantastic 1933 afternoon when he simply ran all the way from midtown Manhattan up to our Harlem apartment, shouting out the news: A job! He had found a job!

11  And throughout my childhood I cannot recall even one utterance of disappointment, or bitterness with America. In fact, my parents hid away any newspaper or magazine article that dealt with "jim crow" or "lynchings" or "discrimination." These were terms of taboo status neither to be spoken nor explained to me. Instead I was given a child's biography of Abraham Lincoln and the Bible stories of Daniel and David, and, from my father, I learned about Marcus Garvey and George Washington Carver and Mary McLeod Bethune. The focus was relentlessly upbeat. Or, as Jimmy Cliff used to sing it, "You can make it if you really try."

12  My mother's emphasis was more religious, and more consistently race-conscious, and she was equally affirmative: God would take care of me. And, besides, there was ("C'mon, Joe! C'mon!") the Brown Bomber, Joe Louis, and then, incredibly, Jackie Robinson who, by himself, elevated the Brooklyn Dodgers into a sacred cult worshipped by apparently dauntless Black baseball fans.

13  We had a pretty rich life. Towards the end of the 1960s I was often amazed by facile references to Black communities as "breeding grounds of despair" or "culturally deprived" or "ghettos." That was not the truth. There are grounds for despair in the suburbs, evidently, and I more than suspect greater cultural deprivation in economically and racially and socially homogeneous Long Island commuter towns than anything I ever had to overcome!

14  In Bedford-Stuyvesant, I learned all about white history and white literature, but I lived and learned about my own, as well. My

father marched me to the American Museum of Natural History and to the Planetarium, at least twice a month, while my mother picked up "the slack" by riding me, by trolley car, to public libraries progressively farther and farther away from our house. In the meantime, on our own block of Hancock Street, between Reid and Patchen avenues, we had rice and peas and curried lamb or, upstairs, in my aunt and uncle's apartment, pigs' feet and greens. On the piano in the parlor there was boogie-woogie, blues, and Chopin. Across the street, there were cold-water flats that included the Gumbs family or, more precisely, Donnie Gumbs, whom I saw as the inarguable paragon of masculine cute. There were "American Negroes," and "West Indians." Some rented their housing, and some were buying their homes. There were Baptists, Holy Rollers, and Episcopalians, side by side.

15  On that same one block, Father Coleman, the minister of our church, lived and worked as the first Black man on New York's Board of Higher Education. There was Mrs. Taylor, whose music studio was actually a torture chamber into which many of us were forced for piano lessons. And a Black policeman. And a mail carrier. And a doctor. And my beloved Uncle Teddy, with a Doctor of Law degree from Fordham University. And the tiny, exquisite arrow of my aunt, who became one of the first Black principals in the entire New York City public school system. And my mother, who had been president of the first Black class to graduate from the Lincoln School of Nursing, and my father, who earned the traditional gold watch as a retiring civil servant, and Nat King Cole and calypso and boyfriends and Sunday School and confirmation and choir and stickball and roller skates and handmade wooden scooters and marbles and make-believe tea parties and I cannot recall feeling underprivileged, or bored, in that "ghetto."

16  And from such "breeding grounds of despair," Negro men volunteered in droves, for active duty in an army that did not want or honor them. And from such "limited" communities, Negro women, such as my mother, left their homes in every kind of weather, and at any hour, to tend to the ailing and heal the sick, regardless of their color, or ethnicity. And in such a "culturally deprived" house as that modest home created by my parents, I became an American poet.

17  And in the name of my mother and my father, I want to say thanks to America. And I want something more:

18    My aunt has survived the deaths of her husband and my parents in typical, if I may so, West Indian fashion. Now in her seventies, and no longer principal of a New York City public school, she rises at 5 a.m., every morning, to prepare for another day of complicated duties as the volunteer principal of a small Black private academy. In the front yard of her home in the Crown Heights section of Brooklyn, the tulips and buttercups have begun to bloom already. Soon every passerby will see her azaleas and jonquils and irises blossoming under the Japanese maple tree and around the base of the Colorado blue spruce.

19    She is in her seventies, and she tells me:

> I love the United States and I always will uphold it as a place of opportunity. This is not to say that you won't meet prejudice along the way but it's up to you to overcome it. And it can be overcome!

20    Well, I think back to Clonmel, Jamaica, and I visualize my aunt skipping along the goat tracks, fast as she can, before the darkness under the banana tree leaves becomes too scary for a nine-year-old. Or I think about her, struggling to fetch water from the river, in a pail. And I jump-cut to Orange High School, New Jersey, U.S.A., where my aunt maintained a 95 average, despite her extracurricular activities as a domestic, and where she was denied the valedictory because, as the English teacher declared, "You have an accent that the parents will not understand." And I stay quiet as my aunt explains, "I could have let that bother me, but I said, 'Naw, I'm not gone let this keep me down!'"

21    And what I want is to uphold this America, this beckoning and this shelter provided by my parents and my aunt. I want to say thank you to them, my faithful American family.


## Discussion Questions

1. Why does Jordan begin her essay with a lengthy discussion of her father, especially his interest in photography?

2. Explain the symbolism of the Statue of Liberty in Jordan's essay.
3. Characterize Jordan, her father, and her mother.
4. In paragraph 15, Jordan uses a series of fragments beginning with the word *and*. Why do you think Jordan presented the list in such a fashion?
5. In small groups, discuss why Jordan wants to thank the United States.
6. To what extent is Jordan's family different from other American families? Explain your answer.
7. What does Jordan mean when she states in paragraph 21, "And what I want is to uphold this America . . ."? What, exactly, does *this* refer to?

# Writing Assignments

1. In a journal entry, write how Jordan's father and mother would react to her essay.
2. Write an essay in which you pay tribute to your family.
3. In an essay, explore to what extent children are the product of their family heritage or their environment.

# Extended vs. Nuclear Families

## CAROL BLY

Carol Bly (b. 1930) was born in Minnesota. She earned her B.A. from Wellesley College and did graduate study at the University of Minnesota. Bly was the comanager of the magazines *The Fifties, The Sixties,* and *The Seventies.* She has also taught at Carleton College, Mankato State University, University of Wisconsin, University of Minnesota, Syracuse University, Indiana University, University of Iowa, and University of Delaware. Bly has been awarded a Minnesota State Arts Board grant, a Bush Foundation fellowship, and a Friends of American Writers award. In 1992, Northland College honored her with a Doctor of Humane Letters degree. She is the author of *Letters from the Country* (1981), in which the following selection appears; *Backbone: Short Stories by Carol Bly* (1985); *Bad Government and Silly Literature* (1986); *The Passionate, Accurate Story* (1990); *The Tomcat's Wife and Other Stories* (1991); and *Changing the Bully Who Rules the World* (1996). Her short stories have also appeared in such publications as *The New Yorker, American Review*, and *Ploughshares.* Bly addresses a timely topic in the following selection that compares and contrasts extended families and nuclear families.

274

1    I have been thinking about the positive side of a Minnesota blizzard. Another of the blessings is that extended-family occasions come to a halt. Thank goodness. The extended-family dinner is a threat to the pleasure and ease of the American farm family, yet it is hard to say so. In Minnesota we are great protectors of the American family—just as we are one of the last areas in which the small "family farm" idea works and is sacred. We are right about this. The nuclear family is far the best of all the units human beings organize themselves into; when you break it down, its members inevitably pursue lesser, not greater, aims. They settle for cheaper values. Jung says that, when the family breaks, the adult members tend to be frozen at the level of consciousness at the moment of the break. On a less subtle level, people begin following their own noses with more abandon. Experiment takes the place of solid satisfaction; satisfaction takes the place of thinking hard.

2    In the country, *family* means father, mother, children, and the grandparents; *extended family* would mean all the above plus the cousins, the uncles, the grownup in-laws on a lot of sides. These relations tend still to be living near one another, and often a farm couple's first five or six Christmases together will be spent in their presence.

3    The extended-family goals are not the nuclear-family goals; what nourishes extended-family society is starvation fare for the nuclear family. Here is how it works. If people are eccentric and verbal and curious about other lifestyles, then the extended-family dinner plus afternoon plus supper plus afterward is a cheerful, messy, engaging, affectionate business even when it does drag on all day (as it always does). But if people are shy or harassed or not perfectly confident about their accomplishments, then the extended-family holiday is informed by some misery along with the Jell-O and fruit and Rice Krispie bars.

4    My suspicion is that prairie families have been ruing these large, hearty, 100 percent threatening occasions for over a century now, but no one dares say anything because it sounds mean—and it does sound awfully mean to say you don't want the whole family back over this year. If you took a poll with promise of utter secrecy I feel sure the vote would be 98 percent: We Should Have Gathered only two times instead of four times this year because I was never so tense or bored in my life, and 2 percent: Well, Merv and LaVonne had them last year, so we figured it was up to us to have them all this

year. Such remarks never get made aloud, however, because our general cultural stance in the countryside is that we wish people "neighbored" more, the way they used to, and we wish families were sticking together more, the way they used to. Who can imagine Laura Ingalls Wilder wishing the folks were not all going to show up? In other words, we are torn about this.

5    I will describe what works badly in big family occasions. Unlike lions and dogs, we are a dissenting animal. We need to dissent in the same way that we need to travel, to make money, to keep a record of our time on earth and in dream, and to leave a permanent mark. Dissension is a drive, like those drives. Our greatest thinkers, the only ones that do us much good, are the dissenters. (It is the toneless lemmings who keep proffering "sharing" and "affirmation.") Orwell and Tolstoy and Jesus and Rachel Carson and Socrates don't suggest we "share" or "affirm" values. They all beg us to use the part of us that dissents. It is the part that shouts "This is frightful! I want to think about it! I want the frightfulness to sift, leisurely, through me, so I've got the feel of it! Then—and not until then—I'll try to act!"

6    For that kind of thinking and feeling we need gravity. We need a chance to be slow, turbid, and grave. Nothing could be worse for this than to be desperately busy all week, week in, week out, at hard physical work and then have a whole valuable, holy holiday taken up by an extended-family occasion. There is little chance to talk about anything. If one says, "Well, the Farmers Union has an interesting project on hand—they're bringing the humanities to nontraditional audiences," a responsible hostess is likely to respond: "Oh—if you're going to talk politics then . . ." And if one says, "You know, I often wonder what happens in that bourn from which no traveller returns—you know? I mean, what dreams'll come when we've shuffled off etc?" a responsible hostess might say, "Oh, for morbid . . ." I don't know why it is that in large family gatherings it is morbid to discuss life after death, whereas it is good, workable smalltalk to discuss accidents involving young fathers and bailing-wire winders on their tractors, or the mutilation of cattle by some occult group.

7    Lions are a more suitable animal for extended-family gatherings than country people. Their time isn't valuable, for one thing. No animal spends less of its time gathering food or contriving shelter than the African lion; no animal spends more of its time in prides (extended-faily excursions), flat on its back napping, paws sticking up.

8    The traditional weapon against time wasting by the extended family was the nineteenth- and twentieth-century prep, or public, school. School was valued as a higher loyalty than the family. Honoring family was a given; a sign of growing up was to have a school to honor. Country was to follow. The loyalty that would have made the young person sit around and nod politely throughout Thanksgiving, Christmas, and New Year's Day, to the cheer of Aunt LaVonne and Uncle Merv, went instead to the school, or to the Army. At its worst, this evolved loyalty went to the school tie and ended there. At its best, I suppose, it went to the eternal communion of writers and their audiences—to whoever made us shout at first reading of him or her, "That's it!" School or army are assumed to be higher loyalties; it is acceptable to rise from a foundering dinner of turkey with "Sorry, people, but I've an exam to study for! Wish I hadn't!" or "Sorry, people, I have to pack, I'm supposed to be at Fort Bragg tomorrow!" whereas it doesn't work the other way round: no one writes Headmaster Sizer that they'll be back at Andover a few days late because Merv and LaVonne and their kids are here from Colorado Springs. And apparently guardhouses and brigs are kept in business by people who try on such explanations in the armed services.

9    A drawback to Midwest rural life has been our serious need to "neighbor," which has locked us into rather more of the extended-family social life than is good for us. We feel torn about this: there was something great in the coming and going of neighbors from pioneer times right up to World War II. Yet it is a terrific relief not to have these invasions—which tend to last for hours. And so we have developed some minor, peripheral social occasions which very few city people could guess at. On Sunday mornings, a couple of men spend an hour parked in one of their snow-cleared farmyards. A farmer drives his heated pickup over to the neighbor's farmyard, and waits for his friend to out and join him in the cab. They sit there for a while, warmed by the heater, listening to the calm engine. They don't want the house; the house is given over to the conventional things—preparation of Sunday dinner, going to Sunday school. They sit with some beer in the pickup. It is very important, because they are outside convention and also free of work. Another place like that, at another season, is the unused stall of the 4-H buildings at the county fair. Somehow people have found a few

straw bales left, and skewed them around into a circle, and they can really talk. In the next stall the heavy Hereford stands; just looking at him you can tell it isn't enough to be *of nature*. We were meant to work out ideas. The city person who retires to country life hasn't the problem of the regular country resident: his situation is free of extended family. No one expects him to show up for New Year's Day dinner and then stay all the afternoon and then eat leftover turkey.

10    There are conversations that can kill:

> "Ja, you can sure tell there's more snow coming from where that came from."

> or

> "You're a lot safer in a jet than you are on U.S. 212 I don't care what they say."

11    The problem with the above remarks is not that they're untrue or dull: it is that one can't reply, "To tell you the truth, I think I'm on the other side of that one." It is impossible to dissent.

12    Why all the fuss about dissenting? Educators, beginning with Piaget, I think, tell us firmly that the mind literally is *changed*, evolved, by the act of conceiving a new idea. It's no longer the same mind. We all need to have this experience; so apparently we need hours and hours of conceptualizing. We have finally got it through our heads, too, that what one class of people needs, all the classes of people have a right to. It isn't just Beethoven who needs silence and gravity: it's all of us. And that means, especially for most of us who are madly moonlighting to make enough money, that it is cruel to waste our precious winter holidays with structured family gatherings.

13    The true good of blizzards is that Mervin and LaVonne get to stay in Colorado Springs and we get to stay at home without them. The schoolbus can't get through, so the children are home. No one can get out to work, so the adults are home. There is no conventional structure for nuclear-family-behavior-during-blizzards, so we face one another with delight and surprise. Anything gets said. The

closeness, as the wind screams around the light pole and builds up its incredible drifts, which later we will tunnel, is absolutely lovely. If whoever of us, like Hamlet, should now wonder aloud how it is without the mortal coil, no one need kill that with "Oh, for morbid!" because the house is full of confidence. Dozens of times I've heard farm men and women mention how cozy it was during the storm—"We did whatever we liked; we talked a lot."

14 Most people have to worry about money most of the time, and then the relations dictate the holiday agenda. There is a lot of conscience in rural Minnesota, too. We stick by the cousins and uncles. So it is wonderful when the blizzards come and set us into an extraordinary situation.

15 Puritans need the extraordinary situation.

# Discussion Questions

1. What is Bly's thesis in this essay?
2. In small groups, discuss the support Bly offers for her position. Which reasons do you find convincing and which are less believable?
3. Describe with examples the tone Bly uses.
4. To what extent do Bly's references to the Midwest strengthen or weaken her argument? Explain your answer.
5. Do you think Bly's comparison of lions and dogs to humans is apt? Why or why not?
6. Explain what Bly means in the last sentence of the essay.

# Writing Assignments

1. In a paper, analyze the strengths and liabilities of nuclear and extended families, explaining why you prefer one kind of family to the other.
2. Write a paper that argues the opposite stance of Bly's essay.
3. In an essay, discuss how other writers in this book might respond to Bly's essay.

# Like Mexicans

## GARY SOTO

Gary Soto (b. 1952) was born in Fresno, California. He earned his B.A. from California State University, Fresno, in 1974 and his M.F.A. from the University of California, Irvine, in 1976. A Mexican American poet and fiction writer, Soto is the author of *The Elements of San Joaquin* (1977), for which he received the United States Award of the International Poetry Forum; *The Tale of Sunlight* (1978), which was nominated for the Pulitzer Prize and the National Book Award; *Father Is a Pillow Tied to a Broom* (1980); *Where Sparrows Work Hard* (1981); *Black Hair* (1985); *Baseball in April and Other Stories* (1990); *A Summer Life* (1990); *Home Course in Religion: New Poems* (1991); *Pacific Crossing* (1992); and *Crazy Weekend* (1992). His books of essays are *Living Up the Street: Narrative Recollections* (1985), which won the American Book Award; *Lesser Evils: Ten Quartets* (1988); and *Small Faces* (1986). In the following essay from *Small Faces*, Soto recalls the advice his grandmother gave him about whom he should marry and the input from his family members that also influenced his life.

1 My grandmother gave me bad advice and good advice when I was in my early teens. For the bad advice, she said that I should become a barber because they made good money and listened to the radio all day. "Honey, they don't work como burros," she would say every time I visited her. She made the sound of donkeys braying. "Like

that, honey!" For the good advice, she said that I should marry a Mexican girl. "No Okies, hijo"—she would say—"Look my son. He marry one and they fight every day about I don't know what and I don't know what." For her, everyone who wasn't Mexican, black, or Asian were Okies. The French were Okies, the Italians in suits were Okies. When I asked about Jews, whom I had read about, she asked for a picture. I rode home on my bicycle and returned with a calendar depicting the important races of the world. "Pues si, son Okies tambien!" she said, nodding her head. She saved the calendar away and we went to the living room where she lectured me on the virtues of the Mexican girl: first, she could cook and, second, she acted like a woman, not a man, in her husband's home. She said she would tell me about a third when I got a little older.

2    I asked my mother about it—becoming a barber and marrying Mexican. She was in the kitchen. Steam curled from a pot of boiling beans, the radio was on, looking as squat as a loaf of bread. "Well, if you want to be a barber—they say they make good money." She slapped a round steak with a knife, her glasses slipping down with each strike. She stopped and looked up. "If you find a good Mexican girl, marry her of course." She returned to slapping the meat and I went to the backyard where my brother and David King were sitting on the lawn feeling the inside of their cheeks.

3    I ignored them and climbed the back fence to see my best friend, Scott, a second-generation Okie. I called him and his mother pointed to the side of the house where his bedroom was a small aluminum trailer, the kind you gawk at when they're flipped over on the freeway, wheels spinning in the air. I went around to find Scott pitching horseshoes.

4    I picked up a set of rusty ones and joined him. While we played, we talked about school and friends and record albums. The horseshoes scuffed up dirt, sometimes ringing the iron that threw out a meager shadow like a sundial. After three argued-over games, we pulled two oranges apiece from his tree and started down the alley still talking school and friends and record albums. We pulled more oranges from the alley and talked about who we would marry. "No offense, Scott," I said with an orange slice in my mouth, "but I would never marry an Okie." We walked in step, almost touching, with a sled of shadows dragging behind us. "No offense, Gary," Scott said, "but I would *never* marry a Mexican." I looked at him: a

fang of orange slice showed from his munching mouth. I didn't
think anything of it. He had his girl and I had mine. But our sev-
enth-grade vision was the same: to marry, get jobs, buy cars and
maybe a house if we had money left over.

5   We talked about our future lives until, to our surprise, we were on
the downtown mall, two miles from home. We bought a bag of popcorn at Penneys and sat on a bench near the fountain watching
Mexican and Okie girls pass. "That one's mine," I pointed with my
chin when a girl with eyebrows arched into black rainbows ambled
by. "She's cute," Scott said about a girl with yellow hair and a
mouthful of gum. We dreamed aloud, our chins busy pointing out
girls. We agreed that we couldn't wait to become men and lift them
onto our laps.

6   But the woman I married was not Mexican but Japanese. It was a
surprise to me. For years, I went about wide-eyed in my search for
the brown girl in a white dress at a dance. I searched the playground
at the baseball diamond. When the girls raced for grounders, their
hair bounced like something that couldn't be caught. When they sat
together in the lunchroom, heads pressed together, I knew they
were talking about us Mexican guys. I saw them and dreamed them.
I threw my face into my pillow, making up sentences that were good
as in the movies.

7   But when I was twenty, I fell in love with this other girl who worried my mother, who had my grandmother asking once again to see
the calendar of the Important Races of the World. I told her I had
thrown it away years before. I took a much-glanced-at snapshot
from my wallet. We looked at it together, in silence. Then grandma
reclined in her chair, lit a cigarette, and said, "Es pretty." She blew
and asked with all her worry pushed up to her forehead: "Chinese?"

8   I was in love and there was no looking back. She was the one. I
told my mother who was slapping hamburger into patties. "Well,
sure if you want to marry her," she said. But the more I talked, the
more concerned she became. Later I began to worry. Was it all a
mistake? "Marry a Mexican girl," I heard my mother say in my
mind. I heard it at breakfast. I heard it over math problems, between
Western Civilization and cultural geography. But then one afternoon while I was hitchhiking home from school, it struck me like a
baseball in the back: my mother wanted me to marry someone of my

own social class—a poor girl. I considered my fiancee, Carolyn, and she didn't look poor, though I knew she came from a family of farm workers and pull-yourself-up-by-your-bootstraps ranchers. I asked my brother, who was marrying Mexican poor that fall, if I should marry a poor girl. He screamed "Yeah" above his terrible guitar playing in his bedroom. I considered my sister who had married Mexican. Cousins were dating Mexican. Uncles were remarrying poor women. I asked Scott, who was still my best friend, and he said, "She's too good for you, so you better not."

9        I worried about it until Carolyn took me home to meet her parents. We drove in her Plymouth until the houses gave way to farms and ranches and finally her house fifty feet from the highway. When we pulled into the drive, I panicked and begged Carolyn to make a U-turn and go back so we could talk about it over a soda. She pinched my cheek, calling me a "silly boy." I felt better, though, when I got out of the car and saw the house: the chipped paint, a cracked window, boards for a walk to the back door. There were rusting cars near the barn. A tractor with a net of spiderwebs under a mulberry. A field. A bale of barbed wire like children's scribbling leaning against an empty chicken coop. Carolyn took my hand and pulled me to my future mother-in-law who was coming out to greet us.

10       We had lunch: sandwiches, potato chips, and iced tea. Carolyn and her mother talked mostly about neighbors and the congregation at the Japanese Methodist Church in West Fresno. Her father, who was in khaki work clothes, excused himself with a wave that was almost a salute and went outside. I heard a truck start, a dog bark, and then the truck rattle away.

11       Carolyn's mother offered another sandwich, but I declined with a shake of my head and a smile. I looked around when I could, when I was not saying over and over that I was a college student, hinting that I could take care of her daughter. I shifted my chair. I saw newspapers piled in corners, dusty cereal boxes and vinegar bottles in corners. The wallpaper was bubbled from rain that had come in from a bad roof. Dust. Dust lay on lamp shades and window sills. These people are just like Mexicans, I thought. Poor people.

12       Carolyn's mother asked me through Carolyn if I would like a *sushi*. A plate of black and white things were held in front of me. I

took one, wide-eyed, and turned it over like a foreign coin. I was biting into one when I saw a kitten crawl up the window screen over the sink. I chewed and the kitten opened its mouth of terror as she crawled higher, wanting in to paw the leftovers from our plates. I looked at Carolyn who said that the cat was just showing off. I looked up in time to see it fall. It crawled up, then fell again.

13    We talked for an hour and had apple pie and coffee, slowly. Finally, we got up with Carolyn taking my hand. Slightly embarrassed, I tried to pull away but her grip held me. I let her have her way as she led me down the hallway with her mother right behind me. When I opened the door, I was startled by a kitten clinging to the screen door, its mouth screaming "cat food, dog biscuits, *sushi. . . .*" I opened the door and the kitten, still holding on, whined in the language of hungry animals. When I got into Carolyn's car, I looked back: the, cat was still clinging. I asked Carolyn if it were possibly hungry, but she said the cat was being silly. She started the car, waved to her mother, and bounced us over the rain-poked drive, patting my thigh for being her lover baby. Carolyn waved again. I looked back, waving, then gawking at a window screen where there were now three kittens clawing and screaming to get in. Like Mexicans, I thought. I remembered the Molinas and how the cats clung to their screens—cats they shot down with squirt guns. On the highway, I felt happy, pleased by it all. I patted Carolyn's thigh. Her people were like Mexicans, only different.

# Discussion Questions

1. How well does Soto describe his relatives and friends? Explain.
2. Explain why it was important to Soto to know his family's and friends' views on marrying within or outside of one's own race.
3. What is the significance of Soto's showing his grandmother the calendar of the Important Races of the World?
4. Explain your understanding of the last line of the essay.
5. What does Soto accomplish using a narrative instead of a more formal argument to make his point?
6. In small groups, discuss whether Soto's mother and grandmother were prejudiced.

# Writing Assignments

1. Write a journal entry in which you describe some good and bad advice your grandmother or grandfather once gave you.
2. In a paper, explore the pros and cons of interracial marriages.
3. Write a paper arguing whether people would be less prejudiced if there were more interracial marriages.

# The Family That Stretches (Together)

## ELLEN GOODMAN

Ellen Goodman (b. 1941) was born in Boston, Massachusetts, and graduated from Radcliffe College in 1963. She worked as a researcher and reporter at *Newsweek* magazine before becoming a feature writer at the *Detroit Free Press.* In 1968, Goodman was named New England Newspaper Woman of the Year by the New England Press Association; she received a Neiman fellow at Harvard University from 1973–74, a media award from the Massachusetts Commission on the Status of Women in 1974, a distinguished writing award from the American Society of Newspaper Editors in 1980, and a Pulitzer Prize for commentary in 1980. Goodman is currently the "At Large" columnist for the *Boston Globe.* Her popular and highly acclaimed columns are compiled in four volumes: *Turning Points* (1979), *At Large* (1981), *Keeping in Touch* (1985), and *Making Sense* (1989). In the following essay from *Keeping in Touch,* representative of the personal and relaxed style of her journalistic essays, Goodman discusses some of the issues the modern family faces.

1    Casco Bay, Maine—the girl is spending the summer with her extended family. She doesn't put it this way. But as we talk on the beach, the ten-year-old lists the people who are sharing the same house this month with the careful attention of a genealogist.

2    First of all there is her father—visitation rights awarded him the month of August. Second of all there is her father's second wife and two children by her first marriage. All that seems perfectly clear. A stepmother and two stepbrothers.

3    Then there are the others, she slowly explains. There is her step-mother's sister for example. The girl isn't entirely sure whether this makes the woman a stepaunt, or whether her baby is a stepcousin. Beyond that, the real puzzle is whether her stepaunt's husband's children by his first marriage have any sort of official relationship to her at all. It does, we both agree, seem a bit fuzzy.

4    Nevertheless, she concludes, with a certainty that can only be mustered by the sort of ten-year-old who keeps track of her own Frequent Flier coupons, "We are in the same family." With that she closes the subject and focuses instead on her peanut butter and jelly.

5    I am left to my thoughts. My companion, in her own unselfconscious way, is a fine researcher. She grasps the wide new family configurations that are neglected by census data takers and social scientists.

6    After all, those of us who grew up in traditional settings remember families which extended into elaborate circles of aunts, uncles, and cousins. There were sides to this family, names and titles to be memorized. But they fit together in a biological pattern.

7    Now, as my young friend can attest, we have fewer children and more divorces. We know that as many as 50 percent of recent marriages may end. About 75 percent of divorced women and 83 percent of divorced men then remarry. Of those marriages, 59 percent include a child from a former marriage.

8    So, our families often extend along lines that are determined by decrees, rather than genes. If the nucleus is broken, there are still links forged in different directions.

9    The son of a friend was asked to produce a family tree for his sixth grade class. But he was dissatisfied with his oak. There was no room on it for his stepgrandfather, though the man had married his widowed grandmother years ago.

10    More to the point, the boy had to create an offshoot for his new baby half-brother that seemed too distant. He couldn't find a proper place for the uncle—the ex-uncle to be precise—whom he visited last summer with his cousin.

11    A family tree just doesn't work, he complained. He would have preferred to draw family bushes.

12    The reality is that divorce has created kinship ties that rival the most complex tribe. These are not always easy relationships. The children and even the adults whose family lives have been disrupted by divorce and remarriage learn that people they love do not necessarily love each other. This extended family does not gather for reunions and Thanksgivings.

13    But when it works, it can provide a support system of sorts. I have seen the nieces, nephews—even the dogs—of one marriage welcomed as guests into another. There are all sorts of relationships that survive the marital ones, though there are no names for these kinfolk, no nomenclature for this extending family.

14    Not long ago, when living together first became a common pattern, people couldn't figure out what to call each other. It was impossible to introduce the man you lived with as a "spouse equivalent." It was harder to refer to the woman your son lived with as his lover, mistress, housemate.

15    It's equally difficult to describe the peculiar membership of this new lineage. Does your first husband's mother become a mother-out-law? Is the woman no longer married to your uncle an ex-aunt? We have nieces and nephews left dangling like participles from other lives and stepfamilies entirely off the family tree.

16    Our reality is more flexible and our relationships more supportive than our language. But for the moment, my ten-year-old researcher is right. However accidentally, however uneasily, "We are in the same family."

## Discussion Questions

1. Explain why in the title the word *together* is in parentheses.
2. What is Goodman's attitude toward the new family? What leads you to your answer?
3. Explain the distinction that the young boy makes between family trees and family bushes.
4. Throughout her essay, Goodman returns to the example of the young girl. Explain the effectiveness of this rhetorical technique.
5. In small groups, discuss why using language is problematic in describing the new family composition.

# Writing Assignments

1. Write a journal entry discussing what term an adult should use to refer to a person she or he is seriously dating.
2. Survey your friends and classmates to determine if they live in extended, nuclear, blended, or single-parent families. In a paper, report on their feelings about their different family structures and include any observations you have made based on the survey.
3. In a paper, compare and contrast the makeup of the traditional family and the new family, explaining why one is preferable.
4. Write a paper on how language has adapted—positively or negatively—to reflect changing family structures.

# Can the American Family Survive?

## MARGARET MEAD

Margaret Mead (1901–1978) was born in Philadelphia, Pennsylvania, and grew up in New York. She received a B.A. from Barnard College, as well as an M.A. and a Ph.D. from Columbia University. She was a professor at Columbia University for many years and was also a visiting professor or lecturer at such schools as Harvard University, Yale University, Emory University, the University of Colorado, and Stanford University. Mead also worked as a curator at the American Museum of Natural History in New York City. In 1925, Mead made her first of many pilgrimages to the South Pacific Islands to do anthropological research. Her six-month stay on the Samoan island of T'ai resulted in *Coming of Age in Samoa* (1928), a book on the maturation of Samoans from adolescence to adulthood. The book won Mead great acclaim and established her as one of the United States most respected anthropologists. A prolific writer, Mead is the author of more than thirty books, the most famous of which are *Growing Up in New Guinea* (1930), *Sex and Temperament in Three Primitive Societies* (1935), *And Keep Your Powder Dry* (1942), *Male and Female* (1949), *An Anthropologist at Work* (1959), *Culture and Commitment* (1970), and *Blackberry Winter: A Memoir* (1972). In all of her work, Mead acknowledges the biological factors that affect people, while emphasizing the powerful role culture has in shaping human behavior. Using her skills as an anthropologist and expert in social relations, Mead examines in the following essay, which originally appeared in *Redbook* in 1977, the difficulties that the modern American family faces.

1    All over the United States, families are in trouble. It is true that there are many contented homes where parents are living in harmony and raising their children responsibly, and with enjoyment in which the children share. Two out of three American households are homes in which a wife and husband live together, and almost seven out of ten children are born to parents living together in their first marriage.

2    However, though reassuring, these figures are deceptive. A great many of the married couples have already lived through one divorce. And a very large number of the children in families still intact will have to face the disruption of their parents' marriage in the future. The numbers increase every year.

3    It is also true that the hazards are much greater for some families than for others. Very young couples, the poorly educated, those with few skills and a low income, Blacks and members of other minority groups—particularly if they live in big cities—all these are in danger of becoming high-risk families for whose children a family breakdown is disastrous.

4    But no group, whatever its status and resources, is exempt. This in itself poses a threat to all families, especially those with young children. For how can children feel secure when their friends in other families so like their own are conspicuously lost and unhappy? In one way or another we all are drawn into the orbit of families in trouble.

5    Surely it is time for us to look squarely at the problems that beset families and to ask what must be done to make family life more viable, not only for ourselves now but also in prospect for all the children growing up who will have to take responsibility for the next generation.

# The Grim Picture

6    There are those today—as at various times in the past—who doubt that the family can survive, and some who believe it should not survive. Indeed, the contemporary picture is grim enough.

- Many young marriages entered into with love and high hopes collapse before the first baby is weaned. The very young parents, on whom the whole burden of survival rests, cannot make it entirely on their own, and they give up.
- Families that include several children break up and the children are uprooted from the only security they have known. Some children of divorce, perhaps the majority, will grow up as stepchildren in homes that, however loving, they no longer dare to trust fully. Many—far too many—will grow up in single-parent homes. Still others will be moved, rootless as rolling stones, from foster family to foster family until at last they begin a rootless life on their own.
- In some states a family with a male breadwinner cannot obtain welfare, and some fathers, unable to provide adequately for their children, desert them so that the mothers can apply for public assistance. And growing numbers of mothers, fearful of being deserted, are leaving their young families while, as they hope and believe, they still have a chance to make a different life for themselves.
- As divorce figures have soared—today the proportion of those currently divorced is more than half again as high as in 1960, and it is predicted that one in three young women in this generation will be divorced—Americans have accepted as a truism the myth that from the mistakes made in their first marriage women and men learn how to do it better the second time around. Sometimes it does work. But a large proportion of those who have resorted to divorce once choose this as the easier solution again and again. Easily dashed hopes become more easily dashed.
- At the same time, many working parents, both of whom are trying hard to care for and keep together the family they have chosen to bring into being, find that there is no place at all

where their children can be cared for safely and gently and responsibly during the long hours of their own necessary absence at their jobs. They have no relatives nearby and there is neither a daycare center nor afterschool care for their active youngsters. Whatever solution they find, their children are likely to suffer.

## The Bitter Consequences

7    The consequences, direct and indirect, are clear. Thousands of young couples are living together in some arrangement and are wholly dependent on their private, personal commitment to each other for the survival of their relationship. In the years from 1970 to 1975 the number of single persons in the 25-to-34-year age group has increased by half. Some couples living together have repudiated marriage as a binding social relationship and have rejected the family as an institution. Others are delaying marriage because they are not sure of themselves or each other; still others are simply responding to what they have experienced of troubled family life and the effects of divorce.

8    At the end of the life span there are the ever-growing numbers of women and men, especially women, who have outlived their slender family relationships. They have nowhere to turn, no one to depend on but strangers in public institutions. Unwittingly we have provided the kind of assistance that, particularly in cities, almost guarantees such isolated and helpless old people will become the prey of social vultures.

9    And at all stages of their adult life, demands are made increasingly on women to earn their living in the working world. Although we prefer to interpret this as an expression of women's wish to fulfill themselves to have the rights that go with money earned and to be valued as persons, the majority of women who work outside their homes do so because they must. It is striking that ever since the 1950s a larger proportion of married women with children than of married but childless women have entered the labor force. According to recent estimates some 14 million women with children—four out of ten mothers of children under six years of age and

more than half of all mothers of school-age children—are working, the great majority of them in full-time jobs.

10    A large proportion of these working women are the sole support of their families. Some 10 million children—more than one in six—are living with only one parent, generally with the mother. This number has doubled since 1960.

11    The majority of these women and their children live below the poverty level, the level at which the most minimal needs can be met. Too often the women, particularly the younger ones, having little education and few skills, are at the bottom of the paid work force. Though they and their children are in great need, they are among those least able to demand and obtain what they require merely to survive decently, in good health and with some hope for the future.

12    But the consequences of family trouble are most desperate as they affect children. Every year, all over the country, over 1 million adolescents, nowadays principally girls, run away from home because they have found life with their families insupportable. Some do not run very far and in the end a great many come home again, but by no means all of them. And we hear about only a handful whose terrifying experiences or whose death happens to come into public view.

13    In homes where there is no one to watch over them, elementary-school children are discovering the obliterating effects of alcohol; a growing number have become hard-ease alcoholics in their early teens. Other young girls and boys, wanderers in the streets, have become the victims of corruption and sordid sex. The youngsters who vent their rage and desperation on others by means of violent crimes are no less social victims than are the girls and boys who are mindlessly corrupted by the adults who prey on them.

14    Perhaps the most alarming symptom of all is the vast increase in child abuse, which, although it goes virtually unreported in some groups, is not limited to any one group in our population. What seems to be happening is that frantic mothers and fathers, stepparents or the temporary mates of parents turn on the children they do not know how to care for, and beat them—often in a desperate, inarticulate hope that someone will hear their cries and somehow bring help. We know this, but although many organizations have been set up to help these children and their parents, many adults do not know what is needed or how to ask for assistance or whom they may expect a response from.

15    And finally there are the children who end their own lives in absolute despair. Suicide is now third among the causes of death for youngsters 15 to 19 years old.

# What Has Gone Wrong?

16    In recent years, various explanations have been suggested for the breakdown of family life.

17    Blame has been placed on the vast movement of Americans from rural areas and small towns to the big cities and on the continual, restless surge of people from one part of the country to another, so that millions of families, living in the midst of strangers, lack any continuity in their life-style and any real support for their values and expectations.

18    Others have emphasized the effects of unemployment and under-employment among Blacks and other minority groups, which make their families peculiarly vulnerable in life crises that are exacerbated by economic uncertainty. This is particularly the case where the policies of welfare agencies penalize the family that is poor but intact in favor of the single-parent family.

19    There is also the generation gap, particularly acute today, when parents and their adolescent children experience the world in such very different ways. The world in which the parents grew up is vanishing, unknown to their children except by hearsay. The world into which adolescents are growing is in many ways unknown to both generations—and neither can help the other very much to understand it.

20    Then there is our obvious failure to provide for the children and young people whom we do not succeed in educating, who are in deep trouble and who may be totally abandoned. We have not come to grips with the problems of hard drugs. We allow the courts that deal with juveniles to become so overloaded that little of the social protection they were intended to provide is possible. We consistently underfund and understaff the institutions into which we cram children in need of re-education and physical and psychological rehabilitation, as if all that concerned us was to get them—and keep them—out of our sight.

21    Other kinds of explanations also have been offered.

22    There are many people who, knowing little about child development, have placed the principal blame on what they call "permis-
siveness"—on the relaxing of parental discipline to include the child
as a small partner in the process of growing up. Those people say
that children are "spoiled," that they lack "respect" for their parents
or that they have not learned to obey the religious prohibitions that
were taught to their parents, and that all the troubles plaguing family life have followed.

23    Women's Liberation, too, has come in for a share of the blame. It
is said that in seeking self-fulfillment, women are neglecting their
homes and children and are undermining men's authority and men's
sense of responsibility. The collapse of the family is seen as the
inevitable consequence.

24    Those who attribute the difficulties of troubled families to any
single cause, whether or not it is related to reality, also tend to advocate panaceas, each of which—they say—should restore stability to
the traditional family or, alternatively, supplant the family. Universal
day care from birth, communal living, group marriage, contract
marriage and open marriage all have their advocates.

25    Each such proposal fastens on some trouble point in the modern
family—the lack of adequate facilities to care for the children of
working mothers, for example, or marital infidelity, which, it is
argued, would be eliminated by being institutionalized. Others,
realizing the disastrous effects of poverty on family life, have advo-
cated bringing the income of every family up to a level at which
decent living is possible. Certainly this must be one of our immediate aims. But it is wholly unrealistic to suppose that all else that has
gone wrong will automatically right itself if the one—but very complex—problem of poverty is eliminated.

## A Look at Alternatives

26    Is there, in fact, any viable alternative to the family as a setting in
which children can be successfully reared to become capable and
responsible adults, relating to one another and a new generation of

children as well as to the world around them? Or should we aim at some wholly new social invention?

27    Revolutionaries have occasionally attempted to abolish the family, or at least to limit its strength by such measures as arranging for marriages without binding force or for rearing children in different kinds of collectives. But as far as we know, in the long run such efforts have never worked out satisfactorily.

28    The Soviet Union, for instance, long ago turned away from the flexible, impermanent unions and collective child-care ideals of the early revolutionary days and now heavily emphasizes the values of a stable family life. In Israel the kibbutz, with its children's house and carefully planned, limited contact between parents and children, is losing out to social forms in which the family is both stronger and more closely knit. In Scandinavian countries, where the standards of child care are very high, serious efforts have been made to provide a viable situation for unmarried mothers and the children they have chosen to bring up alone; but there are disturbing indices of trouble, expressed, for example, in widespread alcoholism and a high rate of suicide.

29    Experience suggests that we would do better to look in other directions. Two approaches may be rewarding. First we can look at other kinds of societies—primitive societies, peasant societies and traditional complex but unindustrialized societies (prerevolutionary China, for example)—to discover whether there are ways in which families are organized that occur in all societies. This can give us some idea of needs that must be satisfied for families to survive and prosper.

30    Second we can ask whether the problems that are besetting American families are unique or are instead characteristic of families wherever modem industrialization, a sophisticated technology and urban living are drawing people into a new kind of civilization. Placing our own difficulties within a wider context can perhaps help us to assess what our priorities must be as we attempt to develop new forms of stability in keeping with contemporary expressions of human needs.

31    Looking at human behavior with all that we know—and can infer—about the life of our human species from earliest times, we have to realize that the family, as an association between a man and

a woman and the children she bears, has been universal. As far as we know, both primitive "group" marriage and primitive matriarchy are daydreams—or nightmares, depending on one's point of view—without basis in historical reality. On the contrary, the evidence indicates that the couple, together with their children, biological or adopted, are everywhere at the core of human societies, even though this "little family" (as the Chinese called the nuclear family) may be embedded in joint families, extended families of great size, clans, manorial systems, courts, harems or other institutions that elaborate on kin and marital relations.

32    Almost up to the present, women on the whole have kept close to home and domestic tasks because of the demands of pregnancy and the nursing of infants, the rearing of children and the care of the disabled and the elderly. They have been concerned primarily with the conservation of intimate values and human relations from one generation to another over immense reaches of time. In contrast, men have performed tasks that require freer movement over greater distances, more intense physical effort and exposure to greater immediate danger; and everywhere men have developed the formal institutions of public life and the values on which these are based. However differently organized, the tasks of women and men have been complementary, mutually supportive. And where either the family or the wider social institutions have broken down, the society as a whole has been endangered.

33    In fact, almost everywhere in the world today societies are endangered. The difficulties that beset families in the United States are by no means unique. Families are in trouble everywhere in a world in which change—kinds of change that in many cases we ourselves proudly initiated—has been massive and rapid, and innovations have proliferated with only the most superficial concern for their effect on human lives and the earth itself. One difference between the United States and many other countries is that, caring so much about progress, Americans have moved faster. But we may also have arrived sooner at a turning point at which it becomes crucial to redefine what we most value and where we are headed.

34    Looking to the past does not mean that we should return to the past or that we can undo the experiences that have brought us where we are now. The past can provide us only with a base for judging what threatens sound family life and for considering whether our

social planning is realistic and inclusive enough. Looking to the past is not a way of binding ourselves but of increasing our awareness, so that we are freer to find new solutions in keeping with our deepest human needs.

35    So the question is not whether women should be forced back into their homes or should have an equal say with men in the world's affairs. We urgently need to draw on the talents women have to offer. Nor is there any question whether men should be deprived of a more intimate family role. We have made a small beginning by giving men a larger share in parenting, and I believe that men and children have been enriched by it.

36    What we need to be sure of is that areas of caretaking associated in the past with families do not simply drop out of our awareness so that basic human needs go unmet. All the evidence indicates that this is where our greatest difficulties lie. The troubles that plague American families and families all over the industrialized world are symptomatic of the breakdown of the responsible relationship between families and the larger communities of which they are part.

37    For a long time we have worked hard at isolating the individual family. This has increased the mobility of individuals; and by encouraging young families to break away from the older generation and the home community, we have been able to speed up the acceptance of change and the rapid spread of innovative behavior. But at the same time we have burdened every small family with tremendous responsibilities once shared within three generations and among a large number of people—the nurturing of small children, the emergence of adolescents into adulthood, the care of the sick and disabled and the protection of the aged. What we have failed to realize is that even as we have separated the single family from the larger society, we have expected each couple to take on a range of obligations that traditionally have been shared within a larger family and a wider community.

38    So all over the world there are millions of families left alone, as it were, each in its own box—parents faced with the specter of what may happen if either one gets sick, children fearful that their parents may end their quarrels with divorce, and empty-handed old people without any role in the life of the next generation.

39    Then, having pared down to almost nothing the relationship between families and the community, when families get into trouble

because they cannot accomplish the impossible we turn their problems over to impersonal social agencies, which can act only in a fragmented way because they are limited to patchwork programs that often are too late to accomplish what is most needed.

40    Individuals and families do get some kind of help, but what they learn and what those who work hard within the framework of social agencies convey, even as they try to help, is that families should be able to care for themselves.

# What Can We Do?

41    Can we restore family stability? Can we establish new bonds between families and communities? Perhaps most important of all, can we move to a firm belief that living in a family is worth a great effort? Can we move to a new expectation that by making the effort, families can endure? Obviously the process is circular. Both optimism and action are needed.

42    We shall have to distinguish between the things that must be done at once and the relations between families and communities that can be built up only over time. We shall have to accept willingly the cost of what must be done, realizing that whatever we do ultimately will be less costly than our present sorry attempts to cope with breakdown and disaster. And we shall have to care for the failures too.

43    In the immediate future we shall have to support every piece of Federal legislation through which adequate help can be provided for families, both single-parent families and intact poor families, so that they can live decently and safely and prepare their children for another kind of life.

44    We shall have to support Federal programs for day care and after-school care for the children of working mothers and working parents, and for facilities where in a crisis parents can safely leave their small children for brief periods; for centers where the elderly can be cared for without being isolated from the rest of the world; for housing for young families and older people in communities where they can actually interact as friendly grandparents and grandchildren might; and for a national health program that is concerned not with

fleecing the Government but with health care. And we must support the plea of Vice-President Walter F. Mondale, who, as chairman of the Senate Subcommittee on Children and Youth, called for "family impact" statements requiring Government agencies to account for what a proposed policy would do for families—make them worse off or better able to take care of their needs.

45 Government-funded programs need not be patchwork, as likely to destroy as to save. We need to realize that problems related to family and community life—problems besetting education, housing, nutrition, health care, child care, to name just a few—are interlocked. To solve them, we need awareness of detail combined with concern for the whole, and a wise use of tax dollars to accomplish our aims.

46 A great deal depends on how we see what is done—whether we value it because we are paying for it and because we realize that the protection given families in need is a protection for all families, including our own. Committing ourselves to programs of care—instead of dissociating ourselves from every effort—is one step in the direction of reestablishing family ties with the community. But this will happen only if we accept the idea that each of us, as part of a community, shares in the responsibility for everyone, and thereby benefits from what is done.

47 The changes that are needed cannot be accomplished by Federal legislation alone. Over a longer time we must support the design and building of communities in which there is housing for three generations, for the fortunate and the unfortunate, and for people of many backgrounds. Such communities can become central in the development of the necessary support system for families. But it will take time to build such communities, and we cannot afford just to wait and hope they will happen.

48 Meanwhile we must act to interrupt the runaway belief that marriages must fail, that parents and children can't help but be out of communication, that the family as an institution is altogether in disarray. There still are far more marriages that succeed than ones that fail; there are more parents and children who live in trust and learn from one another than ones who are out of touch; there are more people who care about the future than we acknowledge.

49 What we need, I think, is nationwide discussion—in magazines, in newspapers, on television panel shows and before Congressional

committees—of how people who are happily married can help those
who are not, how people who are fortunate can help those who are
not and how people who have too little to do can help those who
are burdened by too much.

50    Out of such discussions can come a heightened awareness and
perhaps some actual help, but above all, fresh thought about what
must be done and the determination to begin to do it.

51    It is true that all over the United States, families are in trouble.
Realizing this should not make us cynical about the family. It should
start us working for a new version of the family that is appropriate to
the contemporary world.

# Discussion Questions

1. Twenty years have passed since Mead wrote this article. In small
   groups, discuss whether families in the United States are still in trouble.
2. Do you agree with Mead's observation in paragraph 4: "In one way
   or another we are all drawn into the orbit of families in trouble"?
   Why or why not?
3. Do you agree with the cause-effect relationship Mead draws
   between the "grim picture" and the "bitter consequences"? Explain.
4. Mead examines various reasons for the breakdown of the family.
   Identify those with which you agree and disagree, and explain your
   thinking.
5. Does Mead blame any one person or thing for the deterioration of
   the American family? Explain.
6. Are the alternatives and solutions that Mead offers realistic? If so,
   why? If not, can you recommend others?

# Writing Assignments

1. Write a letter to Mead describing what has happened to the
   American family in the years since she wrote her essay.

2. Do you think too much attention is being given to the troubles of the contemporary American family and not enough to its strengths? Write a paper that supports your perspective.
3. Recent political campaigns have focused largely on "family values." In a paper, compare and contrast your own definition of family values with others you have read or heard.
4. Write an essay in which you argue whether federal legislation alone is sufficient to change the problems of the modern American family.

# Acknowledgments

Anderson, Sherwood. From *Sherwood Anderson's Memoirs: A Critical Edition*, edited by Ray Lewis White. Copyright © 1969 by the University of North Carolina Press. Used by permission of the publisher.

Ascher, Barbara Lazear. From *The Habit of Loving* by Barbara Ascher. Copyright © 1989 by Barbara Ascher. Reprinted by permission of Random House, Inc.

Bly, Carol. "Extended vs. Nuclear Families" from *Letters from the Country* by Carol Bly. Copyright © 1973, 1974, 1975, 1977, 1978, 1979, 1981 by Carol Bly. Reprinted by permission of HarperCollins Publishers, Inc.

Carver, Raymond. "My Father's Life" by Raymond Carver. Reprinted by permission of International Creative Management, Inc. Copyright © by Raymond Carver.

de Beauvoir, Simone. From *Memoirs of a Dutiful Daughter* by Simone de Beauvoir. Copyright © 1958 by Librairie Gallimard. Reprinted by permission of HarperCollins Publishers, Inc.

Didion, Joan. "On Going Home" from "Personals" from *Slouching Towards Bethlehem* by Joan Didion. Copyright © 1968 and copyright renewed © 1996 by Joan Didion. Reprinted by permission of Farrar, Straus & Giroux, Inc.

Dorris, Michael. "A Second Adoption" from *Paper Trail* by Michael Dorris. Copyright © 1994 by Michael Dorris. Reprinted by permission of HarperCollins Publishers, Inc.

Dorris, Michael. "Foreword" by Louise Erdrich from *The Broken Cord* by Michael Dorris. Copyright © 1989 by Michael Dorris. Reprinted by permission of HarperCollins Publishers, Inc.

Goodman, Ellen. "The Family That Stretches (Together)" by Ellen Goodman from *Keeping in Touch* by Ellen Goodman. © 1985 The Boston Globe Newspaper Co./Washington Post Writers Group. Reprinted with permission.

Jordan, June. "For My American Family" from *Technical Difficulties* by June Jordan. Copyright © 1992, 1994 by June Jordan. Reprinted by permission of Pantheon Books, a division of Random House, Inc.

Lessing, Doris. "My Father" from *A Small Personal Voice* by Doris Lessing. Copyright © 1963 Doris Lessing. Reproduced by kind permission of Jonathan Clowes Ltd., London, on behalf of Doris Lessing.

Lopez, Barry. "Searching for Ancestors" by Barry Lopez. Reprinted by permission of Sterling Lord Literistic, Inc. Copyright © 1988 by Barry Holstun Lopez.

Mairs, Nancy. "On Being Raised by a Daughter" by Nancy Mairs. From *Plaintext* by Nancy Mairs. Copyright © 1986 by University of Arizona Press. Reprinted by permission of the publisher.

McCarthy, Mary. Excerpt from "Ask Me No Questions" in *Memories of a Catholic Girlhood*, copyright © 1957 and renewed 1985 by Mary McCarthy, reprinted by permission of Harcourt Brace & Company.

Mead, Margaret and Rhoda Metraux. "Can the American Family Survive?" from *Aspects of the Present* by Margaret Mead and Rhoda Metraux. Copyright © 1980 by Catherine Bateson Kassarjian and Rhoda Metraux. Reprinted by permission of William Morrow & Company, Inc.

Montaigne, trans. by Donald M. Frame. "Of the affection of fathers for their children" by Montaigne. Reprinted from *The Complete Essays of Montaigne* translated by Donald M. Frame with the permission of the publishers, Stanford University Press. © 1958 by the Board of Trustees of the Leland Stanford Junior University.

Ozick, Cynthia. "The Seam of the Snail" from *Metaphor & Memory* by Cynthia Ozick. Copyright © 1989 by Cynthia Ozick. Reprinted by permission of Alfred A. Knopf, Inc.

Porter, Katherine Anne. "The Necessary Enemy" by Katherine Anne Porter from *The Collected Essays and Occasional Writings of Katherine Anne Porter*. Reprinted by permission of The Trustee for the Literary Estate of Katherine Anne Porter.

Quindlen, Anna. From *Living Out Loud* by Anna Quindlen. Copyright © 1988 by Anna Quindlen. Reprinted by permission of Random House, Inc.

Rodriguez, Richard. From *Hunger of Memory* by Richard Rodriguez. Reprinted by permission of David R. Godine, Publisher, Inc. Copyright © 1982 by Richard Rodriguez.

Sanders, Scott Russell. "The Inheritance of Tools" by Scott Russell Sanders. Copyright © 1986 by Scott Russell Sanders; first appeared in *The North American Review*; reprinted by permission of the author and the Virginia Kidd Agency, Inc.

Soto, Gary. "Like Mexicans" from *Small Faces* by Gary Soto. Copyright © 1986 by Gary Soto. Used by permission of the author and Bookstop Literary Agency. All rights reserved.

Staples, Brent. "A Brother's Murder" by Brent Staples, *The New York Times*, March 30, 1986. Copyright © 1986 by The New York Times Co. Reprinted by permission.

Welty, Eudora. Reprinted by permission of the publishers from Eudora Welty, *One Writer's Beginnings*, Cambridge, Mass.: Harvard University Press, Copyright © 1983, 1984 by Eudora Welty.

Wideman, John Edgar. From *Brothers and Keepers* by John Edgar Wideman, © 1984 by John Edgar Wideman. Reprinted by permission of Henry Holt & Co., Inc.

Yu, Connie Young. From *Making Waves* by Asian Women United of California. © 1989 by Asian Women United of California. Reprinted by permission of Beacon Press, Boston.

# Index of Authors and Titles